QUALITATIVE DISCOURSE ANALYSIS
IN THE SOC?

Also by Ruth Wodak

Methods of Text and Discourse Analysis (with S. Titscher, M. Meyer and
   E. Vetter)
Methods of Critical Discourse Analysis (with M. Meyer)
Discourse and Discrimination (with M. Reisigl)
Critical Discourse Analysis: Theory and Interdisciplinarity (with G. Weiss)
A New Agenda in (Critical) Discourse Analysis (with P. Chilton)
The Discursive Construction of History (with H. Heer, W. Manoschek and
   A. Pollak)

Also by Michał Krzyżanowski

*(Un)Doing Europe: Discourses and Practices of Negotiating the EU
   Constitution* (with F. Oberhuber)
The Politics of Exclusion: Debating Migration in Austria (with R. Wodak)
Discourse and Transformation in Central and Eastern Europe (with
   A. Galasińska)

Qualitative Discourse Analysis in the Social Sciences

Edited by

Ruth Wodak and Michał Krzyżanowski

First published 2008 by
PALGRAVE MACMILLAN
Houndmills, Basingstoke, Hampshire RG21 6XS and
175 Fifth Avenue, New York, N.Y. 10010
Companies and representatives throughout the world

PALGRAVE MACMILLAN is the global academic imprint of the Palgrave Macmillan division of St. Martin's Press, LLC and of Palgrave Macmillan Ltd. Macmillan® is a registered trademark in the United States, United Kingdom and other countries. Palgrave is a registered trademark in the European Union and other countries.

ISBN-13: 978-0-230-01986-7   hardback
ISBN-10: 0-230-01986-2   hardback
ISBN-13: 978-0-230-01987-4   paperback
ISBN-10: 0-230-01987-0   paperback

This book is printed on paper suitable for recycling and made from fully managed and sustained forest sources. Logging, pulping and manufacturing processes are expected to conform to the environmental regulations of the country of origin.

A catalogue record for this book is available from the British Library.

A catalog record for this book is available from the Library of Congress.

10   9   8   7   6   5   4   3   2   1
17   16   15   14   13   12   11   10   09   08

Transferred to Digital Printing in 2011

Contents

List of Tables

List of Figures

Notes on the Contributors

Jackie Abell is Lecturer and Director of the MSc Programme in Psychological Research Methods at the Department of Psychology, Lancaster University, UK. Further information: http://www.psych.lancs.ac.uk/people/JackieAbell.html

Helmut Gruber is Associate Professor at the Department of (Applied) Linguistics, University of Vienna, Austria. Further information: http://www.univie.ac.at/linguistics/personal/helmut

Michal Krzyżanowski is Research Fellow in the Department of Linguistics and English Language, Lancaster University, UK, and Assistant Professor in the School of English, Adam Mickiewicz University, Poznań, Poland. He was previously Research Associate at the Department of Linguistics and the Research Centre 'Discourse, Politics, Identity' at the University of Vienna. Further information: http://www.ling.lancs.ac.uk/profiles/309/

Gerlinde Mautner is Full Professor and Director at the Institute for English Business Communication, Vienna University of Economics and Business Administration. She has spent a year as a visiting scholar at the linguistic departments of each of the universities of Birmingham, Lancaster and Cardiff. Further information: http://www.wu-wien.ac.at/ebc/faculty/mautner

Greg Myers is currently Professor of Rhetoric and Communication at the Department of Linguistics and English Language, Lancaster University, UK. He previously worked at the Department of English, University of Texas, and at the Department of Modern Languages at University of Bradford. Further information: http://www.ling.lancs.ac.uk/profiles/297/

Florian Oberhuber was in 2006–7 Jean Monnet Fellow at the European University Institute. He was previously Research Associate at the Research Centre 'Discourse, Politics, Identity' and a collaborator for the Dictionary of Political Language in Austria. Florian has also been teaching at the Universities of Salzburg and Vienna.

Alexander Pollak is Research Manager at the European Fundamental Rights Agency (FRA), Vienna. He previously lectured at the Department of Linguistics University of Vienna and was Research Associate at the Research Centre 'Discourse, Politics, Identity' of the University of Vienna.

Martin Reisigl is APART Research Fellow of the Austrian Academy of Sciences, Visiting Fellow at the Institute for Human Sciences, Vienna, and Lecturer at the Department of Linguistics, University of Vienna. He was previously Research

Fellow of the Alexander von Humboldt Foundation at the Free University of Berlin and Assistant Lecturer at the Department of Linguistics, University of Vienna.

Ruth Wodak is Distinguished Professor of Discourse Studies at Lancaster University. Besides various other prizes, she was awarded the Wittgenstein Prize for Elite Researchers in 1996. She is the author of numerous works in the field of critical discourse studies and co-editor of *Journal of Language and Politics* and *Critical Discourse Studies*. Further information: http://www.ling.lancs.ac.uk/profiles/265/

Introduction: Discourse Studies – Important Concepts and Terms

Ruth Wodak

Introduction

> Discourse Studies is the discipline devoted to the investigation of the relationship between form and function in verbal communication. (Renkema 2004:1)

The notions of *text* and *discourse* have been subject to a hugely proliferating number of usages in the social sciences. Almost no paper or article is to be found which does not revisit these notions while quoting Michel Foucault, Jürgen Habermas, Chantal Mouffe, Ernesto Laclau or many others.[1] Thus, *discourse* means anything from a historical monument, a *lieu de mémoire*, a policy, a political strategy, narratives in a restricted or broad sense of the term, text, talk, a speech, topic-related conversations, to language *per se*. We find notions such as racist discourse, gendered discourse, discourses on un/employment, media discourse, populist discourse, discourses of the past, and many more – thus stretching the meaning of *discourse* from a genre to a register or style, from a building to a political programme. This causes and must cause confusion – which leads to much criticism and many misunderstandings.[2]

However, we rarely find *systematic definitions and operationalizations* of these concepts. Even less frequently – although sometimes brief text materials (interview sequences or small quotes of press articles) are given – are the respective terms applied in an explicit and consistent way. Usually, in the social sciences, text sequences are used as illustrations, sentences are taken out of context, and specific text sequences are used to validate or reject claims without relating them to the entire textual material and without providing any explicit justification or external evidence for their selection.

Comment

Until recently, for example, 'open questions' in questionnaires and hour-long debates in focus groups have often been subjected to quantitative methods of 'content-' or 'frame-analysis', thus neglecting the contextualized detailed argumentative patterns in such debates as well as the evolving group dynamics in discussions.[3]

Because of both the *linguistic* and *cultural turns* in sociology, political science, anthropology and history, texts and discourses have become more than a means for quantitative analysis, for example content analysis of media or other printed materials, or some kind of illustrative and mostly paraphrased analysis of narrative interviews.

Comment

New communication technology (for example, email lists, internet debate forums, websites, and so forth) which has evolved in recent years involves interesting hybrid texts, a mix of visuals and written data. Thus new methodologies had to be created. These new texts and genres (see below) have usually been subjected to mostly quantitative analysis, not taking into account the impact of the visual which necessarily interacts with textual meanings. Thus, we have to add one more *turn*, the *visual turn*, to our scholarly debates, and incorporate toolkits for the analysis of the visual (*multimodality*; *hypermodality*).

Many scholars have recently become aware of the intricacies of textual materials and are searching for more adequate methodologies. They are turning to discourse analysts for information and expertise. This is why we decided to write this book: to provide researchers with the most important concepts, discovery procedures, strategies, methods and tools to analyze a range of *genres of texts and talk* which researchers and students come across when studying complex social phenomena: *political speeches, focus groups, media, the internet, interviews, policy documents* and so forth.

Discourse analysis provides a general framework to *problem-oriented social research*. It allows the integration of different dimensions of *interdisciplinarity* and multiple perspectives on the object investigated. Every interview, focus group debate, TV debate or visual symbol is conceived as a *semiotic entity*, embedded in an *immediate, text-internal co-text and an intertextual and socio-political* context. Analysis thus has to take into account the *intertextual and interdiscursive relationships* (see below) between utterances, texts, genres and discourses, as well as the extralinguistic social/sociological variables, the *history and archaeology of an organization*, and institutional frames of a specific *context of situation*.

Intertextuality refers to the fact that all texts are linked to other texts, both in the past and in the present. Such links can be established in different ways: through continued reference to a topic or main actors; through reference to the same events; or by the transfer of main arguments from one text into the next. The latter process is also labelled *recontextualization*. By taking an argument and restating it in a new context, we first observe the process of decontextualization, and then, when the respective element is implemented in a new context, of recontextualization. The element then acquires a new meaning because meanings are formed in use (see Wittgenstein 1967). *Interdiscursivity*, on the other hand, indicates that discourses are linked to each other in various ways. If we define discourse as primarily topic-related, that is a discourse on X, then a discourse on un/employment often refers for example to topics or subtopics of other discourses, such as gender or racism: arguments on systematically lower salaries for women or migrants might be included in discourses on employment (see below for definitions of text and discourse).

Van Dijk (2007) summarizes the history of *Discourse Studies* (DS) in a very precise way, and emphasizes that 'the "core" of the new discipline remains *the systematic and explicit analysis of the various structures and strategies of different levels of text and talk*'. Thus, DS must draw on anthropology, history, rhetoric, stylistics, conversation analysis, literary studies, cultural studies, pragmatics, philosophy, sociolinguistics and so forth. The history of the field is summarized in detail in Renkema (2004) and Van Dijk (forthcoming).

In the chapters of this volume, each dedicated to different *genres* and *methods* for the analysis of these genres, we illustrate through our examples how the field of DS is now organized in various subdisciplines that have become more or less independent. The methods for the analysis of *text* and *talk*, that is *text in context,* also cover a whole range of grammatical and multimodal approaches which will be discussed extensively throughout this book (see also Titscher *et al.* 2000).

Taking van Dijk's historical summary of the field of DS further (van Dijk, 2007), we can identify the following developments: Between the mid 1960s and the early 1970s, new, closely related disciplines emerged in the humanities and the social sciences. Despite their different disciplinary backgrounds and a vast diversity of methods and objects of investigation, some parts of the new fields/paradigms/linguistic subdisciplines of *semiotics, pragmatics, psycho- and sociolinguistics, ethnography of speaking, conversation analysis and discourse studies* deal with discourse and have at least seven dimensions in common (see ibid.: xxii–xxiii):

- An interest in the properties of *'naturally occurring' language use* by real language users (instead of a study of abstract language systems and invented examples).
- A focus on *larger units than isolated words and sentences,* and hence new basic units of analysis: texts, discourses, conversations, speech acts or communicative events.

▦   The extension of linguistics *beyond sentence grammar* towards a study of action and interaction.

▦   The extension to *nonverbal (semiotic, multimodal, visual) aspects* of interaction and communication: gestures, images, film, the internet and multimedia.

▦   A focus on dynamic (socio)-cognitive or interactional moves and strategies.

▦   The study of the functions of (social, cultural, situative and cognitive) *contexts of language use*.

▦   Analysis of a vast number of *phenomena of text grammar and language use*: coherence, anaphora, topics, macrostructures, speech acts, interactions, turn-taking, signs, politeness, argumentation, rhetoric, mental models and many other aspects of text and discourse.

Comment

Throughout this volume, many of the dimensions mentioned above will be discussed in detail. For example, when analyzing interviews, we view the interview as a dialogue between interviewer and interviewee (the genre), and analyze many features of spoken discourse, such as politeness charateristics, turn-taking, actors and agencies, topics, coherence, strategic moves, and so forth. Thus, in each of the following chapters, the specific genre-related features will be defined and adequate methods of analysis illustrated – step by step, with examples which should allow readers to understand the analysis as well as to learn *how to do it*.

Discourse and text

Discourse

Discourse is what makes us human. (Graesser *et al.* 1997:165)

First it is important to explain some of the many different meanings of *discourse*, several of which are discussed extensively later on, throughout this volume. The term *discourse analysis* stems etymologically from the Greek verb *analuein* 'to deconstruct' and the Latin verb *discurrere* 'to run back and forth'.

The term *discourse analysis* has in recent decades penetrated many disciplines, such as sociology, philosophy, history, literary studies, cultural studies, anthropology, psychology and linguistics. In all these disciplines the term carries distinct meanings, including a social science methodology, the label for a whole field, a subdiscipline of linguistics, a critical paradigm and so forth. Reisigl (2004) lists twenty-three meanings of *discourse* used by Michel Foucault throughout his famous lecture in the Collège de France on *orders of discourse*. In his seminal lecture, Foucault formulates a number of crucial axioms about the nature and contexts of discursive events (*énoncés*):

> I make the assumption that the production of discourse is at once controlled, selected, organized and canalized in every society – and that this is done by way of certain procedures whose task it is to subdue the powers and dangers of discourse, to evade its heavy and threatening materiality. (Foucault 1984:10–11)

Although Foucault refers to many definitions of *discourse* in the course of his famous lecture, it is equally important to note what discourse is not supposed to mean in Foucault's work – specifically, that it is neither defined thematically nor by a strict system of concepts, and that it is not an object but rather a set of relationships existing between discursive events. These stipulations open the door to a dedicated functional approach, enabling the cultural critic to identify both static and dynamic relationships between discursive events and to address the causes and consequences of historical change.[4]

However, and in contrast with Foucault's more abstract notion, in the tradition of Wittgenstein's *language games* (1967) and Austin's *speech acts* (1962), *discourse* is mainly understood as *linguistic action*, be it written, visual or oral communication, verbal or nonverbal, undertaken by social actors in a specific setting determined by social rules, norms and conventions.

Comment

For example, if I say 'I promise to bring the book tomorrow', I make the speech-act of 'promising', which underlies very explicit, socially defined, rules, norms and sanctions in Western societies (thus, people get angry if I do not keep my promise), and I specify what I promise: to bring the book tomorrow.

As early as 1990, while distinguishing discourse analysis from *text linguistics*, van Dijk (1990:164) defined *discourse* as *text in context*; the latter concept probably being one of the most complex, vague and challenging notions for research in DS.[5] Utz Maas (1989) demonstrates, moreover, that the meaning of *discourse* has shifted from 'scholarly deliberation' to 'dialogue' in recent years (see also Wodak 1996: 20ff.), in particular when drawing on the Habermasian theory on discourse and communication (Habermas 1981).

Furthermore, language-specific meanings exist as well as distinct uses within the Anglo-American academic community on the one hand, and European scholarship on the other. For example, in British research, the term *discourse* is frequently used synonymously with *text*, meaning authentic, everyday linguistic communication. The French *discours*, however, is more focused on the connection between language and thought, for instance meaning 'creation and societal maintenance of complex knowledge systems' (Ehlich 2000:162). In German, in functional pragmatics *Diskurs* denotes 'structured sets of speech

acts' (ibid.). In the analysis of discourse, the meaning of *discourse* is therefore closely linked to the particular research context and theoretical approach.

It is not within the scope of this introduction to elaborate further on the many, frequently undefined uses of *discourse*. Nor is it – unfortunately – feasible to discuss the relevant philosophical debates between for example Michel Foucault and Jürgen Habermas here (but see Wodak 1996; Torfing 1999). It is important, however, to acknowledge that discourse analysts and scholars employing various methods of discourse analysis should be required to present their theoretical background and consider other approaches beyond the necessarily limited scope of their school, discipline or academic culture.

Comment

This broader perspective implies, especially for linguists who by nature should be competent in more than one language, including literature from different research paradigms in different cultures, in languages other than English. Unfortunately, this is rarely the case in the Anglo-American world, where references are more often than not restricted to research published in English by authors of British, American, Canadian or Australian origin, interspersed with a few translations from prominent, often 'trendy' scholars.

Following the most important traditions in text linguistics and Discourse Studies,[6] we distinguish between *discourse* and *text* in this volume and take Jay Lemke's definition (1995: 7ff.) as a starting-point:

> When I speak about discourse in general, I will usually mean the social activity of making meanings with language and other symbolic systems in some particular kind of situation or setting . . . On each occasion when the particular meaning characteristic of these discourses is being made, a specific text is produced. Discourses, as social actions more or less governed by social habits, produce texts that will in some ways be alike in their meanings . . . When we want to focus on the specifics of an event or occasion, we speak of the text; when we want to look at patterns, commonality, relationships that embrace different texts and occasions, we can speak of discourses.

In other words, *discourse* is defined on a different, more abstract, level as *text*. *Discourse* implies patterns and commonalities of knowledge and structures whereas a *text* is a specific and unique realization of a discourse. Texts belong to genres. Thus a discourse on New Labour could be realized in a potentially huge range of genres and texts, for example in a TV debate on the politics of New Labour, in a New Labour manifesto, in a speech by one of New Labour's representatives and so forth.

Text

Texts are often considered to be longer pieces of writing. The word text itself evokes the idea of a book, a letter or a newspaper. The decisive contribution of linguistics in this respect has been to introduce a concept of text that includes every type of communicative utterance and which relates to the more abstract notion of discourse presented above in complex ways. Clear criteria ultimately decide whether or not something can be viewed as text or discourse (Fairclough 1992:3ff.). These criteria are purely linguistic in nature and relate to the syntactic and semantic relations within a text. A text may be an inscription on a tombstone, a part of a conversation, a book or a newspaper article. On the one hand, this indicates a very broad concept of communication that regards language and speech as forms of action and derives from Wittgenstein's *language games* (see above); on the other, it suggests a notion of *sign*, as used in modern semiotics. The concept of *semiosis* (meaning-making) relates to any sign (including for instance a traffic sign) that according to social conventions is meaningful (Halliday 1978). Hence, the answer to of what a text is must always be theory-dependent.

Sanders and Sanders (2006:598) define *text* in the following way:

> We consider a text to be a monological stretch of written language that shows coherence. The term 'text' derives from the Latin verb texere 'to weave' (hence the resemblance between the words 'text' and 'textile'). But what makes a text a text? This question has been at the centre of attention of the fields of discourse studies and text linguistics, especially since the 1970s.

And they continue (ibid.:599):

> At present, the dominant stance is that 'coherence' explains best the connectedness shown by texts. Coherence is considered a mental phenomenon; it is not an inherent property of a text under consideration. Language users establish coherence by relating different information units in the text.

Hence, Sanders and Sanders (2006) also recur to the seminal, first *Introduction to Text Linguistics* 1981, by Robert de Beaugrande and Wolfgang Dressler. In what follows I first list the seven criteria proposed by de Beaugrande and Dressler (1981) for the definition of texts (see also Titscher *et al.* 2000: 14ff. for an extensive discussion). This taxonomy is widely adopted and accepted, and for this reason I present it as a first working definition. Below, I examine each of the criteria in turn:

Cohesion concerns the components of the textual surface that signal the

text-syntactic connectedness. The linear sequence of linguistic elements in a text is in no way accidental, but obeys grammatical rules and dependencies. All the functions applied to create relationships between surface elements are categorized as *cohesion*. Cohesion is achieved *inter alia* by:

- *Recurrence*: repetition of lexical elements, sentence components and other linguistic elements
- *Anaphora* and *cataphora*: anaphora directs attention to what has previously been said or read (for example, through the use of pro-forms, such as *s/he* referring to a person previously introduced), while cataphora points to what is to come (for example through the use of deictic elements, such as *then*, *there*, when the site of interaction or the time of the interaction will be specified later on).
- *Ellipsis:* normally unintelligible without the communicative situation and the shared world knowledge (presuppositions) of participants in a conversation.
- *Conjunctions:* these signal relations or connections between events and situations. There are conjunctions (linking sentence structures of the same status), disjunctions (linking sentence structures with differing status), contra-junctions (linking sentence structures of the same status that seem to be irreconcilable, such as cause and unexpected effect) and subordinations (used where one sentence structure is dependent on another).

Coherence (or textual semantics) constitutes the meaning of a text (see above). This often refers to elements that do not necessarily require a linguistic realization. For example, cognitive linguistics assumes cognitive structures in recipients that are actualized through a text and help to determine interpretations (Chilton 2005; van Dijk 2005). Similarly, under certain circumstances, elements of knowledge that are not expressed in a text may also be implied and may likewise influence reception (like Grice's concept of *implicature* or many devices in pragmatics – see Sperber and Wilson 1995; Brown and Yule 1973). De Beaugrande and Dressler (1981) suggest that *concepts* (meanings) are bound through logical, cognitive or semantic *relationships* and then realized in the textual surface.

Comment

For example, causality is a relationship: this affects the manner in which an event of situation may influence other events or situations in a direct way. In 'Jack fell down and broke his crown' – *fall* is the cause of the event *break*.

A text creates no sense in itself but only in connection with knowledge of the world and of the text (Van Dijk 2003, 2005). This implies that in the process

of language acquisition certain ways of structuring both reality and texts also have to be acquired.

Intertextuality has to be mentioned again at this point: every text relates both synchronically and diachronically to other texts, and this is the only way it achieves meaning.

Intentionality relates to the attitude and purpose of text-producers. What do they want and intend with the text? Accordingly, talking in one's sleep would not count as a text, whereas a telephone directory would.

Acceptability is the mirror of *intentionality*. A text must be recognized as such by recipients in a particular situation (*dialogicality* of texts, implying that every text necessarily addresses an audience, is thus by nature dialogic; for example Bakhtin 1982). This criterion is related to conventionality. Acceptability therefore concerns the degree to which hearers and readers are prepared to expect and understand a text that is useful or relevant. Acceptability is therefore context-dependent (see below).

Informativity refers to the quantity of new or expected information in a text. This also addresses the quality of what is offered: how is the new material structured, and using what cohesive means?

Situationality means that the talk-constellation and speech situation play an important role in text production. Only particular varieties or types of text, speech styles or forms of address are both situational and culturally appropriate.

An additional important feature of all definitions of text is expressed in the seven text criteria: the first two criteria (cohesion and coherence) might be viewed as text-*internal*, whereas the remaining criteria are text-*external*. In this way a first distinction may be made between traditional *text linguistics* and *discourse analysis*. In those approaches which are purely *text linguistic* in orientation, the investigation and modelling of cohesion and coherence are predominant (text-grammar); all the text-external factors, in the sense of intervening variables, are in the background. In DS, however, it is precisely these external factors that play an essential role, and texts (that is cohesion and coherence phenomena) are viewed as a manifestation and result of particular combinations of factors. Recent approaches emphasize the functional aspect (Renkema 2004).

Comment: Text criteria

Unlike de Beaugrande and Dressler (1981), I believe that these criteria concern different textual dimensions and should therefore not be considered equally important. Cohesion and coherence should be characterized as constitutive of texts: every text must satisfy these two criteria, independently of co-text and context (see below).

However, *intentionality, informativity, acceptability* and *situationality* are context-dependent. *Intertextuality*, for example, is directly related to the assumption that every text is embedded in a context and is synchronically and diachronically related to many other texts (see the section 'Context' below).

> A linguistic text analysis is therefore defined by its focus on cohesion and coherence, unlike other (sociological) methods of text analysis that select only a few instances of one of these two dimensions. Classical content analysis for example restricts itself to the level of the lexicon (that is to one dimension of semantics). The focus is therefore on the semantic level. Syntax is used merely to support the selection of units of analysis. A linguistic text analysis, however, incorporates syntactic, semantic and pragmatic levels. Most of the sociological methods, on the other hand, stay with only one of these semiotic categories.

Context

The concept of *context* has been associated with text linguistics, pragmatics, sociolinguistics and DA for a considerable time (see de Beaugrande and Dressler 1981; Cicourel 1992; Duranti and Goodwin 1992; Wodak 1996; 2000a). By contrast, Noam Chomsky restricted his examples in the field of generative grammar to context-free individual sentences; *context* was seen as a quasi-wastebasket consisting of unsystematic, unpredictable factors (Chomsky 1965).

In the early days of sociolinguistics, however, context was initially defined in terms of sociological variables such as age, sex, class and so on, and linguistic units were statistically correlated with these variables.

Pragmatics, on the other hand, did investigate speakers, hearers and the communicative setting, but in such microlinguistic examinations other contextual factors were often ignored. This is despite the concepts of presupposition (that is assumed knowledge) and implicature (implied assumptions) requiring significant theoretical assumptions about context (see Titscher *et al.* 2000).

Conversation analysis (CA), particularly in the debates between Schegloff/Wetherell and Billig (*Discourse and Society* 1998), takes account of only those nonverbal contexts which can be explicitly deduced from the sequence under investigation (see Schegloff 1998). Everything else is discounted as speculative and purely interpretative.

Recent theoretical approaches, for example that of Teun van Dijk (2001, 2005), see context in cognitive terms, and assume 'context models' which lead to the recognition and knowledge of contextual information. As such, in the course of our socialization we acquire the necessary knowledge to interpret, understand and remember language behaviour, at least in our own culture(s). Van Dijk further claims that it is possible to describe these 'context models' only in terms of a theory of 'knowledge'. He has not yet detailed how such a theory is constructed. This kind of knowledge and these kinds of contextual models can be based only on implicit or explicit theories which draw on related disciplines, by means of integrative interdisciplinarity (see Weiss and Wodak 2003). In a given case (or text sequence), we have to draw on this theoretical background to construct our interpretation and analysis coherently and transparently. If we encounter an unfamiliar situation, we have first to find out more about it and establish the rules and norms – otherwise we might misunderstand a great deal. We also have to be able to evaluate contexts, or else we might miss incorrect or inappropriate linguistic behaviour. For example, a defendant in a trial may, according to the norms of our courts, answer a judge, but may not ask questions.

The concept of 'context' is thus an inherent part of DA and contributes significantly to how systematically it can be applied as part of interdisciplinary approaches (see Wodak and Weiss 2004). In the course of investigating complex social problems it is necessary to draw on multiple theoretical approaches to analyze given contexts and relate these to texts. To make this possible in a meaningful way, decisions must be made about the theoretical foundations and interdisciplinarity of discourse analysis. In other words, whether 'context' is included in linguistic analysis and the definition of 'context' are dependent on prior theoretical decisions. It is not possible to go into further detail about these decisions here, but see Wodak and Weiss (2004). In any case, context is a central concept in our discourse analysis approach.

Let me illustrate these claims with some brief instances, beginning with Example 1.1; I claim that many instances of everyday conversation need a lot of background information to be understood. When we return home from a holiday, we often do not understand TV or radio news items. The intertextuality is missing and we can not update our information.

EXAMPLE 1.1

In the election campaign by the Austrian Freedom Party (FPÖ) – a right-wing populist party close to Le Pen's party in France – in September 1999, a poster was displayed in Vienna bearing the slogan 'Two real Austrians'. It also showed Jörg Haider, the then leader of the FPÖ, and the then vice-president of the Freedom Party, Thomas Prinzhorn, who was the principal candidate in the election and became the vice-president of the Austrian parliament until 2006. How should such a slogan be understood? Discourse analysts need theories and methodologies to be able to analyze such texts. In this case, many factors are relevant, such as the election campaign and the ongoing discussion about who might be defined as a 'real' Austrian or as a foreigner, which touches on a presupposed and ideologically constructed Germanic–Aryan chauvinistic tradition of German-speaking Austrians; moreover, this poster alludes to an incident that happened many years ago (1970) in which a similar slogan was used by the Austrian People's Party against the then chancellor of the Social-Democratic Party, Bruno Kreisky, who was defined as a 'not-real' Austrian, because he was of Austrian-Jewish origin.

A more pragmatic approach, like that of Nicos Mouzelis, seems suitable for the analysis of such multilingual meanings. In his recent book *Sociological Theory: What Went Wrong?* (1995), Mouzelis introduces the idea of 'conceptual pragmatism' as a possible way out of the theory crisis in the social

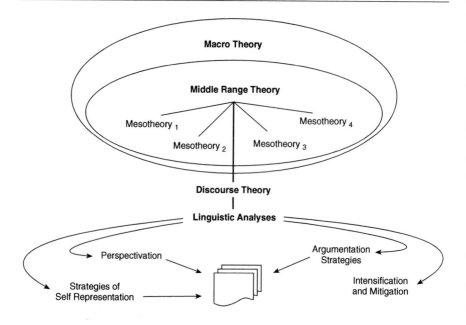

Figure 1.1   Levels of theories and linguistic analysis

sciences. According to Mouzelis, social theory 'has as its major task to clarify conceptual tools and to construct new ones by following criteria of utility rather than truth' (1995:9). Such a pragmatic approach to theory does not purport to provide a catalogue of context-free propositions and generalizations, but rather relates questions of theory formation and conceptualization closely to the specific problems to be investigated. In this sense, the first question we have to address as researchers is not whether we need a grand theory but rather which conceptual tools are relevant for a given problem and context. Although the former question might invite exciting speculations, it leads away from problem-oriented science.

One methodical way for discourse analysts to minimize the risk of critical bias is to follow the principle of *triangulation* (Cicourel 1969). One of the most salient features of the *discourse-historical approach* (which is illustrated with reference to specific genres in Chapters 4, 5 and 8 of this volume; see also Wodak 2001, 2004), for example, is its endeavour to work interdisciplinarily, multimethodically and on the basis of a variety of different empirical data. Depending on the object of investigation, it attempts to transcend the purely linguistic dimension and to include more or less systematically the historical, political, sociological and/or psychological dimensions in the analysis and interpretation of a specific discursive event. Thus, the triangulatory approach is based on a concept of *context* which takes into account four levels (see also Figure 1.1):

1. the immediate, language or text internal co-text;
2. the intertextual and interdiscursive relationship between utterances, texts, genres and discourses;
3. the extralinguistic social/sociological variables and institutional frames of a specific *context of situation* (middle-range theories);
4. the broader socio-political and historical contexts, to which the discursive practices are embedded in and related (macro theories).

In Examples 1.2 and 1.3, I will illustrate each level of context and make the required steps for a sequential analysis transparent.

EXAMPLE 1.2   Identifying different layers of context

To illustrate this context-dependent approach, I would like to discuss some of the many layers of discourse investigated in the study of the *Waldheim Affair*. The background is that during the Austrian presidential election in 1986, Kurt Waldheim at first denied active involvement with Nazism and Nazi military operations in the Balkans (the German Army – the *Wehrmacht* – was heavily involved in war crimes in the Balkans during the second World War, and was also found guilty of supporting the deportation of over 60,000 Jews from Thessaloniki, Greece, to extermination camps in Poland; see Heer *et al.* 2003, 2008). The data were collected every day during the whole election campaign, covering the three months from 3 March 1986 to 6 June 1986.[7]

- There were documents of the Wehrmacht about the war in the Balkans in general, as well as documents relating specifically to Waldheim's activities there.
- There were also several statements by and interviews with other Wehrmacht veterans who had served with Waldheim.
- One step removed from these was the research by historians on the Balkan war in general, and on Waldheim's wartime role specifically.
- At still another level there were the reports in Austrian newspapers on the Balkan war, on Waldheim's past and on the historical research into war and Waldheim's role.
- There were reports in newspapers on Waldheim's own explanation of his past; on the other hand there was the reporting of all these previously mentioned aspects in foreign newspapers, especially in the *New York Times*.
- Simultaneously, the press releases and documents of the World Jewish Congress provided an autonomous informational and discursive source.
- Finally, apart from these, there were statements of and interviews with politicians, as well as the *vox populi* on all these topics.

Though sometimes tedious and very time-consuming, such an approach made it possible to record the varying perceptions, selections and distortions of information, that is the *recontextualization* of anti-Semitic *topoi*.[8] As a result, we were able to trace in detail the constitution of an anti-Semitic stereotyped image, or *Feindbild*, of 'the others', which emerged in the public discourse of Austria in 1986.

EXAMPLE 1.3   Analyzing different layers of context

The linguistic analysis of pragmatic devices in a particular setting, in the aforementioned case, which involved political discourse expressing anti-Semitic prejudice (speeches and media) during the *Waldheim Affair* of 1986,[9] would thus have to draw on a range of analytical tools selected for that specific purpose. In the concrete case I am addressing here, the following procedures and stages lend themselves to an explicit analysis:

- *Historical analysis* of anti-Semitism and its verbal expressions (that is 'coded language').
- *Socio-cognitive analysis* of collective memories and frames guiding the acquisition of specific Knowledge to be able to understand the 'coded language'.
- *Socio-political analysis* of the election campaign, the ongoing debates and the political parties taking part – these two dimensions forming the *broader context.*
- *Genre theory;* the functions of political speeches (persuasive strategies, positive
- Self-presentation/negative other-presentation and so on).
- The *setting,* speakers and so on of the concrete utterances; this is the more *narrow context.*
- The *co-text* of each utterance.
- Finally, the verbal expressions have to be analyzed with regard to *linguistic pragmatic/*grammatical approaches (presuppositions; insinuations; implicatures; and so on as relevant characteristics of the specific 'coded anti-Semitism' in postwar Austria).

Such linguistic devices (in this case) are embedded in *discursive macrostrategies* of *positive self* and *negative other presentation;* these strategies employ various other linguistic features, rhetorical tropes and argumentation/legitimization patterns. In our case, moreover, we have to contextualize this election campaign against other discourses on how to cope with the Nazi past, on Jews, minorities and other marginalized groups in Austria to be able to grasp the interdiscursivity, intertextuality and recontextualization of certain[10] and arguments throughout many genres and public spheres[11].

Genre

A *genre* may be characterized, following Norman Fairclough, as the conventionalized, more or less schematically fixed use of language associated with a particular activity, as 'a socially ratified [RW: that is socially accepted] way of using language in connection with a particular type of social activity' (Fairclough 1995:14).

Corbett (2006:26ff.) presents the scholarly history of research on *genre,* beginning with Aristotle (*Poetics,* chapter 6) up to literary studies as exemplified by William Hazlitt in his *Lectures on the English Poets* (1933 [1818]). Russian Formalists (Propp 1968; and later Bakhtin 1986) elaborated notions of genre. Most recently, functional systemic linguistics, studies on language in the professions, DS and applied linguistics have extensively discussed the concept of genre.[12]

Aristotle and two thousand years later Hazlitt were concerned with the structure of tragedies; the segmentation into plots, characters, diction, thought, spectacle and song. Propp, in the early 1920s, focused, by contrast, on functions: the constitutive functions to be fulfilled by any story or narrative, an early *actor analysis* (van Leeuwen 1996). Bahktin (1952–3 [1986]:60; cited in Corbett 2006:27) defines genre in the following way:

> Each separate utterance is individual, of course, but each sphere in which language is used develops its own *relatively stable types* of these utterances. These we may call *speech genres*.

In functional systemic linguistics, Gunter Kress (1985:19) argues that – as most situations are conventional and rule-governed – they produce texts that have to be regarded as 'generic':

> The social occasions of which texts are a part have a fundamentally important effect on texts . . . The situations are always conventional . . . They range from entirely formulaic and ritualized occasions, such as royal weddings, sporting encounters, committee meetings, to family rituals such as breakfasts or barbecues or fights over who is to do the dishes. Other, probably fewer occasions are less ritualized, less formulaic; casual conversations may be an example.

John Swales's (1990) theoretical approach is quite similar to that of Kress. He also takes situations and their conventions as a starting-point, and proposes the concept of *discourse community* as constitutive for the use and creation of genres. Discourse communities are defined inter alia through a broadly agreed set of common public goals, through mechanisms of intercommunication among its members; through their own genres; through their own lexis; and through a suitable degree of relevant content and discursive expertise (see also Corbett 2006:29). Hence, each peer-group or subgroup will develop their own goals, their own styles, their own genres and their own values. Such a definition relates well with scientific communities, their journals, their publication rules, their writing requests, professional lexicon and terminology, and their argumentation devices. David Barton (1994) elaborates Swales's approach and integrates the notion of discourse communities into literacy studies.

In sociolinguistics, Labov and Waletzky (1967) have also – building on Propp and on literary studies – detected the most common structure of oral narratives while analyzing stories in interviews with their informants. This seminal article has certainly influenced both sociolinguistics and DS ever since.

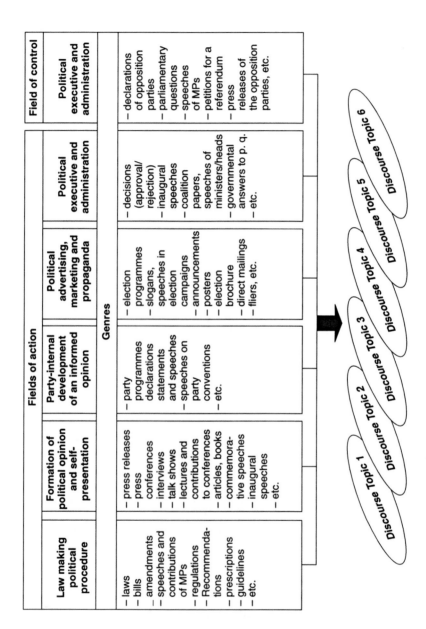

Fields of action					Field of control
Law making political procedure	Formation of political opinion and self-presentation	Party-internal development of an informed opinion	Political advertising, marketing and propaganda	Political executive and administration	Political executive and administration
		Genres			
– laws – bills – amendments – speeches and contributions of MPs – Recommenda-tions – regulations – prescriptions – guidelines – etc.	– press releases – press conferences – interviews – talk shows – lectures and contributions to conferences – articles, books – commemora-tive speeches – inaugural speeches – etc.	– party programmes – declarations statements and speeches on party conventions – etc.	– election programmes – slogans, speeches in election campaigns – announcements – posters – election brochure – direct mailings – fliers, etc.	– decisions (approval/rejection) – inaugural speeches – coalition papers, speeches of ministers/heads – governmental answers to p. q. – etc.	– declarations of opposition parties – parliamentary questions – speeches of MPs – petitions for a referendum – press releases of the opposition parties, etc.

Discourse Topic 1 Discourse Topic 2 Discourse Topic 3 Discourse Topic 4 Discourse Topic 5 Discourse Topic 6

Figure I.2 Selected dimensions of discourse as social practice

Basically, they deconstruct each story into orientation (the introduction), exposition (introducing events), culmination (the *point* of the story – the surprising occurrence) and the coda (the morale as the summary of the story). This structure has, of course, been elaborated in many studies; but the basic story line seems to fit many spontaneous and fictional narratives (see Schiffrin 1994).

In sum, we can observe a move from inherent textual characteristics, through a more functional approach, to, finally, an approach focused on social practices, conventions, rules and norms governing certain sets or groups of speakers and hearers (viewers/listeners).

A proposal, for example a policy paper on combating unemployment, is a manifestation of certain rules and expectations according to social conventions. The proposal itself follows certain textual devices, the contents follow certain ideological concepts put forward by a specific political group (like the trade unions) (see Wodak 2000b).

Fields of action (Girnth 1996), taking Pierre Bourdieu's notion of *field* as a starting-point, may be understood as segments of the respective societal *reality*, which contribute to constituting and shaping the *frame* of a discourse. Thus for example in the area of political action we distinguish between the *functions* of legislation, self-presentation, the manufacturing of public opinion, developing party-internal consent, advertising and vote-getting, governing as well as executing, and controlling as well as expressing (oppositional) dissent (see Figure 1.2).

Hence, a discourse about a specific topic (un/employment) can find its starting-point within one field of action and proceed through another one. Discourses and discourse topics *spread* to different fields and discourses. They cross between fields, overlap, refer to each other or are in some other way socio-functionally linked with each other. We can represent the relationship between fields of action, genres and discourse topics with the example of the field of politics.

Each genre which relates to one of the macrofunctions defined above thus follows conventions defined culturally and politically (see Example 1.4).

EXAMPLE 1.4   Identifying genres in a debate on language policies

Which genres are we dealing with when analyzing debates on *language policies?* Debates about languages or language policies occur in very different settings. Politicians rarely mention language (language choices; linguistic choices) or language policies/politics in their speeches (see de Cillia and Wodak 2006); however written policy papers of various kinds (treaties, constitutions, proposals, declarations, and so on) sometimes contain statements on language policies.

In parliamentary resolutions, for example, policies and proposals are stated in a declarative mode; in the constitution, we are dealing with legal language; in speeches, politicians use persuasive rhetoric to convince their audience of certain measures, justify some and reject others. Specific rhetorical tropes and figures are thus preferred, as well as strategies of argumentation, which are typical for political discourse. Finally, in spontaneous conversations, in semi-private publics, pragmatic and linguistic rules of dialogue/conversation prevail.[13]

If we, on the other hand, experimentally elicit certain language data which relate to the macrotopic 'language policies/language politics', then we deal with interviews (semi-structured, narrative, standardized), questionnaires (with open and closed questions), focus groups (on video and on tape), tests and so on (see Wodak 2005c).

(a) Legal and other official genres
In analyzing some of the aforementioned genres while focusing on the arguments for and against specific language policies, it makes sense to start by analyzing the policy papers and existing legal framework in the European Union.

In a declaration by the European parliament (*European Parliament Resolution 28.10. 1988, AI-0218/88 OOJC 326p282–9*) some of the most important policies in respect to language are summarized:

> 22. [The European parliament] [c]onsiders it essential for the European cultural identity that the specific regional characteristics existing within each Member State be given scope for expression, by making the most of their specific characteristics and thus respecting the interests, aspirations and linguistic and cultural heritage of each region; and by facilitating trans frontier or interregional linguistic and cultural cooperation in the case of linguistic and cultural heritages which extend beyond existing administrative divisions.

The *genre of a parliamentary resolution* is characterized by the declarative mode; however, there should be enough room for each region (in this case) to implement the resolution according to its specificities. Thus, we are confronted with vagueness in this text, which is expressed in abstract terms, nominalizations and many positively connoted, prestigious nouns, such as 'aspirations, cultural heritage, cultural cooperation' and evaluative verbs, such as 'respecting, facilitating'. These nouns define general phenomena, which would need to be specified. They are 'grammatical metaphors' in Halliday's sense (Halliday 1994): actions are transformed and substituted by nouns, thus agents are deleted. The most important part of the resolution is to be found in the last clause: linguistic and cultural boundaries are seen as more important then administrative boundaries. These linguistic features, analyzed in a functional systemic way, are typical for this genre. The text is not argumentative; the main proposal is not justified or accounted for, contrasting positions are not presented here. This resolution is, of course, the end of a textual chain, a recontextualization of many debates, which has been acclaimed and accepted (see Wodak 2000b).[14]

Looking at a second genre, *political speeches*, we are surprised that language policies are rarely mentioned on the European level (see de Cillia 2003; Wodak 2003a). However, they are manifested in the speeches of national and regional politicians. This is not surprising when we conside the context of national identity and the role of language in nation states (Wodak *et al.* 1999; Ricento 2003). When analyzing speeches of politicians, traditional rhetoric suggests itself, in combination with argumentation theory (see Reisigl 2004).

A third genre is *media texts.* Newspapers recontextualize the arguments which politicians have put forward. The selection of quotes, reported speech, gives new meanings to the arguments, which are written/talked about. A comparison of *topoi* and arguments in these three genres becomes possible. Which arguments and with what frequency are used, when and where, by whom? How are they realized linguistically? Which *topoi* are selected to underline the persuasiveness of certain argumentation modes?

(b) Focus group debates: semi-public genres
It is important to investigate other public spaces and settings, where more spontaneous debates occur (see above). On the one hand, *TV debates* are an obvious option, because invited speakers tend to get involved in a debate; on the other hand, *focus group discussions* could be set up to explore certain groups of the population and to trigger topic-oriented discussions (see Chapter 8). In both cases, the moderator of the discussion is the most influential person because s/he determines the macrotopics, and is allowed to interrupt and to start or end interventions. S/he is also allowed to give away turns. Of course, depending on the specific media event, the rules can be more or less restrictive (see Myers 2004; Wodak 2005c).

Discussions or debates are conversations or face-to-face interactions. The organization of conversation follows certain rules which conversation analysis as well as pragmatics have successfully described and precisely categorized over the last few decades. In such cases, the selection of methods depends on the specific research question.

Most importantly, linguists view the whole discussion as one text. The single turns depend on each other, conflicts evolve throughout the development of the whole debate, and group dynamics play a decisive role. The first important step in analyzing such discussions or debates, after having transcribed the video or tape, might be an attempt to lay out a *semantic network* (see Figure 1.3). Such a semantic network heuristically grasps the flow of topics in a conversation and the influence of certain speakers (for details see Benke 2003; Kovács and Wodak 2003).

The semantic network describes the thematic connections made in the discussion of a focus group, consisting of four Viennese families (comprising different generations), who are discussing security problems and Austrian neutrality. While constructing the networks according to the macrotopics mentioned and constructed and their relationships with each other, we analyzed the transcripts sequentially and noted various topics and their argumentative development. For each topic (of sufficient relevance and importance) identified, we introduced a new node and drew lines showing the discursive connections (links) between the existing topics. ATLAS.ti provides certain predefined relationships, but in principle it is possible to define further relationships if necessary. Such a diagram enables the researcher to formulate initial hypotheses about the dynamics of the interaction and the flow of arguments. Of course, it would be possible to analyze a whole set of linguistic features in detail in the debates we illustrate elsewhere in this book (for more analytic details of semantic networks see Benke 2003).

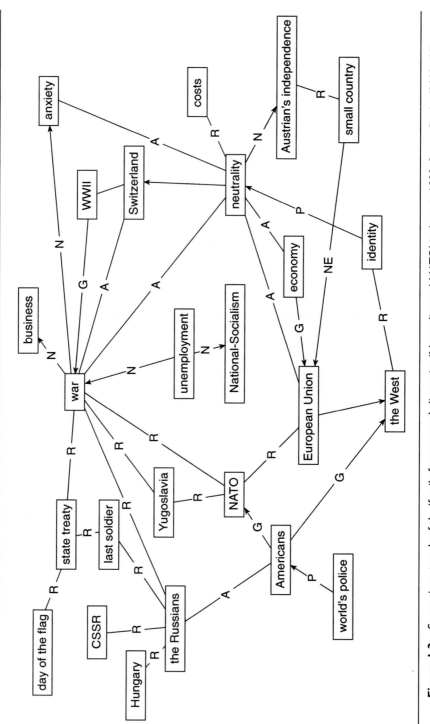

Figure 1.3 Semantic network of the 'family focus group', discussing 'Neutrality and NATO' in Austria 1998. *Source:* Benke (2003:403)

Outline of the volume

Before briefly presenting the outline of this volume, I would like to emphasize what the above introductory remarks clearly illustrate: that all the concepts and terms discussed are defined differently in the large number of approaches to DA. Thus, it is important to be very precise when attempting an analysis; to define one's concepts and to provide working definitions; to be aware of the epistemological background of each approach which one might employ; and to consider carefully whether the framework selected makes sense in relation to both the data being investigated and the theoretical claims and research questions which necessarily guide every analysis.

The volume starts out with a first part on methods of analyzing very common and also traditional genres: press reporting, diverse new media genres (for example email or text messages), broadcast political debates, TV documentaries and political rhetoric.

Gerlinde Mautner (Chapter 2) focuses on the use of print media as a data source in social science projects. First, she investigates and discusses different types of print media, and why they are of interest to those engaged in social enquiry. Second, she turns to newspapers and magazines, in order to consider their particular role in changing media landscapes, as well as how they are produced and read. Moreover, she summarizes the practicalities of developing research designs and collecting the texts to be studied. Finally, key components of a basic analytical toolkit are laid out, drawing on the traditions of both critical discourse analysis (CDA) and corpus linguistics. The latter perspective allows the combination of both qualitative and quantitative methods and methodologies when analyzing press reports.

In Chapter 3, Helmut Gruber deals with communication in the new media by discussing why it is interesting and relevant for social scientists to investigate 'new' communicative forms such as email, chat or text messaging. The chapter first provides a theoretically informed view on the interplay of media and forms of communication (defined as configurations of certain technical and situational features). Then, issues such as, for example, how to compile a corpus of new media texts and which ethical aspects to consider are addressed in detail. Further, a sample pilot research project is undertaken in which readers are able to trace the process of analyzing key features of email texts. That second part of the chapter also provides an overview of relevant textual and discursive characteristics of new media text genres and the ways in which those genres are/should be investigated and analyzed.

The next chapter, by Alexander Pollak (Chapter 4), functions as guide to the analysis of television documentaries. Focusing on the genre of historical documentaries, a five-step approach towards a meaningful analysis of documentaries is developed and the question of how representations are discursively constructed through TV documentary films is addressed. In this context, the chapter deals with questions of authenticity and truth – questions that always accompany the perception of the documentary genre – a genre growing in importance in its function of providing more information than short news items. Finally, the chapter will also discuss problematic aspects related to the analysis of audiovisual material.

Following this, Chapter 5 focuses on political rhetoric, analyzing speeches and other genres from the field of politics – a field much investigated across the disciplines, but often enough without any adequate tools. In the chapter Martin Reisigl focuses particularly on right-wing populist rhetoric as an example and case-study. Reisigl rightly claims that both political scientists interested in issues of language and linguists or rhetoricians interested in political issues have only rarely analyzed political rhetoric in detail. Consequently, studies in linguistics or rhetoric and political science have frequently been amateurish with respect to their use of theory, methods and methodology. In this chapter, it is illustrated that a remedy for the many shortcomings in this area can be found in a transdisciplinary, 'politolinguistic' approach that connects rhetoric, critical discourse analysis and concepts in political science.

Finally, in this first part of the volume we have included a chapter – Chapter 6 – which focuses on the broadcast political debates, such as those that are a regular part of presidential elections in the United States. As Greg Myers shows in that chapter, broadcast political debates have so far been heavily studied in terms of their content, rhetorical appeals, format and so on, and he argues for an approach that focuses on the interactions in the debates between the candidates, audiences and moderator, considering questions and answers, address, quotation, timing and tone. He uses an analysis of one debate to place this genre in a wider context of broadcast genres in political campaign discourse.

The next part of the volume turns to three distinct methodologies frequently applied in the social sciences but rarely analyzed in detail as communicative interactions: interviews, ethnography and focus groups. These contributions attempt to close this gap – namely that between employing a methodology in naïve ways without taking their interactive features into account, and the often very detailed linguistic analyzes which neglect methodological aims and accompanying social structures.

Jackie Abell and Greg Myers (Chapter 7) illustrate in which ways interviews could be analyzed in a much more fruitful and stimulating manner when approaching them from a discourse-analytical perspective. Interview transcripts are often treated as quarries for carefully excavated chunks of telling quotation. But interviews can also be analyzed in detail as interactions in which interviewer and interviewee respond to one another, collaboratively shaping the topic, doing face-work, using arguments, telling narratives and shifting the frame of the encounter. Discourse analysis has been used in such fields as sociology, social psychology, anthropology, cultural studies and oral history, as well as linguistics; the different disciplines share some approaches, but have different emphases on ordering of social interaction, construction of versions of reality, methodology of social research and the ethical and episte-mological issues raised by interviews. The chapter offers an overview based on the four levels of context in which a given utterance might be analyzed (see above): the co-text (the rest of that interview), the intertextual links (including reported speech and topoi), the context of situation (all the conditions of par-ticipants, setting and genre surrounding the event) and the historical and socio-political conditions in which the event takes place.

As Michał Krzyżanowski (Chapter 8) is able to demonstrate in detail in his chapter, *focus groups* have recently become one of the key methods of qualita-tive exploration in the social sciences. Focus groups have been used for different purposes in a variety of (disciplinary and interdisciplinary) research settings, and depending on those purposes may be defined in a variety of ways. Nonetheless, there are several core definitions of focus groups which, pointing to their main advantages and virtues, describe the actual 'what' of the focus group research. In contrast to many studies which analyze focus groups purely from the perspec-tive of content analysis, Krzyżanowski proposes a variety of methods which serve to investigate subgenres in focus groups (such as debates, narratives and so forth) from a discourse-analytical point of view. Such detailed and systematic analysis, he claims, achieves more reliable results.

Finally, we turn to the last chapter – Chapter 9, by Florian Oberhuber and Michał Krzyżanowski – on ethnography, which has crossed many discipli-nary boundaries in recent years. Once associated with studies of (the cul-tures of) distant, that is non-European 'others', ethnography has now firm-ly established its place 'at home'. The ethnographic way of looking at the world itself is conceived in terms of 'taking a distance' within day-to-day life and is thus constitutive for the salient choices every empirically oriented scholar has to take when entering a new terrain. Ethnography has also crossed disciplinary boundaries. 'Going into the field' is no longer the exclu-sive property of professional anthropologists. Other disciplines increasingly accommodate and adapt ethnographic methods for their own purposes: sociology, sociolinguistics, discourse studies, education, administrative stud-ies, nursing, cultural studies, social psychology and other disciplines now routinely integrate elements of the ethnographic toolbox into their own approaches and research designs. The focus of this chapter is limited to research on (political, corporate, media, administrative and so on) organiza-tions. This object-field lends itself particularly well for demonstrating how the study of discourse can be enhanced by an ethnographic analysis of par-ticular socio-cultural locales.

Notes

1. See Panagl and Wodak (2004); Van Dijk (2006); Wodak (2006a).
2. See Gee (2003); Reisigl (2004); Wodak (2006b); Blommaert (2005); van Dijk (2007).

3. See van Dijk (1997); Barbour and Kitzinger (1999); Myers and Macnaghten (1999); Schiffrin, Tannen and Hamilton (2001); Wodak and Meyer (2001); Fairclough (2003); Kovács and Wodak (2003); Wodak and Meyer (2003); Renkema (2004); Sanders and Sanders (2006).
4. See Lemke (1999); Wodak and Wright (2006); Kress and Van Leeuwen (2001); Van Leeuwen (2005); Norris (2004).
5. See Fairclough (1992); Ensink and Sauer (2003); Heer *et al.* (2003); Martin and Wodak (2003); Blommaert (2005); Wodak (2005a); Wodak (2005b); Heer *et al.* (2008).
6. See Duranti and Goodwin (1992); Wetherell *et al.* (2001); Howarth (2000); Johnstone (2002); van Dijk (2003); Panagl and Wodak (2004); van Dijk (2005).
7. See de Beaugrande and Dressler (1981); Titscher *et al.* (2000: Chapter 1); Sanders and Sanders (2006:598ff.); Van Dijk (forthcoming) for more extensive discussions.
8. See Wodak *et al.* (1990); Mitten (1992); Wodak (2003a).
9. Within argumentation theory, *topoi* or *loci* can be described as parts of argumentation which belong to default premises which are either explicit or inferable. They are the 'content-related warrants or *conclusion rules* which connect the argument or arguments with the conclusion, the claim. As such, they justify the transition from the argument or arguments to the conclusion' (Kienpointner (1992: 194).
10. See Pelinka and Wodak (2002); Wodak and Pelinka (2002); Wodak and Reisigl (2002).
11. See note 9.
12. See Reisigl and Wodak (2001); Wodak (2001, 2004a) for precise definitions of these concepts which are central to many approaches in CDA. See below for brief definitions and the glossary of specific linguistic terms.
13. See Bazerman (1988); Myers (1990); Swales (1990); Bhatia (1993); Halliday and Martin (1993); Chilton and Schäffner (2002); Gruber and Muntigl (2005); Fairclough (2006).
14. I have not mentioned the specific national/minority/majority language, which is used in a text; the choice of language has a huge impact on linguistic realizations. See Clyne (2003); Bellier (2002) for features of written genres in different languages.
15. Of course, the text analysis could be much more detailed from the point of view of systemic grammar. I have restricted myself to some illustrative points, because the focus of this chapter is on methods in general.

References

Austin, J.L. *How To Do Things With Words*, ed. J.O. Urmson (Oxford: Clarendon, 1962).
Bakhtin, M. *The Dialogic Imagination: Four Essays* (Austin: University of Texas Press, 1982).
Bakhtin, M. *Speech Genres and Other Late Essays* (Austin: University of Texas Press, 1986).
Barbour, R.S. and Kitzinger, J. (eds) *Developing Focus Group Research: Politics, Theory and Practice* (London: Sage, 1999).

Barton, D. *Literacy: An Introduction to the Ecology of Written Language* (Oxford: Blackwell, 1994).

Bazerman, C. *Shaping Written Knowledge: The Genre and Activity of the Experimental Article in Science* (Madison: University of Wisconsin Press, 1988).

Bellier, I. 'European Identity, Institutions and Languages in the Context of the Enlargement', *Journal of Language and Politics* 1(1) (2002), 85–114.

Benke, G. 'Somehow Emotionally – If We Lose Neutrality That Makes Me Afraid', in A. Kovács and R. Wodak (eds) *NATO, Neutrality and National Identity* (Vienna: Böhlau, 2003), pp. 347–407.

Bhatia, V. *Analysing Genre: Language Use in Professional Settings* (London: Longman, 1993).

Blommaert, J. *Discourse: A Critical Introduction* (Cambridge University Press, 2005).

Brown G. and G. Yule *Discourse Analysis* (Cambridge University Press, 1973).

Chilton, P. and Schäffner, C. (eds) *Politics as Text and Talk: Analytic Approaches to Political Discourse* (Amsterdam: Benjamins, 2002).

Chilton. P. 'Missing Links in Mainstream CDA: Modules, Blends and the Critical Instinct', in R. Wodak and P. Chilton (eds) *A New Research Agenda in Critical Discourse Analysis: Theory and Interdisciplinarity* (Amsterdam: Benjamins, 2005), pp. 19–51.

Chomsky, N. *Aspects of the Theory of Syntax* (New York: Harper & Row, 1965).

Cicourel, A.V. *Method and Measurement in Sociology* (New York University Press, 1969).

Cicourel, A.V. 'The Interpenetration of Communicative Contexts: Examples from Medical Encounters', in A. Duranti and C. Goodwin (eds) *Rethinking Context: Language as an Interactive Phenomenon* (Cambridge University Press, 1992), pp. 291–310.

Clyne, M. 'Towards Intercultural Communication in Europe without Linguistic Homogenisation', in R. de Cillia, H.J. Krumm and R. Wodak (eds) *Die Kosten der Mehrsprachigkeit – Globalisierung und sprachliche Vielfalt* (Vienna: ÖAW, 2003), pp. 39–47.

Corbett, J. 'Genre and Genre Analysis', in K. Brown (ed.) *Encyclopaedia of Language and Linguistics*, vol. 5 (Amsterdam: Elsevier, 2006), pp. 26–32.

de Beaugrande, R. and Dressler, W.U. *Introduction to Text Linguistics* (London: Longman, 1981).

de Cillia, R. 'Grundlagen und Tendenzen der europäischen Sprachenpolitik', in M. Mokre, G. Weiss and R. Bauböck (eds) *Europas Identitäten: Mythen, Konflikte, Konstruktionen* (Frankfurt am Main: Campus, 2003), pp. 231–56.

de Cillia, R. and R. Wodak. *Ist Österreich ein 'deutsches' Land? Sprachenpolitik und Identität in der Zweiten Republik* (Innsbruck: Studien Verlag, 2006).

Discourse and Society 9(3 and 4)(1998), 307–570.

Duranti, A. and Goodwin, C.(eds) *Rethinking Context: Language as an Interactive Phenomenon* (Cambridge University Press, 1992).

Ehlich, K. 'Diskurs', in H. Glück (ed.) *Metzler Lexikon Sprache* (Stuttgart: Metzler, 2000), pp. 162–3.

Ensink, T. and Sauer, C. (eds) *Framing and Perspectivising in Discourse* (Amsterdam: Benjamins, 2003).

Fairclough, N. *Discourse and Social Change* (Cambridge: Polity, 1992).

Fairclough, N. *Critical Discourse Analysis* (London: Longman, 1995).

Fairclough, N. *Analysing Discourse: Textual Analysis for Social Research* (London: Routledge, 2003).

Fairclough, N. 'Genres in Political Discourse', in K. Brown (ed.) *Encyclopaedia of Language and Linguistics*, vol. 5 (Amsterdam : Elsevier, 2006), pp. 32–8.

Foucault, M. 'The Order of Discourse', in M.J. Shapiro (ed.) *Language and Politics* (Oxford: Blackwell, 1984), pp. 108–38.

Gee, J.P. *An Introduction to Discourse Analysis: Theory and Method* (London: Routledge, 2003).

Girnth, H. 'Texte im politischen Diskurs. Ein Vorschlag zur diskursorientierten Beschreibung von Textsorten', *Muttersprache* 1 (1996), 66–80.

Graesser, A.C., Millis, K.K. and Zwaan, R.A. 'Discourse Comprehension', *Annual Review of Psychology* 48 (1997), 163–89.

Gruber, H. and Muntigl., P. *Approaches to Genre* (special issue of *Folia Linguistica*) (Berlin: de Gruyter, 2005).

Habermas, J. *The Theory of Communicative Action* (London: Beacon, 1981).

Halliday, M.A.K. *An Introduction to Functional Grammar* (London: Arnold, 1994).

Halliday, M.A.K. and Martin., J.R. *Writing Science: Literacy as Discursive Power* (London: Falmer, 1993).

Halliday, M.A.K. *Language as Social Semiotic* (London: Arnold, 1978).

Hazlitt, W. *Lectures on the English Poets* (Oxford University Press, 1933 [1818]).

Heer, H., Manoschek, W. Pollak, A. and Wodak, R. (eds) *Wie Geschichte gemacht wird. Zur Konstruktion von Erinnerungen an Wehrmacht und Zweiten Weltkrieg* (Vienna: Czernin, 2003)

Heer, H., Manoschek, W. Pollak, A. and Wodak, R. (eds) *The Discursive Construction of History: Remembering the Wehrmacht's War of Annihilation*, revised edn; English translation by S. Fligelstone (Basingstoke: Palgrave Macmillan, 2008).

Howarth, D. *Discourse* (Buckingham: Open University Press, 2000).

Johnstone, B. *Discourse analysis* (Malden, MA: Blackwell, 2002).

Kienpointner, M. *Alltagslogik: Struktur und Funktion von Argumentationsmustern* (Stuttgart: Frommann-Holzboog, 1992).

Kovács, A. and Wodak, R. (eds) *NATO, Neutrality and National Identity* (Vienna: Böhlau, 2003)

Kress, G. *Linguistic Processes in Sociocultural Practice* (Geelong: Deakin University Press, 1985).

Kress, G. and van Leeuwen, T. *Multimodal Discourse: The Modes and Media of Contemporary Communication* (London: Arnold, 2001).

Labov, W. and Waletzky, J. 'Narrative Analysis: Oral Versions of Personal Narratives', in J. Helm (ed.) *Essays on the Verbal and Visual Arts: Proceedings of the 1966 Annual Spring Meeting of the American Ethnological Society* (Seattle: University of Washington Press, 1967), pp. 12–44.

Lemke, J. *Textual Politics: Discourse and Social Dynamics* (London: Taylor & Francis, 1995).

Lemke, J. 'Typological and Topological Meaning in Diagnostic Discourse', *Discourse Processes* 27 (2) (1999), 173–85.

Maas, U. *Sprachpolitik und politische Sprachwissenschaft: Fünf Studien* (Frankfurt am Main: Suhrkamp, 1989)

Martin, J.R. and Wodak, R. (eds) *Re/Reading the Past: Critical and Functional Perspectives on Time and Value* (Amsterdam: Benjamins, 2003).

Mitten, R. *The Politics of Antisemitic Prejudice: The Waldheim Phenomenon in Austria* (Boulder, CO: Westview, 1992).

Mouzelis, N. *Sociological Theory: What Went Wrong? Diagnosis and Remedies* (London: Routledge, 1995)

Myers, G. *Writing Biology: Texts in the Social Construction of Scientific Knowledge Science and Literature Series* (Madison: University of Wisconsin Press, 1990).

Myers, G. *Matters of Opinion: Talking about Public Issues* (Cambridge University Press, 2004).

Myers, G. and Macnaghten, P. 'Can Focus Groups Be Analysed as Talk?', in R.S. Barbour and J. Kitzinger (eds) *Developing Focus Group Research: Theory and Practice* (London: Sage, 1999), pp.173–85.

Norris, S. *Analysing Multimodal Interaction: A Methodological Framework* (London: Routledge, 2004).

Panagl, O. and Wodak, R.(eds) *Text und Kontext: Theoriemodelle und methodische Verfahren im transdisziplinären Vergleich* (Würzburg: Königshausen und Neumann, 2004).

Pelinka, A. and Wodak, R. (eds) *'Dreck am Stecken', Politik der Ausgrenzung* (Vienna: Czernin, 2002).

Propp, V. *Morphology of the Folktale* (Austin: University of Texas Press, 1968).

Reisigl, M. 'Wie man eine Nation herbeiredet. Eine diskursanalytische Untersuchung zur sprachlichen Konstruktion österreichischen Nation und österreichischen Identität in politischen Fest- und Gedenkreden', PhD thesis, University of Vienna, 2004.

Reisigl, M. and R. Wodak. *Discourse and Discrimination* (London: Routledge, 2001).

Renkema, J. *Introduction to Discourse Studies* (Amsterdam: Benjamins, 2004).

Ricento, T. ' The Discursive Construction of Americanism', *Discourse and Society* 14(5) (2003), 611–37.

Ricento, T (ed.) *An Intoduction to Language Policy: Theory and Method* (Oxford: Blackwell, 2005).

Sanders, T. and Sanders, J. 'Text and Text Analysis', in K. Brown (ed.) *Encyclopaedia of Language and Linguistics*, vol. 12 (Amsterdam: Elsevier, 2006), pp. 597–607.

Schegloff, M. 'Reply to Wetherell', *Discourse and Society* 9 (3) (1998), 413–16.

Schiffrin, D. *Approaches to Discourse. Language as Social Interaction* (Cambridge, MA: Blackwell, 1994).

Schiffrin, D., Tannen, D. and Hamilton, H.E. *The Handbook of Discourse Analysis* (Oxford: Blackwell, 2001).

Sperber, D. and Wilson, D. *Relevance: Communication and Cognition* (Oxford: Blackwell, 1995).

Swales, J. *Genre Analysis. English in Academic and Research Settings* (Cambridge University Press, 1990).

Titscher, S., Meyer, M. Wodak, R. and Vetter, E. *Methods of Text and Discourse Analysis* (London: Sage, 2000).

Torfing, J. *New Theories of Discourse: Laclau, Mouffe, and Zizek* (Oxford: Blackwell, 1999).

van Dijk, T.A. 'The Future of the Field: Discourse Analysis in the 1990s', *TEXT* 10(1990), 133-156.

van Dijk, T.A. *Discourse Studies. A Multidisciplinary Introduction,* vols. 1 and 2 (London: Sage, 1997).

van Dijk, T.A. 'Multidisciplinary CDA: A Plea for Diversity', in R. Wodak and M. Meyer (eds) *Methods of Critical Discourse Analysis* (London: Sage, 2001), pp. 95–120.

van Dijk. T.A. 'The Discourse–Knowledge Interface', in G. Weiss and R. Wodak (eds) *Critical Discourse Analysis: Theory and Interdisciplinarity* (Basingstoke: Palgrave Macmillan, 2003), pp. 85–109.

van Dijk, T.A. 'Contextual Knowledge Management in Discourse Production. A CDA Perspective', in R. Wodak and P. Chilton (eds) *A New Agenda in (Critical) Discourse Analysis* (Amsterdam: Benjamins, 2005), pp. 71–100.

van Dijk, T.A. 'Introduction: Discourse, Interaction and Cognition', *Discourse Studies* 8 (2006), 5–7.

van Dijk, T.A. 'The Study of Discourse – An Introduction', in T.A. van Dijk (ed.) *Discourse Studies*, Vol. 1 (London: Sage, 2007), pp. xix–xlii.

van Leeuwen, T. 'The Representation of Social Actors', in: C.R. Caldas-Coulthard and M. Coulthard (eds) *Texts and Practices: Readings in Critical Discourse Analysis* (London: Routledge, 1996), pp. 32–70.

van Leeuwen, T. *Introducing Social Semiotics* (London: Routledge, 2005).

Weiss, G., and Wodak, R. (eds) *Critical Discourse Analysis: Theory and Interdisciplinarity* (Basingstoke: Palgrave Macmillan, 2003).

Wetherell, M., Taylor, S. and Yates, S.J. (eds) *Discourse as Data* (London: Sage, 2001)

Wittgenstein, L. *Philosophische Untersuchungen* (Frankfurt am Main: Suhrkamp, 1967).

Wodak, R. *Disorders of Discourse* (London: Longman, 1996).

Wodak, R. 'La Sociolingüística necesita una teoría social? Nuevas perspectivas en el análisis crítico del discurso', *Discurso y Sociedad*. 2(3) (2000a), 123–47.

Wodak, R. 'From Conflict to Consensus: The Co-Construction of a Policy Paper', in P. Muntigl, G. Weiss and R. Wodak *European Union Discourses on Un/employment* (Amsterdam: Benjamins, 2000b), pp. 73–114.

Wodak, R. 'The Discourse-Historical Approach', in R. Wodak and M. Meyer (eds) *Methods of Critical Discourse Analysis* (London: Sage, 2001), pp. 63–95.

Wodak, R. 'Auf der Suche nach europäischen Identitäten: Homogene und/oder multiple sprachliche Identitäten', in R. de Cillia, H.J. Krumm and R. Wodak (eds) *Die Kosten der Mehrsprachigkeit – Globalisierung und sprachliche Vielfalt* (Vienna: ÖAW, 2003a), pp. 125–34.

Wodak, R. 'Discourses of Silence: Anti-Semitic Discourse in Post-War Austria', in L. Thiesmeyer (ed.) *Discourse and Silencing: Representation and the Language of Displacement* (Amsterdam: Benjamins, 2003b), pp. 179–209.

Wodak, R. 'Critical Discourse Analysis', in C. Seale, G. Gobo, J.F. Gubrium and D. Silverman (eds) *Qualitative Research Practice* (London: Sage, 2004), pp. 197–213.

Wodak. R. 'Linguistic Analyses in Language Policies', in T. Ricento (ed.) *An Intoduction to Language Policy: Theory and Method* (Oxford: Blackwell, 2005), pp. 170–93.

Wodak, R. 'Discourse Analysis (Foucault)', in D. Herman, M. Jahn and M.-L. Ryan (eds) *Routledge Encyclopaedia of Narrative Theory* (London: Routledge 2005a), pp. 112–14.

Wodak, R. 'Understanding and Explaining Social Change: "Déjà-Vu" Experiences', *International Journal of Applied Linguistics* 15(2) (2005b), 240–3.

Wodak, R. 'Review Article: Dilemmas of Discourse (Analysis)', *Language in Society* 35 (2006a), 595–611.

Wodak, R. 'Mediation between Discourse and Society – Assessing Cognitive Approaches in CDA', *Discourse and Society* 8(1) (2006b), 179–90.

Wodak, R. and Meyer, M.(eds) *Methods of Critical Discourse Analysis* (London: Sage, 2001).

Wodak, R. and Pelinka, A. (eds) *The Haider Phenomenon in Austria* (New Brunswick, NJ: Transaction Publishers, 2002).

Wodak, R. and Reisigl, M. ' "Wenn einer Ariel heist . . ."': Ein linguistisches Gutachten zur politischen Funktionalisierung antisemitischer Ressentiments in Österreich', in A. Pelinka and R. Wodak (eds) *Dreck am Stecken* (Vienna: Czernin, 2002), pp. 134–72.

Wodak, R. and Meyer, M. (eds) *Métodos de Análisis Crítico del Discurso* (Barcelona: Gedisa, 2003).

Wodak, R. and Weiss, G. 'Möglichkeiten und Grenzen der Diskursanalyse: Konstruktionen europäischer Identitäten', in O. Panagl and R. Wodak (eds) *Text und Kontext: Theoriemodelle und methodische Verfahren im transdisziplinären Vergleich* (Würzburg: Königshausen & Neumann, 2004), pp. 67–85.

Wodak, R. and Wright, S. 'The European Union in Cyberspace: Multilingual Democratic Participation in a Virtual Public Sphere?', *Journal of Language and Politics* 5(2) (2006), 251–75.

Wodak, R., Nowak, P., Pelikan, J., Gruber, H., de Cillia, R. and Mitten, R. *'Wir sind alle unschuldige Täter!' Diskurshistorische Studien zum Nachkriegsantisemitismus* (Frankfurt am Main: Suhrkamp, 1990).

Wodak, R. de Cillia, R., Reisigl, M. and Liebhart, K. *The Discursive Construction of National Identity* (Edinburgh University Press, 1999).

Analyzing Newspapers, Magazines and Other Print Media

Gerlinde Mautner

2

Introduction

This chapter focuses on the use of print media as a data source in social science projects. We look first at different types of print media, and why they are of interest to those engaged in social enquiry. Second, we focus on newspapers and magazines, in order to consider their particular role in the media landscape, as well as how they are produced and read. We then turn to the practicalities of developing research designs and collecting the texts to be studied. Finally, key components of a basic analytical toolkit are laid out, drawing on the traditions of both critical discourse analysis (CDA) and corpus linguistics.[1]

Laying the foundations: what are print media?

Activity

To prepare for this chapter, ask yourself the following questions:

- Which print media are you exposed to regularly?
- Apart from books and magazines, what other printed text can you spot if you take a look around your immediate surroundings? (Try this exercise both at home and while you are walking along a street or sitting in a café.)

Most people are likely to associate 'print media' primarily with books, newspapers and magazines. In fact the range is much wider; print media come, quite literally, in many different shapes and sizes. Before tackling a research project that aims to investigate 'print', it is therefore worth surveying the scene to make sure that in selecting data you make an informed choice. If we take 'print medium' to refer to any medium that uses paper and ink, a more comprehensive (though still not exhaustive) list would look something like this:

- Books
- Newspapers
- Magazines
- Academic journals
- Billboards
- Posters
- Flyers
- Mail order catalogues
- Theatre programmes
- University prospectuses
- Company annual reports[2]
- Restaurant menus and paper placemats with writing on them
- Instruction manuals provided with household appliances, electronic gadgets and the like
- Postcards[3]

If we include print on three-dimensional carriers and also relax the 'paper' criterion, the range becomes wider still and includes, for example, consumer goods packages, signage in public space, on shopfronts and on vehicles, carrier bags, printed T-shirts, bags and merchandising articles with promotional messages (such as mousemats, pens, keyrings and umbrellas). Because the printing process is mechanical, it can be repeated indefinitely at low cost and with little effort, so that the product is no longer unique. Arguably, that is the whole point. The technological, social and political revolution wrought by the printing press was enabled precisely by the twin phenomena of mass production and widespread availability.

While these factors continue to ensure the success of print, the advent of electronic media is certainly having a significant impact. As on so many other levels (spatial, temporal, social) here, too, it is the internet that is the great dissolver of boundaries. It is undoubtedly a medium in its own right, with specific 'affordances' (Lemke 2002), or 'possible actions that the properties of the medium make available to users' (Bucy and Affe 2006: 228). And yet there are numerous links, spillover effects and processes of two-way hybridization between print and the Web. For one thing, there are, as Baker (2006) reminds us, 'many texts which originally began life in written form' (p. 31) but can now be found on websites. In the most straightforward cases, as with self-contained and 'static' pdf documents, what you download is an exact replica of the original paper copy. In other, more complicated cases, such as online newspapers (see Li 2002), the transfer of content from print to Web involves substantial recontextualization (essentially, new intertextual relationships with surrounding material), dynamization (through clickable hypertext links) and upgraded interactivity, for instance through email links and discussion fora (see Rusch 2006). Arguably, what happens in such cases is less a simple 'transfer' than a metamorphosis, resulting not only in manifestly different textualities but also, on the audience's side, in different uses and gratifications (Lin and Salwen 2006). What is more, semiotic conventions originating in electronic discourse have made their way into print. Icons, cursor symbols and pull-down menus are now appearing, for example, in advertisements, flyers and reference works.[4] It is too soon to judge whether this heralds a lasting and substantial colonization of print by the semiotics of the Web, but what such imports do show is that electronic literacies are increasingly being taken for granted.

Why study print media?

In reply to the question 'Why study media language?' Bell (1991) heads his detailed list of reasons with an answer as laconic as it is to the point: 'First, because it is there' (p. 3). This applies equally to print media. Their very ubiquity, coupled with intensity of usage, public attention and political influence, should generate an intrinsic interest among social scientists. In addition, print offers very real practical advantages over other media. It is infinitely easier to collect than audiovisual data and more permanent than most Web material.[5] It is already 'out there', ready to be gathered, and does not require time-consuming transcription before analysis. Also, the observer's paradox is not an issue. Unlike, say, informants' elicited responses or structured interviews, printed material is not in danger of changing just because it is being observed.

Practicalities apart, there are of course cogent substantive reasons for wanting to investigate print media, and in particular newspapers and magazines. One is that the print media, at least of the high-circulation, 'glossy' and professional variety, very much reflect the social mainstream (or *a* mainstream, given that in pluralistic societies there is generally more than one). If you are interested in dominant discourses, rather than dissident or idiosyncratic voices, the major dailies and weeklies are obvious sources to turn to. Another and closely related reason for the value of these media to social research lies in their impact. While it is regarded as axiomatic within the CDA paradigm that *all* discourse is not only socially constituted but also constitutive (Fairclough 1995:55; Phillips and Jørgensen 2002:61), this dialectic is clearly of particular relevance in the case of the mass media, including print. Dissemination to large audiences enhances the constitutive effect of discourse – its power, that is, to shape widely shared constructions of reality. For social scientists, therefore, print media represent a key data source.

Production and consumption

Naturally, patterns of production and reception vary considerably depending on which medium is involved. The questions needed to capture the specifics of each case relate to the following issues:

- The economic, political and legal background.
- The institutional environment in which the print medium is produced.
- Authorship (individual or collaborative).
- The production process, including the use of sources, writing and editing.
- The demographics and lifestyles of the audience (in terms of age, education, social class, preferred leisure activities and so on).
- The audience's literacy practices.[6]

Guided by the factors bulleted here, the researcher can explore the contexts in which individual print media are situated. In the case of news media, for example, there are two main areas that deserve particular attention: news values and news sources. Both concepts are crucial to an appreciation of the fact that between an event and its appearing (or not appearing) in print there lies a chain of selection processes. Selection is conditioned by economic, political, cultural and social structures made evident through institutional practices so highly routinized that the result appears normal and inevitable.

Essentially, news values are factors that make it more likely for events to be considered newsworthy. In their seminal 1965 paper, Galtung and Ruge identified twelve such factors.[7] Although still widely quoted and influential, Galtung and Ruge's taxonomy has since been modified by several authors, including van Dijk (1988:119–24) and Bell (1991:155–60). A recent critique and subsequent revision is Harcup and O'Neill's (2001) set of ten news values – arguably clearer, more up-to-date, more versatile and easier to apply than the original twelve. Harcup and O'Neill's news values are (1) reference to the power elite, (2) celebrity, (3) entertainment, (4) surprise, (5) bad news, (6) good news, (7) magnitude (that is impact), (8) relevance (to the intended audience, that is), (9) follow-up (whatever is already in the news is more likely to be reported on again) and (10) the individual newspaper's agenda.

As far as the sources of news are concerned, journalists draw on information they themselves elicit, and on that which they are offered – by news agencies, in press conferences, press releases, previous stories on the topic and a variety of other documents such as reports and minutes (Bell 1991:56–65).[8] A substantial proportion of the input journalists use comes from organizational sources that have 'organized relationships with the press' (van Dijk 1988:120). If you turn briefly to the two articles reproduced on pages 39–40, you will spot a number of references to such sources, notably government spokespersons, committee reports and 'leaked papers'. Journalists' newsgathering routines thus invariably tilt the balance in favour of powerful élite sources (Bell 1991:59) – news actors, that is, capable of 'pushing their agendas and frames of understanding into the media' (Tuchman 2002:89). 'The result', Fairclough argues, 'is a predominantly establishment view of the world' (1995:49). What discourse analysis aims to do is to show how language is instrumental in constructing this view and to challenge it through deconstruction.

Getting started and engaging with your data

Suppose you, the researcher, were to start on a project with the working title 'Discursive Representations of Shopping in British Monthly Magazines'. The kind of texts that first made you realize that you might be 'on' to something interesting may have been similar to the editor's letter in the British women's magazine *eve*, from which the extract in Example 2.1 is taken.

EXAMPLE 2.1   eve, September 2006, p. 6 (bold print added)

Just as we're getting used to one season's trends, like summer's city shorts, chiffon dresses and jewelled sandals, in come the glittery knits, delicious hide-all-sins woollen coats, and a cornucopia of boots and shoes in rich shades of burgundy, moss green and chocolate brown. Suddenly, **all the clothes we've optimistically bought for the hot weather look old hat compared to the glory of the new winter collections.** That's why we can't wait to show you the very best of the new fashion trends while you're still lying on the beach, Solero in hand.

In this month's 80-page fashion special, you'll find the new trends that work for real women (the grey over-the-knee pop socks **went straight into the bin),** the most luxurious designer buys and **the high-street must-haves** that'll give you the look without the price tag . . .

I hope you'll join us in celebrating the new season ahead by perusing at your leisure, marking the looks you love and **then heading out to the shops confident you're going to snap up all the great buys before anyone else.** But then you know you can always rely on eve to deliver, whether it's fashion, beauty, homes or features. **See you on the high street.** Until next month, Sara Cremer, editor.

From the extract in Example 2.1, we can pick out a number of points that would be worth following up. We can see for example that non-essential items are constructed as necessities (*the high-street must-haves*) and that shopping is described as a competitive activity (*confident you're going to snap up all the great buys before anyone else*). The new season's collection is talked up (*delicious, rich shades, most luxurious, glory*) and the old one down (*old hat, went straight into the bin*). This results in an evaluative dichotomy that neatly reflects the relentless dynamics of consumerism, which could be summed up, with Orwellian bluntness, as 'new is good, old is bad'. Also, we can see the writer explicitly establishing commonality of experience between herself and the 'implied reader' (Reah 2002:40), who, on several occasions, is addressed directly in the second person (*That's why we can't wait to show you; I hope you'll join us; See you on the high street*). Furthermore, the text endorses a particular constellation of female qualities, attitudes and behaviour. The implied reader relaxes *lying on a beach*, is weight-conscious and therefore thought to be interested in *hide-all-sins woollen coats* (note the moral and religious implications of referring to the causes of excess body fat as *sins*). The fashion trends mentioned, the editor argues, *work for real women*, a somewhat spurious claim given that scores of 'real women' (this author included) are rarely spotted in 'glittery knits' and 'jewelled sandals'.

Such first impressions are a valuable source of inspiration, indicating what one might look for in a larger text corpus, and indeed providing some guidance for the corpus-building process itself.

Corpus-building

Before beginning to build your corpus, you will need to identify the material that potentially constitutes data for your project. This is referred to as the 'population', 'universe of discourse' (Bell 1991:10) or 'universe of possible texts' (Titscher *et al.* 2000:33). Next, you will require a sample representative of the whole. For qualitative projects, attempts at random sampling ('take every *n*th element') are generally not appropriate (Bauer and Aarts 2000:19), first because the size of the population is frequently not known (using the above example, the total number of magazine articles about shopping 'out there' is unknown) and second because the variety of representations, such as particular motifs or argumentative patterns, should not in fact be determined *a priori* (Bauer and Aarts 2000:33). Instead of random sampling, therefore, a cyclical process has been recommended (see Figure 2.1.). The idea here is that you begin by selecting a small but relevant and homogeneous corpus, analyze it and on the basis of your findings select again (Bauer and Aarts 2000:31). More material is added up to the point when, following the law of diminishing returns, new data no longer yield up new representations. The corpus can then be said to have reached 'saturation' (Bauer and Aarts 2000:34). In other words, you continue looking until it becomes evident that what you find is simply more of the same. It follows from this that the more homogeneous a corpus is, the smaller it can be, because saturation point is reached more quickly.

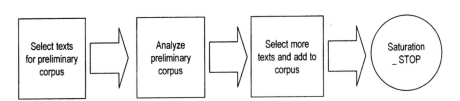

Figure 2.1 Cyclical corpus-building for qualitative research. *Source*: Bauer and Aarts (2000:31–4)

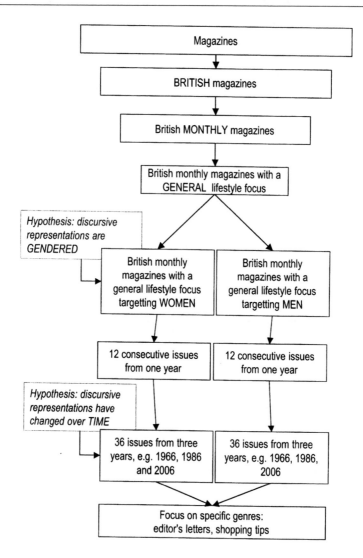

Figure 2.2   An example of selecting media by progressive specification and reduction

Alternatively, a top-down approach may be used, starting out from the 'universe of possible texts' and progressively narrowing down one's choices. Returning to the example introduced in the previous section, the selection process might look like the one shown in Figure 2.2.

The result would be a specialized, topic-oriented and diachronic corpus (see Baker 2006:26–9). Even if one uses such an approach, it is a good idea to interrupt data collection occasionally and do small-scale sample analyzes. The results can lead to the modification and/or creation of hypotheses which may influence selection decisions further along the flowchart and, crucially, can prevent data collection from going down a dead end – amassing data, that is, that turn out to be unsuitable for answering your research questions.

Clearly, no matter which method of corpus-building is used, different research questions and hypotheses ought to lead to different selection decisions.[9] For example, if the discursive representations related to a particular event were to be investigated – such as elections, a particular court trial or a natural disaster – an obvious structuring criterion could be time and you would go for, say, newspaper reports published during a certain period before and after the event. If, on the other hand, an issue is polarized politically, you would have to make sure that print media associated with different political camps are selected. Likewise, if a public debate revolves around an ideologically loaded keyword – such as *political correctness* (Johnson *et al.* 2003) or *entrepreneurial university* (Mautner 2005a) – then the first selection criterion to be applied has to be the occurrence of that word in the texts to be collected.

Throughout this process, researchers must be at pains to resist the temptation of skewed sampling, that is, cherry-picking texts that support their personal views and ignoring those that do not. When, for the reasons given above, it does not make sense to select texts mechanically and randomly, then other checks and balances are necessary. Ultimately, choosing data always involves an element of subjective judgement, and it is precisely because this cannot be completely avoided that subjectivity needs to be counterbalanced by rigour and choices exposed to critical scrutiny. The key correctives are transparency and accountability. These, in turn, can be safeguarded best by using a reasoned step-by-step approach to sampling and forcing oneself to spell out and justify the choices made along the way.

Finally, you will need to tackle the mundane question of cataloguing and storing your data in a way that allows quick identification, retrieval and source referencing. A computer-based corpus is the obvious answer. Beyond the self-evident efficiency gains, the electronic format has the advantage of enabling one to process a much larger purpose-built corpus than would be possible without computer assistance. Programs such as Wordsmith[10] and Wordpilot[11] compile frequency data and produce keyword-in-context ('KWIC') concordances which highlight collocational patterns. The use of concordances originated in corpus linguistics, but also has significant potential for applications in qualitative discourse analysis (Hardt-Mautner 1995; Stubbs 1996–2001; Koller and Mautner 2004; Baker 2006; Mautner 2007). Even if you restrict yourself to manual analysis of a small corpus, comparative data from large electronically held corpora can help substantiate your analysis. This technique will be illustrated in the section below entitled 'Checks and balances: comparative evidence from reference corpora'.

Key resources for textual analysis

ACTIVITY 2.1

Read the two articles from the *Sun* in Figures 2.3 and 2.4, 'Why Reid [the Home Secretary] Will Fail on Crime and Illegals' and '45,000 Crooks on Way Here'. Next,

▨ determine the articles' key message and point of view; and
▨ identify the linguistic devices you consider instrumental in conveying that message and stance (as many as you can).

That our two articles from the *Sun* support an anti-EU-enlargement agenda is obvious enough. Yet one looks in vain for any explicit statement to this effect. This is where the discourse analyst comes in, unpacking the mechanisms at work in the text with the help of a specifically linguistic repertoire of analytic devices.

On the level of *lexis*, the analyst will try to identify patterns in the choice of words, and in particular those with a distinctive 'evaluative meaning' (Hunston 2004:157), also called 'evaluative polarity' (Channell 2000:41). In our two texts, the *labelling of news actors* is a case in point (see also: Reisigl and Wodak, 2001; Matouschek *et al.* 1995). The expressions used to refer to Eastern European migrants have an unequivocally negative semantic load: *crooks, gangsters, mob, undesirables, Europe's criminal underclass, criminal gangs* and *ex-lags*. Furthermore, adjectives with negative polarity contribute to heightening the sense of urgency and crisis – see *soaring violence and rampant immigration* (more on *rampant* below) – and serve to sweepingly disparage whole countries: *in corrupt Romania and Bulgaria*. Adjectival and verbal choices are used to accuse the government and government agencies of helplessness, incompetence and indeed corruption (*new Home Secretary John Reid flails around for solutions; the shambolic immigration service; border patrols will be powerless; The rot* [inside the immigration service] *is now so entrenched . . .*).

Also, *figures* are used for rhetorical effect, emphasizing the threat allegedly posed by migrants. The headline reads *45,000 crooks on way here*, with *45,000* printed in a font twice as large as the rest of the sentence. Other figures, sounding equally ominous, are scattered liberally throughout the two articles: *662,000 came here in the past two years; with official forecasts of more than SEVEN million more on their way* (with the block capitals adding further emphasis); *a staggering 10,000 foreign prisoners are clogging our jails; one-in-ten citizens in cities like Plymouth and Southampton are from Poland; up to 140,000 will flock here.* Note how in the last quote a large number is not only mentioned explicitly but also implied in the semantics of the verb: *flocking* is something that only large groups can do, as a search on the Web or in a computerized reference corpus will quickly show.[12] (See the following section for further details on this technique.) The sense of threat is further

TREVOR Kavanagh

ON MONDAY

WELCOME LONDON EQUAL CRIME OPPORTUNITIES FOR ALL

LATVIA · ROMANIA · BULGARIA · STOP

B.C.

Why Reid will fail on crime and illegals

AS new Home Secretary John Reid flails around for solutions to soaring violence and rampant immigration, I make two predictions.

First, he will fail on both counts. Second, he won't be around long enough to carry the can.

The Government will **NOT** build two prisons in five years.

It will **NOT** deport thousands of illegal immigrants — or stop millions more entering this country.

Indeed the reverse will happen. Crime is rising — especially street violence and Home Office insiders admit there is nothing they can do to stop it.

Immigration is out of control with official forecasts of more than **SEVEN** million more on their way over coming years.

The two issues are directly linked.

A staggering 10,000 foreign prisoners are clogging our jails — one-in-eight of the total.

A startling BBC probe claims ex-Communist states are exporting their criminals to Britain.

Thousands of ex-lags from Poland, Latvia and other new EU states have moved to London and are helping those in cells back home to head this way when they get out.

In addition, 45,000 known "undesirables" in corrupt Romania and Bulgaria are packing their bags for the day when they join the EU — with plenty more to follow.

Free-and-easy Britain is fast becoming the organised crime capital of the world.

According to security services, criminal gangs have infiltrated the sharp end of the immigration service to wave through those who pay with cash.

More than 700 have been caught, but more are working

the system from the inside. The rot is now so entrenched that virtually nothing can be done to reverse or eradicate it.

Home Office officials privately admit crime figures are going to keep climbing.

And this time, the Government cannot send thuggish Tony McNulty on to the airwaves to deny it.

Damning

It was McNulty who scoffed at The Sun's sex-for-visas scoop, claiming it was an "isolated incident". Now we know there are hundreds like that.

The damning facts on crime and immigration come from the Government's own sources — either the Home Office itself or the all-party Home Affairs Committee of MPs.

The independent think tank, Reform, says street crime is now spreading from inner cities to leafy suburbs.

And it rejects John Reid's claim that muggings are the result of affluent youngsters carrying expensive iPods and MP3 players. "In America, just

as many youngsters have mobile technology, but there has been a fall in robberies," says Reform director Andrew Haldenby.

Today's report by MPs on immigration is devastating.

It stresses the right of a "modern sovereign state to control who enters it" — and slams the Government for failing to do so.

It blames penny-pinching on frontline services, failure to enforce rules and deport illegals and a refusal to outlaw firms who use illegal

FOR all his sins and crass behaviour, John Prescott still has some pride left. Friends say he is nowhere near as thick-skinned as enemies claim and feels every new barb of criticism like a freshly twisted knife. So why doesn't he do himself and the rest of us a favour now — and leave the stage with at least a few shreds of dignity intact?

labour. None of this will surprise anyone in Britain with eyes to see.

Ministers have been warned for years that illegal immigration and crime go hand in hand. Even legal immigration has reached absurd levels when one-in-ten citizens in cities like Plymouth and Southampton are from Poland.

The only consolation for John Reid is that none of this is his fault.

This is his eighth ministerial job in nine years. He hasn't been around long enough to make his mark in any of them.

The Home Secretary — along with the rest of us — is reaping the whirlwind of a government in thrall to human rights, gender awareness and ethnic diversity at the expense of public safety.

For ten years it has turned its face against the tough measures he is now promising.

Short of cash, short of time, short of political will, does anyone believe it has the guts to put those promises into effect now?

● Read my blog at thesun.co.uk ● Email: trevorblog@the-sun.co.uk ● Write: Trevor Kavanagh, The Sun, 1 Virginia St, London E98 1SL

Figure 2.3 *Why Reid Will Fail on Crime and Illegals. Source: the Sun, 24 July 2006*

Figure 2.4 *45,000 Crooks on Way Here. Source: the Sun, 24 July 2006*

enhanced by the use of *metaphors*; immigrants are conceptualized as an invading army (*new EU invasion*; *an army of 45,000 crooks and gangsters is set to invade Britain*) and as an uncontrollable natural force (*Fears that Britain will be flooded . . .*; *the new wave of migrants*; *the huge flood of migrants*).

At the interface of the lexical and syntactic levels the system of *transitivity* is located, 'a resource for construing our experience in terms of configurations of a process, participants and circumstances' (Martin *et al.* 1997:102). Developed originally within the tradition of systemic-functional grammar (seminally, by Halliday 2004), the concept is now widely applied in critical discourse analysis.[13] With rather bold oversimplification we can say that transitivity is about asking how events are described: who does what to whom, and what happens without intervention from actors. Four different process types are distinguished (Simpson 1993:95): verbal ('saying'), mental ('sensing'), relational ('being') and material ('doing'). In material processes, the actor is 'the one that does the deed' (Halliday 2004:179). The 'goal', on the other hand, is the participant that is 'impacted by the performance of the Process by the Actor' (Martin *et al.* 1997:118). Transitivity helps us capture the difference between, to use a manufactured example, *The immigrant left*, *The immigrant was deported* and *Immigration officials deported the immigrant* – one and the same event, but clearly different constructions of reality. In our two articles from *The Sun*, the majority of processes in which migrants occupy the role of actor describe movement that is purposeful and self-directed (rather than induced by adverse circumstances such as poverty): see *will head here*; *have already tried to enter the UK*; *will flock here*; *came here*; *[are] on their way*; *have moved to London*; *are packing their bags*. In those cases where migrants occupy the semantic role of 'goal', the verbal processes involved centre on the theme of rejection and expulsion. It makes no difference that in some cases the authorities, cast in the role of actor, are criticized for not succeeding in exclusionary practices – the underlying theme is still the same. Examples include: *border patrols will be powerless to stop them settling here*; *those who have already been turned away*; *it would be impossible to ban or remove undesirables*; *they have been removed*; *It [the government] will NOT deport thousands of illegal immigrants – or stop millions more entering this country*; *failure to enforce rules and deport illegals*. Note also how migrants are implicitly dehumanized by verbs that would generally collocate with objects rather than people: *use* and *export* (for example *firms using illegal workers*; *ex-Communist states are exporting their criminals to Britain*). In a similar vein, migrants are said *to have been removed*.

Another analytical dimension that bridges syntax and lexis is *modality*. As Stubbs puts it, modality refers to

> the ways in which language is used to encode meanings such as degrees of certainty and commitment, or alternatively vagueness and lack of commitment, personal beliefs versus generally accepted or taken for granted knowledge. (1996:202)

Markers of modality include modal verbs (for example *can, might, must*) and modal adverbials (for example *perhaps, certainly*). Depending on which markers are deployed, the result may be a hedged, tentative proposition that the speaker is not sure about ('low' modality, as in *he might leave* and *perhaps they are too old*) or one that the speaker fully commits herself to ('high' modality, as in *he must have left* and *they are definitely too old*). Unmodalized declaratives, on other other hand (for example *he has left*), express the strongest form of affinity and commitment, with the speaker fully supporting the truth value inherent in the assertion.[14] Patterns of modality usage may correlate with certain discursive practices. In advertisements, for example, product claims are typically realized through non-modal declaratives,[15] whereas academic writing, notorious for its reluctance to peddle 'truths', has been found to have a very high incidence of *may* (Biber *et al.* 1999:491). Tabloids, on the other hand, present black-and-white pictures of the world and express strong editorial opinion. The two articles from the *Sun* are no exception. In Figure 2.3, 'Why Reid Will Fail on Crime and Illegals', modality is instrumental in presenting migrant movements as fact rather than prediction (for example *The mob will head here; border patrols will be powerless to stop them settling here*). A certain degree of distancing is achieved through *source attribution* (*Fears that . . . are revealed; They warn that . . .*), but in these instances, too, the embedded propositions are couched in high-affinity modality (*Fears that Britain will be flooded with Europe's criminal underclass . . .; They warn that up to 140,000 will flock here . . .*). The other article, Figure 2.4, '45,000 Crooks on Way Here', makes similar modality choices in criticizing the government and painting a grim picture of crime on the rise, alternating between the high level of certainty expressed by *will*-predictions (for example *Why Reid Will Fail on Crime and Illegals*; *It* [the government] *will NOT deport thousands of illegal immigrants*) and unmodalized, categorical assertions (for example *Free-and-easy Britain is fast becoming the organized crime capital of the world*). Again, occasional source attribution achieves some distancing, but because the sources are presented as credible (for example *According to security services . . .; A startling BBC probe claims . . .; Home Office officials privately admit . . .*), the overall effect of certainty is not impaired. In fact, references to élite sources serve a legitimizing function, supporting the author's point of view and bolstering his credibility.

Moving on to the higher level of *text*, we can now look at larger meaning-making structures. In the two articles from the *Sun*, for example, a key argumentative strategy is to denounce immigration by linking it to crime. This is achieved in Figure 2.3, 'Why Reid Will Fail on Crime and Illegals' partly through devices on the local, below-sentence level, notably coordination: see *soaring violence and rampant immigration; crime and illegals; The damning facts on crime and immigration*. Then, in Figure 2.4, '45,000 Crooks on Way Here', there are statements explicitly establishing the connection: *The two issues are directly linked* and *Ministers have been warned for years that illegal immigration and crime go hand in hand*. Finally, and this is the tactic hardest to pin down, the text oscillates between the two themes, with the link arising simply because they co-occur in successive paragraphs. In some cases that link is reinforced by *cohesive ties*, that is 'text-connecting features' (Hoey 2001:41) such as repetition, paraphrase, co-reference and ellipsis. In the first seven paragraphs of 'Why Reid Will Fail on Crime and Illegals', for example, a cohesive chain is established by the co-referring news actor labels *crooks and gangsters, mob, 'undesirables', criminals, criminal underclass* and *up to 140,000*. In the eighth paragraph, *migrants* first appears. That we assume *migrants* and all the preceding negative labels to refer to the same group of people is due to a web of other cohesive ties: between *flooded* and *wave* (paragraph 6: *flooded with Europe's criminal underclass*; paragraph 8: *wave of migrants*), between *immigration chiefs, criminals* and *migrants* (see paragraph 4: *compiled by immigration chiefs from records of criminals*) and between, on the one hand, *the secret blacklist, records* and *Whitehall papers* (all of which are mentioned in connection with criminals) and *one document* (which is said to talk about migrants, thus performing the referential switch from criminals to migrants).

Another argumentative device located on the textual level is the establishment of *rapport between author and reader*. This is achieved for example through the use of rhetorical questions (for example *does anyone believe it* [the government] *has the guts to put those promises into effect now?*), appealing to the supposedly unifying force of common sense (for example *None of this will surprise anyone in Britain with eyes to see*) and the construction of a 'we' group built on the commonality of interest and solidarity that exists between author and reader (*The Home Secretary – along with the rest of us . . .*) (see also: Krzyżanowski and Wodak, 2008).

Last but not least, textual analysis ought to turn to *nonverbal message components*. Key parameters include visuals, page layout, frames, boxed inserts, font style and size (witness my earlier comment on the use of a very large font in the headline which supports the rhetorical use of figures). in '45,000 Crooks on Way Here' features a map showing the route that the 'crooks' are following through Europe, and, in keeping with the metaphor of invasion, it does so in the style of a military deployment plan. 'Why Reid Will Fail on Crime and Illegals' is accompanied by a cartoon depicting lorries labelled *Romania* and *Bulgaria* full of hooded figures with masked faces, thus encouraging the association of migrants with criminals.[16]

Although the sample analysis presented here has tried to move step-by-step from smaller to larger units, it should also have become clear that such an approach must not be allowed to obscure the many interrelations between levels. Evaluative stance, for example, is realized on the microlevel through lexical items, but also emerges on the textual macro level as the sum total of many other choices (Bednarek 2006), including the strategic use of sequencing, quotations and illustrations. Likewise, metaphor is located at the lexical level because it is tied to words, but chains of related metaphors may extend over longer stretches of text, creating powerful cohesion, which is a textual and not merely lexical phenomenon. Also, as the multimodal realization of the invasion theme showed, metaphors may be realized simultaneously in the verbal and visual modes. In essence, none of the devices discussed above functions completely independently. Rather, they are all intertwined and mutually reinforcing, working together to create overall textual meaning and perspective (see also Chapter 1 by Wodak).

To sum up, the linguistic resources we looked at in our qualitative discourse analysis included the following:

- Lexis (evaluative meaning; news actor labels; rhetorical use of figures; metaphors).
- Transitivity ('who does what to whom'; types of verbal processes, for example 'doing' versus 'happening').
- Modality (expressing certainty vs. vagueness; 'high' vs. 'low' commitment to propositions on the part of the speaker as expressed for example through modal verbs and modal adverbials).
- Source attribution and presence of different 'voices' in the text.
- Textual coherence and cohesion.
- Argumentative devices establishing rapport between author and reader (for example rhetorical questions; appeals to common sense; discursive construction of 'we' groups).
- Nonverbal message components (for example photographs, charts, page layout, frames, boxed inserts, font size and style).

In keeping with the context-sensitive orientation of discourse analysis (see Chapter 1 by Wodak), a fine-grained linguistic investigation needs to recognize the relevance of the social, cultural, political and economic background against which texts are written and read. In larger-scale projects, this would mean moving back and forth, in recursive cycles, from the microlevel analysis of text to the macroanalysis of discursive and social practice, embedding them in each other and thus acknowledging the fundamental dialectic between language and the social (see Fairclough 2003). At the same time, it is vital not to prejudice the analysis too soon and thus risk finding in the text only what one expected to find. One way of avoiding this pitfall is to consult comparative evidence from large reference corpora, an approach explained in the next section.

Checks and balances: comparative evidence from reference corpora

In the previous section, there were several occasions on which we identified evaluative elements. Mostly they were negative labels designed to denounce migrants, the countries they come from, or the British authorities. In many cases, negativity is not in doubt. We hardly need supportive evidence for our claim that *mob, gangsters, undesirables, rot* or *thuggish*[17] are negative. On the other hand, there are cases where questions of semantic load are not so clear, or where the value judgement adhering to a particular lexical item depends less on the denotative, 'core' meaning of the item itself (as in the case of *undesirables*, for example) but on connotative meaning. Like denotation, connotations are not merely based on individual experience, but 'are also widely shared within a speech community' (Stubbs 2001:35). Using large computer-held corpora such as the British National Corpus[18] or Wordbanks Online[19], we can get fast and easy access to what these shared connotations are, thus putting our judgement of evaluation in perspective and making sure that we neither over- nor underinterpret (O'Halloran and Coffin 2004). This is likely to be as useful to the native-speaker analyst, who may have too many preconceived notions about evaluative load, as to the non-native, who may have too few.

Take the expression *rampant immigration*, for example, which occurs in the lead sentence of 'Why Reid Will Fail on Crime and Illegals'. Its negativity derives, on the one hand, from what O'Halloran and Coffin (2004:285) call 'the dynamism of meaning-meaking as the text proceeds'. Coordination with *soaring violence* clearly plays a role in this, as does the cartoon with its lorryloads of criminals. A few lines further down, items appear that form a cohesive chain with *rampant immigration* but add new elements of meaning: the notion of illegality is introduced (*illegal immigrants*) and *millions more* implicitly corroborates the 'rampant' (that is uncontrolled) quality of immigration. On the other hand, the meaning of *rampant* in *rampant immigration* is derived partly from its collocational behaviour. Words that *rampant* habitually co-occurs with give it a 'consistent aura of meaning', or 'semantic prosody' (Louw 1993:175). Consulting the British sections of Wordbanks Online, a multi-million word corpus of English text,[20] we can see that this aura is consistently negative, with the ten most frequent and most strongly associated collocates of *rampant* including *commercialism, consumerism, materialism, corruption and inflation*.[21] Further examples of nominal collocates, gleaned from a concordance of *rampant*, are *ageism, bigotry, capitalism, crime, homophobia, lesbianism* and *sleaze and cronyism*. (A sample concordance is reproduced in Figure 2.5.) All of these, it is worth noting, describe (or, in the case of *lesbianism*, are to be passed off as) human ills and excesses and most have distinctly moralizing overtones. Thus, in addition to shared negativity, there is also some similarity between common collocates with regard to other semantic features – that is, in terms of 'semantic preference' (Stubbs 2001:88; Partington 2004). To sum up, things are 'rampant' because people make them so (and it is people, therefore, who can put a stop to them), and they are negative in terms of an ethical value judgement. These are meaning elements that *rampant* projects onto the nouns it modifies, in our case *immigration*. Thus, by looking at a word's semantic prosody, we can tease out the specific sources of negativity in a given text.

The second example occurs in the last paragraph but one of 'Why Reid Will Fail on Crime and Illegals'. It reads as follows: 'The Home Secretary – along with the rest of us – is reaping the whirlwind of a government *in thrall to*

```
          will be swallowed whole by the rampant Americans, with Juli Inkster, the
teams." <p> Fulham, ripped apart by rampant Arsenal the previous week, were
down." Psyched up from overseeing a rampant bbcl, his brief is to bring
   direction of US rates. But what do rampant bond yields mean for the UK
        of 73 in partnership with his now rampant buddy Bradman. By the time of the `
      result of harsh dictatorships and rampant corruption. There was no political
     of congress suggesting there was rampant criminality at Enron. ''These
       militant civil rights candidates. Rampant discrimination in the Stormont era
Woods. <p> Kirtley recalled, page 46 Rampant Essex, page 46 Taylor's triumph,
           in a vivid orange hive, breasts rampant, face daubed and drawn and
      away with even greater animation. A rampant federalist, he is Bill Cash in
what he is about and standing up to rampant Frenchmen when resistance is
</dt> <p> PARMA 5 GLOUCESTER 48. <p> RAMPANT Gloucester had this Shield match
          Outside the window, some of the rampant greenery from the back garden
        needed to be done to reign in rampant growth. But Mr Greenspan's
     dying his hair jet-black - and his rampant hypochondria. On Turkmenistan's
  Currency: peso (£1 = 4.65 pesos). Rampant inflation has caused chaos in
He escaped a few weeks later. 1923 Rampant inflation in Germany reached a
        while trying to cope with rampant inflation (hyperinflation in some
         by rising unemployment and rampant inflation. In 1976, under pressure
economic policies aimed at curbing rampant inflation. A BBC correspondent
Prada. <p> But in a profession where rampant insecurity can lead to drug-
      says that prisons are hotbeds of `rampant lesbianism". <h> Big money </h>
   of the carriage was adorned with a rampant lion, its claws ready for war,
2001 </dt> <p> MILLWALL 4 NORWICH 0. Rampant Lions get mcghee warning. SCORE
             over fraud, mismanagement and rampant nepotism in Brussels. It defused
      type of stark comes to mind when rampant nudists skydive out of a plane
   in corporate governance too, with rampant politicking, senior figures
  per email with a cap of $500,000. "Rampant pornography and fraudulent credit
     the Ann Summers bestseller is the Rampant Rabbit vibrator. <p> The pink
of Celtic. And Combe doesn't believe rampant Rangers will slip up in the run-
     exists and it does kill. It is a rampant reaction by the body to the
        A D'Urso Attendance: 35,973 <h1> Rampant Reds storm to top; Football; Match
Union </h1> <subh> Cherries ripe for rampant revival: Gloucester 41 Newcastle
          found themselves swamped by the rampant Rhinos. <p> There was no hint of
an abrupt and brutal end as they hit rampant Robins. <p> City boss Danny Wilson
   could spoil the party for 26,000 rampant Rovers fans. <p> They have
for 10 minutes and try a red-blooded rampant Scot for a change." He swept me
    forth across the landscape by the rampant soldiery. But if you confront any
        is doubly alarming, given the rampant spread of sexually transmitted
          oblivious for a while of the rampant state terrorism. When I got a call
      a sexy name and pretend you're a rampant stranger who can't resist him.
         and Dadaism run parallel in a rampant stream of technological
      With recruitment shortages, and rampant street crime, maybe he wishes he
  the Tour de France last summer for rampant substance abuse. Massacre A
         Sat 09-Jun-2001 </dl> <h1> Lions rampant Taylor injury blow as Henry's men
       <dl> Mon 27-Aug-2001 </dl> <h1> Rampant Thistle shrug off injuries </h1>
     a 2-0 Test series win over Japan. Rampant Wales demolished their hosts 64-10
     crack at avoiding relegation. <p> Rampant Watford twice had shots cleared
     trust sector, the retreat of the rampant waves has exposed holes in the
```

Figure 2.5   Random selection of 50 occurrences of *rampant* followed by a noun from
the British subcorpora of Wordbanks Online

human rights, gender awareness and ethnic diversity at the expense of public
safety [emphasis added].' What we have here is one of those rather interesting
cases where the evaluative load of words depends crucially on who uses them
how and in what context. In fact, one of the key characteristics of such keywords is, precisely, that they are 'nodes around which ideological battles are
fought' (Stubbs 2001:188).[22] One and the same expression may be a 'banner
keyword' for some and a 'stigma keyword' for others (Teubert 2000). For

```
     a sinister fundamentalist church in thrall to a charismatic leader. The attack
          in history can have been so in thrall to a predecessor. <p> But Lady
      a wholly persuasive young officer in thrall to a gambling mania. Perhaps, at
       stabbed in the bath. We were all in thrall to A Tale of Two Cities and we were
           from it. Magnetized by a nose. In thrall to a nose. She felt a giggle
           of British superiority and in thrall to America," explains the Times.
             conservative land deeply in thrall to an ageless past. Mr Putin may be
        of the way in which democracy is in thrall to bankers. It is also an example
         that his government remained in thrall to big business. However, Mr Blair'
      with the idea of Cool Britannia, in thrall to Britpop and increasingly
             became a part of a culture in thrall to chivalry and precedence.
    loved one. <p> Sebold is a writer in thrall to extremity and the confessional -
       to Oxford where he finds a city in thrall to giant international
      find nothing in him to like were in thrall to him. <p> To Pat Eddery, the most
       from his fiancee and to his being in thrall to his own manservant. The story
        of a man lacerated by doubt, but in thrall to his bowels and inexorable sense
         that she felt herself once more in thrall to his presence. As she could see
     turnover of £46 million, had been in thrall to its traditional customer base.
      good cellists, too. <hl> The fans in thrall to Krall; Jazz; First Night </hl>
        the middle ages. Nor is it Iran, in thrall to militant Islam. With one fell
     but not to the print media, a man in thrall to no-one and absolutely in charge
       per cent of viewers who are not in thrall to our sport. <p> Sir Peter O'
     health officials so often seemed in thrall to prejudice and faddism. Party
      creations." <p> We were equally in thrall to Rosemary's "ancient wisdom" as
        of the ruling, fans will remain in thrall to Sky if they wish to follow the
            the industry seems to be in thrall to superstitions about dates and
   But just as the 20th century was in thrall to the 19th, so the 21st century
        power, while musically more in thrall to the Beatles than ever, they
    what can happen to those utterly in thrall to the corrupting power of
         <p> By the early 1980s he was in thrall to the electro-pop of the era. Art
        but in a sense they are all in thrall to the idea that racing is corrupt.
        that too many musicians are in thrall to the past <p> The ghosts are
      and the birth of our own era, in thrall to the sexy power of celebrity. No
           <p> Indeed, far from being in thrall to the torch and twang tradition,
      trade which, she says, is still in thrall to the brutal management techniques
     the pageantry of a warrior class in thrall to the concept of honour. Dhobi
      as financial watchdogs remain in thrall to the industry they are meant to
         are you there Lord Bragg? - in thrall to the mechanistic arguments of
     a few, fitful adolescent months in thrall to the revival of the British
       them. New Labour, which is often in thrall to the US experience, should learn
     had political representatives not in thrall to the likes of Clinton, Bush, and
       of post-colonial guilt and in thrall to the professional "anti-racism"
       brew. Imran Ahmed Two brothers! In thrall to the classicism of the 60s!
    But Wall Street and the City are in thrall to the power of `e". See the impact
      Iad's malevolence had been held in thrall to the 'shu, and by the time it had
    that a number of men are equally in thrall to their waxers. Though in case you'
       the city is too proud, too much in thrall to these old songs. When you wander
         nowhere but spent his life in thrall to those who did belong; a man who
    that this shows the Government is in thrall to unrepresentative special
        man. <pg> 14 </pg> <hl> Duma in thrall to Yeltsin ego </hl> <subh> The
```

Figure 2.6   Random selection of 50 occurrences of *in thrall to* from the British subcorpora of Wordbanks Online

many people, including the proverbial left-wing cosmopolitan liberal, *human rights, gender awareness* and *ethnic diversity* are likely to be positively connoted. In the above extract, however, they are clearly nothing of the kind. Incidentally, the inclusion in this enumeration of *gender awareness* is a particular oddity. Whereas *human rights* and *ethnic diversity* have clear cohesive links with the rest of the article, *gender awareness* does not: gender simply is not an issue here. It appears to have been thrown in for good measure, as it were, to add rhetorical force to this assemblage of specters haunting the right-wing citizen. To say that this is quite simply in keeping with the *Weltbild* of the typical *Sun* reader may be true, but it tells us nothing about the specifically linguistic devices that achieve what O'Halloran and Coffin refer to as 'positioning the reader to accept a particular point of view' (2004:277). What the linguist working within a discourse-analytic paradigm wishes to know is what it is *in* the text that creates and supports such evaluative positioning. In the passage quoted above, two devices are at work. First, *human rights, gender awareness* and *ethnic diversity* are pitted against *public safety*, a positive keyword likely to ring the right bells among a conservative tabloid readership. Anything directly juxtaposed with that is implicitly denigrated, with *at the expense of* suggesting that there is an inevitable trade-off: you cannot have one *and* the other. Second, and more subtly, a negative semantic aura radiates out from *in thrall to*. Again, concordance data extracted from the Wordbanks corpus can help substantiate this. (For a sample, see Figure 2.6.) Specifically, it emerges from the concordance for *in thrall to* that some of the noun phrases that follow, as in our example, do indeed describe something positive – such as *chivalry, glamour, the Protestant work ethic* and *his virile beauty*. On the other hand, instances of negative concepts that one can be 'in thrall to' occur, too. Among these there is a notable semantic preference for extremism and socially deviant behaviour: see *a gambling mania, single-issue fanatics and pressure groups, prejudice and faddism, brutal management techniques*, and *a voracious mistress*. In any case, the use of *in thrall to* expresses the speaker's or writer's disapproval of someone succumbing, unquestioningly and in an exaggerated manner, to people and ideas (be they positive or negative). By implication, the ideas themselves are criticized. In some instances, the negativity of *in thrall to* is reinforced by intensifying adverbs that also have negative polarity: see *abjectly in thrall to glamour*; *unhealthily in thrall to macho pack leader Len*; *utterly in thrall to the corrupting power of celebrity*.[23] With such corpus-based evidence of the semantic prosody of *in thrall to*, we are in a better position to argue that *human rights, gender awareness* and *ethnic diversity*, while clearly positive in other co-texts and contexts, are indeed negatively connotated in the texts under investigation.

Summary

Print media are rich sources of data for research projects in the social sciences. The specific contribution that qualitative discourse analysis can make lies in making explicit the linguistic means through which representations of reality and social relationships are enacted. Textual analysis needs to be underpinned by a thorough understanding of the conditions under which the print medium to be investigated is produced and consumed. In the case of newspapers and magazines, key aspects of production are institutionalized sourcing procedures and selection on the basis of so-called 'news values'.

Before embarking on a project, it pays to delve into a small data sample, collecting initial observations, formulating general hypotheses, identifying promising lines of inquiry, testing your methodological toolkit and honing your analytical skills. Inspired by first and as yet tentative results, you can then proceed to more systematic data-gathering. This can either follow a cyclical path, with data selection and analysis driving each other until saturation point is reached, or proceed in a more top-down and linear fashion, making the sample progressively more focused. In either case, it is advisable to continue to carry out small-scale exploratory studies even before corpus compilation is completed.

The textual analysis of print media aims to identify meaning-making resources on various linguistic levels, focusing in particular on devices used to position readers into adopting a certain point of view. To this end, the inquiry needs to concentrate on the evaluative load of words, including those denoting news actors, as well as on metaphor. At the interface of lexis and syntax, choices from the modality and transitivity systems are investigated. On the level of the coherent text, cohesive ties are examined, as are explicit signals of rapport-building between author and reader. What is more, the analysis has to extend to nonverbal messages such as photographs, charts and cartoons.

Finally, in order to substantiate claims about the evaluative load of words and phrases, comparative evidence can be gleaned from large, computerized reference corpora. These can be trusted to reflect general usage and widely shared connotations, thus providing support for and, if necessary, a corrective to the analyst's own interpretation.

Acknowledgements

Articles on pages 39–40 reprinted with kind permission of the *Sun*. Material from the Bank of English® (pages 46–7) reproduced with the kind permission of HarperCollins Publishers Ltd.

Notes

1. Key literature that needs signposting at this stage includes, for the CDA strand of the account, Fowler (1991); Fairclough and Wodak (1997); Fairclough (2003); Reisigl and Wodak (2001). For introductions to corpus linguistics, and explorations of its practical value for discourse studies, see Stubbs (1996) and Baker (2006).
2. For a linguistic analysis of corporate annual reports see Rutherford (2005).
3. See Östman (2004) for a study of 'the postcard as media'.
4. A recent example of such semiotic hybridization is the *Langenscheidt Explorer Wörterbuch Englisch,* a monolingual English learner's dictionary whose page layout mimics the file manager of Windows Explorer.
5. On the challenges caused by the ephemeral quality of Web-based data, see Mautner (2005b: 817–19).

6. An example of how situated literacy can have an impact on print media design could be observed recently on the British newspaper market. Three broadsheets (*The Independent, The Times* and *The Scotsman*) 'downsized' to tabloid format. One of the key drivers of the change was the reading habits of metropolitan commuters, who had found the traditional large format inconvenient to read while travelling to work on overcrowded trains.

7. A clear summary and critique is given by Fowler (1991:12–17).

8. For an overview of journalists' 'sourcing routines', see Keeble (2006:51–73).

9. For an overview of how to select material for analysis see also chapter 3 in Titscher *et al.* (2000), and in particular the section on sampling on pp. 38–41.

10. For information on Wordsmith access http://www.lexically.net/wordsmith/

11. Information on Wordpilot is available at http://www.compulang.com/

12. For an in-depth, computer-assisted analysis of the semantics of *flock*, see O'Halloran and Coffin (2004:280–7). The topos of numbers is salient for such texts (see, for example, Reisigl and Wodak, 2001: 75ff.). The use of related metaphors is particularly analyzed in Baker *et al.* (2008) and Wodak (2008).

13. For good overviews of the practical analytical value of transitivity for CDA see Simpson (1993:86–118) and Richardson (2006:54–9).

14. On modality in textual analysis, see Fairclough (2003: 164–78) and Richardson (2006:59–62). Detailed systemic-functional accounts are given in Halliday (2004:143–50) and Eggins (2004:172–6).

15. See the following example from a cosmetics ad published in *chatelaine*, a Canadian women's magazine in May 2006): *Biofirm Lift (. . .) visibly **fills** wrinkles (. . .)* **Protects** *the skin's elastic fibre network from deterioration (. . .)* **Gives** *the skin an instant lift effect.* For product claims like this, anything but categorical assertions would be in breach of genre conventions.

16. That the one face that is visible in the cartoon has a moustache ties in with the frequently gendered image of both crime and immigration (see the 'absence of refugee women' identified in a recent report published by Article 19, an international human rights organization, on media representation of refugees and asylum seekers in the UK (Buchanan *et al.* 2003:34–5).

17. *Thuggish* is used in Article B to refer to a Labour MP denying charges of large-scale corruption in the immigration service.

18. For information on the British National Corpus see http://www.natcorp.ox.ac.uk/

19. For information on Wordbanks Online see http://www.cobuild.collins.co.uk/Pages/wordbanks.aspx

20. The British subcorpora of Wordbanks make up a total of 336.6 million words, consisting of books, magazines, ephemera (such as brochures and advertisements), national newspapers (including *the Sun*, the *Guardian,* the *Independent* and the *Times*), regional newspapers and transcribed spoken language (including casual conversation, radio broadcasts and lectures).

21. The statistical measure Wordbanks uses to capture the strength of the collocational bond is the so-called MI (Mutual Information) Score. An MI score of 3 or higher is generally regarded as significant (Hunston 2002:71). The above-mentioned collocates of *rampant* all have MI scores of at least 7.

22. For discussions and applications of the concept of 'keyword', including its conceptual history going back to Firth (1935) and Williams (1976/1983), see Stubbs (1996); (2001); Teubert (2000); Mautner (2005a).

23. On the predominantly negative semantic prosody of *utterly* see Louw (1993:160); Partington (2004:147).

Key readings

Baker, P. *Using Corpora in Discourse Analysis* (London: Continuum, 2006).
Fairclough, N. *Analysing Discourse: Textual Analysis for Social Research* (London: Routledge, 2003).
Fowler, R. *Language in the News: Discourse and Ideology in the Press* (London: Routledge, 1991).
Richardson, J.E. *Analysing Newspapers: An Approach from Critical Discourse Analysis* (Basingstoke: Palgrave Macmillan, 2006).

References

Baker, P. *Using Corpora in Discourse Analysis* (London: Continuum, 2006).
Baker, P., Gabrielatos, C., Khosravinik, M., Krzyżanowski, M., Wodak, R. and McEnery, A., 'A Useful Methodological Synergy? Combining CDA and Corpus Linguistics to Examine Discourses of Refugees and Asylum Seekers in the UK Press', *Discourse and Society*, 19(3), (2008), pp. 273–305.
Bauer, M.W. and B. Aarts, 'Corpus Construction: a Principle for Qualitative Data Collection', in M.W. Bauer and G. Gaskell (eds) *Qualitative Researching with Text, Image and Sound* (London: Sage, 2000), pp. 19–37.
Bednarek, M. *Evaluation in Media Discourse: Analysis of a Newspaper Corpus* (London: Continuum, 2006).
Bell, A. *The Language of News Media* (Oxford: Blackwell, 1991).
Biber, D. *et al. Longman Grammar of Spoken and Written English* (Harlow: Longman, 1999).
Buchanan, S., Grillo, B. and Threadgold, T. *What's the Story? Results from Research into Media Coverage of Refugees and Asylum Seekers in the UK* (Article 19, available at http://www.article19.org/pdfs/publications/refugees-what-s-the-story-.pdf)
Bucy, E.P. and Affe, R.B. 'The Contributions of Net News to Cyber Democracy: Civic Affordances of Major Metropolitan Newspaper Sites', in X. Li (ed.) *Internet Newspapers. The Making of a Mainstream Medium* (Mahwah, NJ: Erlbaum, 2006), pp. 227–42.
Channell, J., 'Corpus-Based Analysis of Evaluative Lexis', in S. Hunston and G. Thompson (eds) *Evaluation in Text: Authorial Stance and the Construction of Discourse* (Oxford University Press, 2000), pp. 38–55.
Eggins, S. *An Introduction to Systemic Functional Linguistics* (London: Continuum, 2004).
Fairclough, N. *Media Discourse* (London: Arnold, 1995).
Fairclough, N. *Analysing Discourse: Textual Analysis for Social Research* (London: Routledge, 2003).
Fairclough, N. and R. Wodak, 'Critical Discourse Analysis', in T.A van Dijk (ed.) *Discourse Studies: A Multidisciplinary Introduction*, vol. 2 (London: Sage, 1997), pp. 258–84.

Firth, J.R. 'The Technique of Semantics', in *Papers in Linguistics 1934–1951* (London: Oxford University Press, 1957; original work published 1935), pp. 7–33.

Fowler, R. *Language in the News: Discourse and Ideology in the Press* (London: Routledge, 1991).

Galtung, J. and Ruge, M. 'Structuring and Selecting News', in S. Cohen and J. Young (eds) *The Manufacture of News: Social Problems, Deviance and the Mass Media* (London: Constable, 1973), pp. 62–72 (originally published in *Journal of International Peace Research* 1 (1965), 64–90).

Halliday, M.A.K. *An Introduction to Functional Grammar*, 3rd edn (London: Arnold, 2004).

Harcup, T. and O'Neill, D. 'What is News? Galtung and Ruge Revisited', *Journalism Studies* 2(2) (2001), 261–80.

Hardt-Mautner, G. *Only Connect. Critical Discourse Analysis and Corpus Linguistics.* http://www.comp.lancs.ac.uk/computing/research/ucrel/papers/techpaper/vol6.pdf (1995).

Hoey, M. *Textual Interaction: An Introduction to Written Discourse Analysis* (London: Routledge, 2001).

Hunston, S., 'Counting the Uncountable: Problems of Identifying Evaluation in a Text and in a Corpus', in A. Partington, J. Morley and L. Haarman (eds) *Corpora and Discourse* (Bern: Peter Lang, 2004), pp. 157–88.

Hunston, S. *Corpora in Applied Linguistics* (Cambridge University Press, 2002).

Johnson, S., Culpeper, J. and Suhr, S. 'From "Politically Correct Councillors" to "Blairite Nonsense": Discourses of "Political Correctness" in Three British Newspapers', *Discourse & Society* 14(1) (2003), 29–47.

Keeble, R. *The Newspapers Handbook* 4th edn (London: Routledge, 2006)

Koller, V. and Mautner, G. 'Computer Applications in Critical Discourse Analysis', in A.C. Hewings, C. Coffin and K. O'Halloran (eds) *Applying English Grammar* (London: Arnold, 2004), pp. 216–28.

Krzyżanowski, M. and Wodak, R. *The Politics of Exclusion: Debating Migration in Austria.* (New Brunswick, NJ: Transaction Publishers, 2008).

Langenscheidt Explorer Wörterbuch Englisch (München: Langenscheidt, 2006).

Lemke, J. 'Travels in Hypermodality', *Visual Communication* 1 (2002), 299–325.

Li, X. (ed.) *Internet Newspapers. The Making of a Mainstream Medium* (Mahwah, NJ: Erlbaum, 2006).

Lin, C.A. and M.B. Salwen, 'Utilities of Online and Offline News Use', in X. Li (ed.) *Internet Newspapers. The Making of a Mainstream Medium* (Mahwah, NJ: Erlbaum, 2006), pp. 209–25.

Louw, B., 'Irony in the Text or Insincerity in the Writer? – The Diagnostic Potential of Semantic Prosodies', in M. Baker, G. Francis and E. Tognini-Bonelli (eds) *Text and Technology: In Honour of John Sinclair* (Amsterdam & Philadelphia: Benjamins, 1993), pp. 157–76.

Martin, J.R., Matthiessen, C.M.I.M., and Painter C. *Working with Functional Grammar* (London: Arnold, 1997).

Matouschek, B., Wodak, R. and Januschek, F. *Notwendige Massnahmen gegen Fremde?* (Vienna: Passagen Verlag, 1995).

Mautner, G., 'The Entrepreneurial University. A Discursive Profile of a Higher Education Buzzword', *Critical Discourse Studies* 2(2) (2005a), pp. 95–120.

Mautner, G., 'Time to Get Wired: Using Web-Based Corpora in Critical Discourse Analysis', *Discourse & Society* 16(6) (2005b), 809–28.

Mautner, G., 'Mining Large Corpora for Social Information: The Case of Elderly', *Language in Society* 36(1) (2007).

O'Halloran, K. and Coffin, C. 'Checking Overinterpretation and Underinterpretation. Help from Corpora in Critical Linguistics', in A. Hewings, C. Coffin and K. O'Halloran (eds) *Applying English Grammar* (London: Arnold, 2004), pp. 275–97.

Östman, J.-O., 'The Postcard as Media', *Text* 24(3) (2004), 423–42.

Partington, A. 'Utterly Content in Each Other's Company. Semantic Prosody and Semantic Preference', *International Journal of Corpus Linguistics* 9(1) (2004), 131–56.

Phillips, L. and Jørgensen, M.W. *Discourse Analysis as Theory and Method* (London: Sage, 2002).

Reah, D. *The Language of Newspapers*, 2nd edn (London: Routledge, 2002).

Reisigl, M. and Wodak, R. *Discourse and Discrimination: The Rhetorics of Racism and Anti-Semitism*. (London: Routledge, 2001).

Richardson, J.E. *Analysing Newspapers: An Approach from Critical Discourse Analysis* (Basingstoke: Palgrave Macmillan, 2006).

Rusch, D. *Online Journalismus. Von den Möglichkeiten der Web-Inszenierung zum audio-visuellen Gesamtereignis am Beispiel online-journalistischer Kulturberichterstattung in Österreich und den USA* (Frankfurt am Main: Peter Lang, 2006).

Rutherford, B.A., 'Genre Analysis of Corporate Annual Report Narratives. A Corpus Linguistics-Based Approach', *Journal of Business Communication* 42(4) (2005), 349–78.

Simpson, P. *Language, Ideology and Point of View* (London and New York: Routledge, 1993).

Stubbs, M. *Text and Corpus Analysis* (Oxford: Blackwell, 1996).

Stubbs, M. *Words and Phrases: Corpus Studies of Lexical Semantics* (Oxford: Blackwell, 2001).

Teubert, W. 'A Province of a Federal Superstate, Ruled by an Unelected Bureaucracy: Keywords of the Eurosceptic Discourse in Britain', in A. Musolff, C. Good, P. Points and R. Wittlinger (eds) *Attitudes Towards Europe: Language in the Unification Process* (Aldershot: Ashgate, 2000), pp. 45–86.

Titscher, S., Meyer, M., Wodak, R. and Vetter, E. *Methods of Text and Discourse Analysis* (London: Sage, 2000).

Tuchman, G., 'The Production of News', in K.B Jensen (ed.) *A Handbook of Media and Communication Research: Qualitative and Quantitatve Methodologies* (London: Routledge, 2002), pp. 78–90.

van Dijk, T.A. *News as Discourse* (Hillsdale, NJ: Erlbaum, 1988).

Williams, R. *Keywords. A Vocabulary of Culture and Society*, 2nd edn (London: Fontana, 1983; original work published in 1976).

Wodak, R. '"Us" and "Them". Inclusion and Exclusion – Discrimination via Discourse', in G. Delanty, P.R. Jones and R. Wodak (eds) *Identity, Migration and Belonging* (Liverpool: Liverpool University Press, 2008), pp. 54–77.

Analyzing Communication in the New Media

Helmut Gruber

3

Introduction

This chapter deals with communication in the new media and why it is interesting and relevant for social scientists to investigate communicative forms such as email, chat or text messaging. We first have a theoretically informed view on the interplay of media and forms of communication (defined as configurations of certain technical and situational features). We then deal with the question of how to compile a corpus of new media texts and which ethical aspects have to be considered. In the remainder of the chapter we conduct a sample-pilot project in which we investigate key features of email texts. This second part of the chapter provides an overview of relevant textual and discursive characteristics of new media text genres and the way they are investigated.

New media: an overview

In the last fifteen years, the rise of information technology has had far-reaching cultural and social impacts. Computer technology and the development of the internet play the main role in this technological revolution, but mobile phone services have an ever increasing part in this process. Together they represent what has been called the 'new media' during the last decade.

New information technologies not only offer the appropriate technological means for meeting the needs of the globalized information society; they also symbolize all the relevant features we associate with twenty-first-century society: decentralization, interactivity, multimodality, transnationality and transculturality (Münker and Roesler 1997). Like the invention of any new technology of writing, the new media have had a tremendous effect on communicative and discursive practices and have fostered the emergence of new communicative styles and genres (Bolter 1997).

But what distinguishes communicative practices in the new media from those in the 'old' media such as newspapers, magazines (see Chapter 2) or radio and TV (see Chapters 4 and 6)? To answer this question, it is useful to distinguish between types of media, communicative forms and genres. Holly (1997) suggests using the term 'medium' for an array of communicative possibilities characterized by:

- the types of signs they can process (for example spoken sounds vs. written signs);
- the direction of communication (monological vs. dialogical);
- the possibilities of transmission and storage of data.

One specific medium may facilitate different communicative forms, characterized by combinations of certain features on these three dimensions. The medium 'computer' – may for instance be used for the production of written, monological, stored (hyper-) texts[1] as well as for engaging in spoken, dialogical (by default) unstored video conferences. It is worth noting here that calling a computer a communicative 'medium' is only a shorthand method for denoting a complex combination of computers, their network connections and specific transmission protocols and software tools which enable users to transmit data between computers. These technical (hardware and software) characteristics of new media communication, however, are relevant for social scientists only in so far as their technological features shape communicative practices of and social relationships between users of these technologies.

Forms of communication are not necessarily associated with one single medium. A monological, written text may for instance be realized as a book, an inscription on a stone or an electronic text. The realization of a form of communication in a specific medium allows however for media-specific variations of these respective forms.

Additionally, forms of communication may be realized as different genres, depending on the communicative purpose they fulfil in a certain situation type (that is a written, monological text may represent the genre of 'cooking recipe' or of 'software manual' depending on the social and communicative function the respective texts serves). As in the case of media-specific realizations of communicative forms, genres may also be realized differently in different media.

In order to characterize communicative forms in the new media,[2] Gruber (2008) split each of Holly's dimensions into two subdimensions as Table 3.1 shows (cf. Herring 2007 for a similar classification grid, especially her dimensions for classifying the 'medium factors'):[3]

The 'sign type' dimension is divided into the subdimensions (1) 'conceptual mode of communication' and (2) 'communicative modality'. Subdimension (1) draws upon a distinction which was introduced by Koch and Österreicher (1994), who assume that the conception of a communicative product as 'spoken' or 'written' is independent from its realization in the oral or written mode – that is a speech delivered orally in front of an audience may have been composed in written mode very carefully by the speaker, having in mind the face-to-face communicative situation of the speech which may result in a

Table 3.1   Specification of Holly's (1997) dimensions for characterizing communicative forms in the new media

Holly's original dimensions	Subdimensions introduced by Gruber (2008)
Types of sign	(1) Conceptual mode
	(2) Semiotic mode
Direction of communication	(3) Primary communicative function
	(4) Number of communication partners
Possibilities of transmission	(5) Degree of intended persistence
	(6) Synchronicity vs. asynchronicity

'writ[ten] to be spoken' (Gregory and Carroll 1978:47) text. The oral delivery of a pronouncement in court, on the other hand, is a typical instance of the oral presentation of a conceptually written text. According to Koch and Österreicher, the conceptually literal pole of communication is associated with interpersonal distance, whereas the conceptually oral pole is associated with closeness between communication partners.

Subdimension (2) (communicative modality) refers to the semiotic modalities which are (in principle) available in the different media and forms of communication. These modalities range from oral through written to pictorial, musical and so on.

Holly's second dimension (direction of communication) is split into the subdimensions of (3) 'monological vs. dialogical communication' and (4) 'number of communication partners'. Subdimension (3) refers to the primary communicative function a certain form of communication has whereas subdimension (4) specifies how many senders prototypically interact with how many addressees by the specific communicative form. Three types of sender–addressee combinations are possible: one to one (1:1; 'private communication'), one to many (1:n; 'broadcasting'), and many to many (n:n; 'communicative networks') communications.

The third dimension (possibilities of transmission and storage of data) is split into the two subdimensions (5) 'degree of intended persistence' and (6) 'synchronous vs. asynchronous communication'. Subdimension (5) takes up a notion of Erickson (1999) who notes that most forms of computer-mediated-communication (CMC henceforth) are intended to persist for a longer time period (that is they can be stored) and argues that this feature compensates for some of the shortcomings of CMC like unclear references between messages in a discussion (or – in more technical terms – 'unclear inter-turn references'). Users may associate different degrees of intended persistence with different forms of communication (for example a hypertext is intended to persist for a longer time than a turn in a chat communication or a text message).

Subdimension (6) specifies whether communicators interact synchronously or asynchronously in a form of communication. Table 3.2 gives an overview

Table 3.2 Characterization of new media as 'communicative forms'. *Source:* Gruber (2008:365)[4]

Subdimension	Hypertext	Email	Chat	Text messages
1. Conceptual mode of communication	Conceptually written	Conceptually written + conceptually spoken	Conceptually written + conceptually spoken	Conceptually written + conceptually spoken
2. Semiotic modality	Multimodal	Primarily textual (hypertext possible)	Textual	Textual
3. Primary communicative function	Monological	Dialogical	Dialogical	Dialogical
4. No. of communication partners	1:n	1:1 (personal communication) 1:n (newsgroups and so on)	n:n (1:1 possible)	1:1 (1:n possible)
5. Degree of intended persistence	High	Medium	Low	Low
6. Synchronicity vs. asynchronicity	Asynchronous	Asynchronous	Synchronous	Asynchronous

of the prototypical specifications of each form of communication on the six subdimensions.

The features of the four forms of communication on the six subdimensions in Table 3.2 show that no clear-cut boundaries divide one from another, but that they rather share different characteristics on different subdimensions. Hypertexts stand out as the most distinctive of the four forms. They share only the feature of asynchronicity with email and text communication. On all other dimensions, hypertexts differ from the others. Hypertexts are conceptually literal, multimodal, monological[5], one-to-many forms of communication with a high degree of intended persistence; that is they are produced to be accessible (yet not unchanged) at least for a certain time rather than designed as one (ephemeral) move in a multi-party communication.

Email, chat and text messaging share the same features on the first three subdimensions (that is they are conceptually written *and* spoken; their primary semiotic modality is textual; and they are dialogical), but differ in the last three. Here, email and text messaging show the same characteristics on subdimensions 4 and 6 (that is they are used primarily for 1:1 communications and they are asynchronous forms of communication), whereas chat and text messaging are similar on subdimension 5 (that is their degree of intended persistence is low).

This preliminary characterization of the four forms of communication shows that they constitute a network which we can expect to share certain discursive features, communicative practices and genres.

Activity 3.1

Ask yourself in which situations and for which purposes you used various forms of communication in the new media during the last two weeks. Then try to imagine how you would have conducted these communications were these media not available. Which communicative practices in which communicative modes could replace them and what effects on different aspects of communication (speed, form and so on) would this have?

Why investigate communication in the new media as a social scientist?

The simplest answer to this question is that researching communication in the new media is most easily done in terms of collecting data. Data of computer-mediated communication (CMC) exist in machine-readable form from the beginning on, they are easy to collect and easy to store, and they can be subjected easily to automatic and semi-automatic routines of analysis by concordance programs and so on (for an overview of freely available concordance programs see David Lee's webpage http://devoted.to/corpora; if you compile a corpus of CMC data you have, of course, to observe ethical considerations –

see below). The availability of CMC data alone is of course no sufficient reason for researching it (empty beer cans are also easily available but only of limited use for social scientists interested in interpersonal communication).

One reason why communication in the new media is interesting for social scientists was already alluded to at the beginning of this chapter: CMC has become ubiquitous at least in modern Western societies and investigating various forms of CMC can therefore provide us with important insights into the 'communicative households' of inhabitants of the twenty-first century. Recall the results of the above activity: one of your results might have been that the speed of your communication might slow down considerably if you did not have access to new communication media: Writing a letter might easily replace sending an email to somebody, but think how long it will take until you receive the reply to your mail. But CMC does not only speed up communication – it also makes possible new forms of communities. Think of chat groups composed of participants from various countries and who 'meet' regularly in their chat room to maintain their social relations. It is almost certain that these people would never have been in touch with each other without CMC. These examples show that CMC is an integral part of modern life and therefore also a worthy object of social science studies.

There is also a further reason why investigating CMC is interesting for social scientists concerned with communication. Although CMC forms of communication are widely used and indispensable for many people in the Western world, they are still new forms of communication compared with printed forms of communication or even to electronically transmitted forms of communication such as television or radio communication. Investigating forms and emerging genres of CMC allows us as social scientists to examine how people appropriate new forms of communications for their social and communicative needs. As was already pointed out in Chapter 2 (p. 33) in reference to printed media and their electronic counterparts, textual and semiotic conventions for communication in new media are never totally new. Text producers rather use their knowledge about already conventionalized genres and their semiotic organization in traditional media in order to communicate in new media. The semiotic and technological affordances of these new media in turn influence and shape the realization of these conventional genres in the new media. Investigating communication in the new media thus allows us to analyze the process of appropriation of new communicative possibilities by people and the emergence of new genres through the interplay of already established generic conventions with new technological and semiotic possibilities.

Compiling a corpus of CMC texts

The technical side of compiling a corpus of CMC texts is – as mentioned above – quite unproblematic. CMC texts are available in machine-readable formats (as plain-text files, rtf files or html files) and they are either stored automatically by the respective programs used to create and exchange them (for example: email programs) or they are easily storable during CMC interaction (as in the case of chat interactions). Thus, if you decide to investigate a certain form of CMC and as soon as you have developed an appropriate research question, the building of a corpus is not difficult at all. Once you have compiled your corpus you can subject it to various forms of automatic or semi-automatic analysis (see Chapter 2).

Apart from the technical ease of data collection in CMC research, there are, however, ethical considerations to be taken into account. As mentioned above, forms of CMC may be realized in different genres (according to the communicative purposes they are used to fulfil) and they may be used in different degrees of publicity. Thus, if a close friend or your lover sends you an email he/she will probably not be very happy (to use a most neutral term) to find this mail included in your collection of CMC texts after some time.

On the other hand, postings to academic email discussion lists freely accessible and often stored and searchable on publicly accessible servers almost share equivalent status with published texts in terms of their quotability, that is you might quote an email posting to a discussion list in a term paper (under certain conditions) and you might also use it as an object of investigation in an academic project.

These two extreme cases should illustrate that in compiling CMC data you have to follow the same ethical considerations as in collecting any kind of discourse data: if you want to use CMC data which come from private contexts and interactions then you have to inform the writers/interactants and gain their consent for using these data. Additionally, you should remove all details from your data which would allow your readers to identify individuals (and sometimes also places and circumstances) of the interaction you investigate; that is you should anonymize your data. This latter advice holds also for publicly available CMC data such as the above-mentioned academic discussion lists. Although these postings are freely available and stored for search and use by others, some people do not like the idea that their texts are objects of investigations rather than sources for intellectual stimulation. Thus, if you quote an email posting in your study because you refer to its content (for example as a backing of one of your arguments or as the point of departure for a counter argumentation) then of course you have to quote it in a scholarly manner (giving full name of author(s), title and date of posting and date of retrieval, name of the mailing list). But if you quote a posting because you want to analyze some of its communicative, linguistic, structural and other properties, it is wise to at least omit the name of the author and also names of others who might be referred to in the message (see Herring 1995, 1996a; for a detailed discussion on the ethics of CMC investigations).

A note on the use of independent variables (background information) in your study of CMC: many social scientists are interested in correlating certain features of the discourse data they investigate with background variables like age, gender, social class, country of origin and so on of the persons who produced data. If you plan such a study using CMC data, you have to be careful about how you obtain the necessary background information. Thus, if you –

for instance – want to conduct a project in which you analyze gender-specific differences of 'flaming' practices (that is heated disputes – Lea *et al.* 1992) on email discussion lists (like Herring, 1996a, did), you cannot rely on the (nick-) names contributors use for deciding which gender the author of a certain message has, because these names are no reliable source for you. On the internet, everybody can choose the identity he/she wants to perform for others: a male may adopt a female identity and vice versa and so on. It is therefore necessary that you base the classification of your CMC data into groups on more robust grounds than on the information you gain from virtual space.

In the remainder of this chapter, I focus on the linguistic properties of the genre of contributions to scholarly email discussion lists because email communication was the earliest available type of CMC and is therefore the most researched form of communication in the new media. I concentrate on postings to scholarly discussion lists because they are a typical example of the generic hybridity of CMC texts in which technical possibilities of the medium interact with already established genre conventions of a discourse community and communicative aims of this community in newly emerging genres and subgenres. What follows is thus a short introduction into key concepts and practices of 'computer-mediated discourse analysis' (CMDA, Herring 2004) – a somewhat misleading term as it is not a discourse analysis mediated by computers but a discourse analysis of computer-mediated discourse. The term is widely used however in present day CMC research.

I first discuss the underlying conception of genre I use and then proceed to show you different linguistic aspects of the mentioned generic hybridity of the postings under discussion. This part of the chapter is intended to show you how a pilot study in the field of CMC research could be conducted.

My examples come from two linguistic discussion lists, the LINGUIST list and the ETHNO list. The LINGUIST list is the oldest discussion list in the area of linguistics and has several thousand subscribers all over the world who are mainly (but not exclusively) language scholars (from students to university professors). The list is moderated and discussions cover all topics of linguistics. The ETHNO list is not moderated and discussion topics are restricted to questions concerning ethno-methodology and conversation analysis.

Activity 3.2

Read the two texts in Figures 3.1 and 3.2. Both texts are postings which were sent during discussions (that is they are 'reactive-postings'); text 1 was posted on the LINGUIST list and text 2 was posted to the ETHNO list. Next,

■   try to determine those linguistic/stylistic features which the two texts have in common, and then

■   try to determine those linguistic/stylistic features which differentiate between the two texts.

Date: Fri, 06 Oct 1995 02:49:10 Re: 6.1334, Disc 2
From: OL2 <OL2 [e-mail address, HG]>
Subject: Re: 6.1334, Disc: 2

On the language/dialect discussion, AL2 says:
> Date: Thu, 28 Sep 1995 16:35:00 PDT
> From: AL2 [e-address, HG] (AL2, full name, HG)
> Subject: Disc 2 (original thread name, HG).more
>
> might want to respond. I am particularly interested in corrections and
> additions to what I say about "Spanish", "castellano" and "Gallego"
> below.
> ...
> A final thought on the above problem is that some people will
> argue on the basis of the standard that, say, there is no
> continuum between Spanish and Portuguese because "Spanish" means
> standard Spanish, also known by the "dialectal" name castellano,
> and Gallego, the Galician transition between Northern "Spanish"
> and Northern "Portuguese" is a separate language, not Spanish.
> ^^^^^^^^^^^

This is indeed an awkward formulation. It pressuposes, by negation, that
Galizan could be considered a dialect of *Spanish*. The use of the
Spanish name "Gallego" for it, instead of the native Portuguese term
"Galego" or either of the English translations Galician/Gallegan (both, by
the way, derived from Spanish "Galicia" and "gallego") reflects a
dubiously informed view about the nature of the native dialects of Galiza
Portuguese.

We may say that, in terms of usages and socio-functional distribution,
Galizan has been (and for the most part continues to be) a *social*
dialect of Spanish -- very roughly.speaking, Spanish varieties for formal
domains, Galizan varieties for informal domains. But structurally, native
Galizan has been, still is, and will presumably continue to be (until it
disappears as a native dialect in the next generations) a part of the
Western Ibero-Romance Block.

The view of Galizan as an "intermediate step" in the Portuguese-Spanish
continuum is only a very rough formulation of the question. We would need
to be more specific as to what specific Galizan dialects we're focusing
on. Urban varieties of Galiza Portuguese are highly 'interferred' by
Spanish. The regularized, formal variety spread through the spoken media
(particularly television) is, curiously enough, a prosodic and phonetic
calque of Spanish, seasoned with a few, highly productive lexical elements
and quaint formulae ("enxebrismos" is the Galizan word) which symbolize
the new "language" -- and discourse on identity. No wonder why speakers
from other areas of the Portuguese domain interpret this sort of TV
Galizan as a "weird Spanish".

Overall, the differences between Galizan, Portuguese, Brazilian and other
clusters of varieties do not warrant the classification of Galizan as a
separate language from a strictly structural viewpoint. It is puzzling to
observe the lack of rigor and consistency on the part of linguists (for
the most part dialectologists) who proclaim the independence of "Galician"
when it comes to applying the same classificatory criteria based on
dialectal variation to other linguistic domains of the world -- including,
of course, Spanish, English, French, or you-name-it. Even Ruhlen's
extensive catalogue _A Guide to the World's Languages_ is not exempt from
this type of inconsistencies.

Finally, as for the written form, the current official attempt to impose
an orthography heavily based on the Spanish model may have serious
negative implications for the very goal the language planners officially
declare to pursue: the "normalization" of the "Galician language". The
unstated official programme is one of pure, unjustified differentialism
from standard Portuguese. As it stands, anything that passes as Spanish
may also pass as "Galician", while anything that sounds "too Portuguese"
is, literally, banned (from officially sanctioned written and oral texts).

Language planners in Galiza have an immense responsibility in reopening an
academic debate about the issue which should have never been closed due to
dogmatism and political reasons. I personally think, simply put, that --
as it happens sometimes in the political spectrum -- there's no viable
linguistic or sociolinguistic space in between Portuguese and Spanish in
the world to come -- as there would be no room for an independent
"Brazilian language". But, paradoxically enough, it is easier to air out
one's disobedient views about Galizan in an international forum like
LINGUIST than in Galiza itself.

OL2
[full institutional address, telephone number, and e-mail address, HG]

Figure 3.1 Text from the LINGUIST list

Tue, 8 Aug 1995 12:32:10 -0800>
Reply-To: Ethnomethodology/conversation analysis <ETHNO@RPITSVM.BITNET>
Sender: Ethnomethodology/conversation analysis <ETHNO@RPITSVM.BITNET>
"Thomas P. Wilson" <wilson@ALISHAW.UCSB.EDU>
Re: disc 2, subthread of disc 1, HG>
X-To:Ethnomethodology/conversation analysis
<ETHNO%RPITSVM.BITNET@PSUVM.PSU.EDU>
To: Multiple recipients of list ETHNO <ETHNO@RPITSVM.BITNET>

CE1 [first name, HG] asks how can we proceed if we reject probabilistic decision theory on the grounds that it is inadequate or incoherent.

However, the task is not to respecify the enterprise of subjective probability or figure out some alternative framework ahead of time. Maybe subjective probability theory is the only formal analysis ready to hand, but that doesn't mean we have to accept its terms before starting to look, nor do we need to specify an alternative a priori framework in advance of inquiry. To insist on this would be to adopt a policy of constructive analysis quite antithetical to ethnomethodology, early and late, and also to conversation analysis.

Instead, at least from a CA point of view, the task is to look at the data to see how the participants manage things so as to produce what they and others orient to as a verdict, hung jury, mistrial, or whatever. And along the way, of course, there's lot's of interesting stuff, such as how participants treat testimony as credible or not, evidence as real or planted or contaminated or ... , how they invoke the law, etc.
The CA literature on educational and medical settings, official hearings, emergency calls, and courtrooms comes to mind. I don't know what's there relevant to this, but I suspect one should have that in hand.

IE1 [full name, HG]

IE 1 + full institutional address, telephone number and e-mail address [HG]

Figure 3.2   Posting to the ETHNO list

What is a genre?

In analyzing genres used in academic contexts, John Swales's genre approach is very useful (Swales 1990; see also Chapter 1). Swales postulates a strong relationship between 'discourse communities' and 'genres' and thus stresses a central feature of recent genre approaches, namely the close interdependence of genres (that is written or spoken texts) and contextual features of their use. He states that *'a discourse community utilizes and hence possesses one or more genres in the communicative furtherance of its aims'* (Swales 1990:26; original emphasis). This as one of six defining features of a 'discourse community'. Browsing through these features suggests at first glance that subscribers of email discussion lists have to be viewed as discourse communities in Swales's sense (Swales 1990:24–6, emphases removed):

'1.   A discourse community has a broadly agreed set of common public goals
       . . .' – This is true for both discussion lists as on subscribing; each new
       subscriber receives a file which spells out the aims of the respective list.[6]

'2.   A discourse community has mechanisms of intercommunication among
       its members . . .' – Obviously the many-to-many communication mode of
       the Listserv software is 'the' mechanism of intercommunication between
       members.

'3.   A discourse community uses its participatory mechanisms primarily to
       provide information and feedback . . .' – This criterion is also met by
       both lists as 'chat' (that is personal communication between subscribers
       with no relevance for the general 'aim' of the list) is explicitly not permit-
       ted or at least negatively sanctioned by other list members.

'4.   A discourse community utilizes and hence possesses one or more genres
       in the communicative furtherance of its aims . . .' – This is the leading
       question of the rest of this chapter. How can we determine whether there
       is a genre which could be coined 'scholarly email discussion list contribu-
       tion' in the same sense as there is the genre 'research paper in the human-
       ities/social sciences'?

'5.   In addition to owning genres, a discourse community has acquired a
       specific lexis . . .' – This is true for both lists, as you will have noticed
       when reading the two sample texts in the Appendices. On the LIN-
       GUIST list terminology from all areas of Linguistics is used, whereas on
       the ETHNO list ethnomethodological and conversation analytic termi-
       nology prevails.

'6.   A discourse community has a threshold level of members with a suitable
       degree of relevant content and discoursal expertise' – That this is the case
       can be seen by the (infrequent) complaints of 'competent' subscribers
       about 'unnecessary' or even 'dumb' questions, which are sometimes put
       on the lists.

The previous considerations have provided us with enough evidence that list
subscribers on both discussion lists can be viewed as 'discourse communities'
in Swales's sense. The next step of our investigation now focuses on their contributions to the two respective lists. We try to find out whether discussion list
contributions realize a distinct genre and if the answer to this question is positive, we will determine the linguistic and communicative properties of this
genre.

Key properties of scholarly email postings

If you do a pilot study to determine the linguistic properties of your text sample you have first to determine which texts you choose for your investigation
as you will want to select most typical texts. How can you proceed in the case
of email discussions?

In many cases, it will be useful to include entire discussions in your database (which is easily done by referring to the thematic thread of the messages).[7] In the next step, you can determine how many messages each discussant contributed to the respective discussion and how often others referred to these messages. This provides you with a first impression about (1) the communicative activity of single contributors and (2) the perceived relevance of their contributions (see Gruber 1998a). You may find out that there are discussants who posted a lot of contributions which were rarely (or even never) reacted to be others, and that there are other discussants whose postings received many reactions (follow-up postings). The former contributions (the unsuccessful ones) will not be interesting for you in the first step of your investigation, in which you want to determine the typical features of the texts in your sample, because for some reason (which you do not yet know) they were 'dead ends' in the discussion under investigation.

You will rather focus on the successful postings at this state of your project, that is on those messages which received many follow-up postings as they seem to have properties which make them interesting and 'reactable' for other members of the discourse community (in a later state of your project – as soon as you have determined the key properties of the genre you are investigating – you may of course also include the unsuccessful postings in your analysis to find out in which respect they differ from the successful ones and in doing so you can find out which linguistic features of your texts are most salient for the genre they represent).

In our sample project, we will concentrate on two postings which occurred during the discussion and which received many direct and indirect reactions (postings which were not immediately sent in response to the respective postings but which referred to them in later contributions in the discussion). First, we will look at the overall structure of the postings and analyze how this structure reflects both technological affordances of CMC and genre conventions of established academic genres.

Herring (1996b) describes the canonical structure of reactive email postings in the following way:

1. link to an earlier message
2. expression of views
3. appeal to other participants (Herring 1996b:91)

where positions 1 and 2 can occur several times within one posting (that is one message can refer to several previous ones). Reactive email postings thus display strong *intertextual relationships* to other texts. *Intertextuality* means that other texts are explicitly present in the text under analysis; they are 'manifestly' marked or cued by features on the surface of the text, such as quotation marks. Note, however, that a text may 'incorporate' another text without the latter being explicitly cued: one can respond to another text in the way one words one's own text, for example. (Fairclough 1992:104)

As the quotation from Fairclough says, there are some crucial differences in the possible *realizations of* intertextuality in our sample texts:

EXAMPLE 3.1   (emphases added)

On the language/dialect discussion, **AL2 (full name,** *H.G.) says:*
> Date: Thu 28 Sep 1995 16:35:00 PDT
> From: AL2 (login name, H.G.)   )
> Subject: Disc 2 (original thread name, H.G).more
>
> might want to respond. I am particularly interested in corrections and
> additions to what I say about 'Spanish', 'castellano' and 'Gallego' below.
> . . .
> A final thought on the above problem is that some people will
> argue on the basis of the standard that, say, there is no
> continuum between Spanish and Portuguese because 'Spanish' means
> standard Spanish, also known by the 'dialectal' name castellano,
> and Gallego, the Galician transition between Northern 'Spanish'
> and Northern 'Portuguese' is a separate language, not Spanish.
*^^^^^^^^^^^*
This *is indeed an awkward formulation.* **It** *pressuposes, by negation, that*
Galizan could be considered a dialect of *Spanish*. The use of the
Spanish name 'Gallego' for it, instead of the native Portuguese term
'Galego' or either of the English translations Galician/Gallegan (both, by the way, derived from
Spanish 'Galicia' and 'gallego') reflects a
dubiously informed view about the nature of the native dialects of Galiza
Portuguese . . . (OL2, 6. Oct, LINGUIST-List, disc. 2)

Example 3.1 represents the beginning of the text from the LINGUIST list (Figure 3.1) which is highly relevant for the following discussion and causes a topic shift from the discussion of 'language and dialect' in general to the discussion of the relationship between Spanish, Portuguese and Galician.

Viewed under a formal perspective, it is an example of 'direct quoting', that is the inclusion of parts of a previous posting in the actual message which is a standard way of including the referred text into the actual message in most email programs. Direct quotes are marked off from the 'auctorial text' by means of an alphanumeric sign ('>') at the beginning of each quoted line. In this case, the author quotes not only the portions of text he refers to and comments on but also the software-generated parts of the message, that is date, sender and subject line (thematic thread), which is rather unusual. But it guarantees that readers may find this previous posting in their own email reader or even retrieve it from the site where the postings are stored. The use of the anaphoric forms '*this*' and '*it*' in the first two sentences of the auctorial text illustrates the tight relation between quoted and auctorial text.

Direct quoting enables any receiver of a posting (1) to check whether the reference to a previous contribution is correct (and the current author is not commenting on a distorted representation of the point of view of his/her opponent) and (2) to trace back a discussion to its origins and thus enables receivers who did not follow a certain discussion from the beginning to join in at a later date. The use of direct quoting is a sign for the awareness of discussants not only that they are communicating with the author of the message(s) they refer to, but also that there is a group of anonymous, silent 'listeners' who might also be interested in the topic under consideration but who might not have followed the discussion from the beginning.

Example 3.2 (from the posting to the ETHNO list, Figure 3.2) shows that the structural position 'link to an earlier message' can be realized very differently.

EXAMPLE 3.2   (emphasis added)

CE1 (first name, H.G.) asks how can we proceed if we reject probabilistic decision theory
on the grounds that it is inadequate or incoherent.
However, the task is not to respecify the enterprise of subjective
probability or figure out some alternative framework ahead of time. Maybe
subjective probability theory is the only formal analysis ready to hand,
but that doesn't mean we have to accept its terms before starting to look,
nor do we need to specify an alternative a priori framework in advance of
inquiry. To insist on this would be to adopt a policy of constructive
analysis quite antithetical to ethnomethodology, early and late, and also
to conversation analysis.
Instead, at least from a CA point of view, the task is to look at the data
to see how the participants manage things so as to produce what they and
others orient to as a verdict, hung jury, mistrial, or whatever. (IE1, 8. Aug, ETHNO-List, disc. 1)

In the first sentence of this posting, the author refers back to a previous message which he comments on in the remainder of his contribution. If we compare the kinds of reference in Examples 3.1 and 3.2 we find marked differences. In Example 3.2, the author obviously does not use the built-in software function for replying but rather paraphrases the previous contribution. Additionally, he mentions only the first name of the author of the previous message without quoting any further information. In the above example, readers only learn that CE1 is the author of the previous posting and then a rough reformulation of a rather lengthy message follows. Readers have to know that CE1 is the first name of the 'dominant contributor' of this discussion and additionally they have to have read all his postings because CE1 sometimes posted several contributions a day.

Both kinds of referring to previous messages are typical for the respective lists as a systematic analysis of communicative practices and generic features of these two lists showed (Gruber 1998a, 1998b) and, of course, both ways of text reference also resemble academic quotation practices. The author of text 1 uses a direct quotation to link his own arguments to another author's position whereas the author of text 2 uses an indirect quotation. In this respect, both texts show typical features of intertextual relationships which can also be found in traditional academic genres (Gruber 2000b). Both texts, however, show specific characteristics typical for the communicative context of the discussion and of the email-text subgenre they realize: The author of text 1 uses a technological feature of his email software for realizing a direct quote that enables all readers to locate the reference message. This shows us how new technologies are appropriated by users in order to realize established generic conventions in an emergent genre.

Text 2 hints at another generic feature of academic email postings which distinguishes them from 'traditional' genres, namely the realization of the *interpersonal function* (Halliday 1994) of communication. The concept of the interpersonal (meta-) function of language refers to the fact that language not only has an *ideational function* (that is it is used to *transmit 'ideas' from one person to another*) but is also used to *establish and maintain social relationships between people*. The use of the first name to refer to the author of the previous message in text 2 indicates a rather personal relationship between the author of text 2 and the author of the message to which he is referring. At the same time, it also indicates that the author of text 2 assumes that all readers of his posting have the same kind of relationship towards the author of the reference message. By using the first name for *person reference*, the author or text 2 thus creates a communicative atmosphere which resembles a face-to-face interaction rather than a written exchange. This is a first indication that genre conventions for scholarly email postings are not exclusively modelled after the 'research paper' genre conventions, but that they combine features of traditional written academic genres with spoken everyday genres. The author of text 1 on the other hand uses the traditional method of written academic prose to refer to the author of the reference posting. In this respect, his posting is closer to the written pole of communication, although we shall see that his text also contains elements of spoken language.

Another aspect of the realization of the interpersonal function is the use of *modality*. Modality is used to express 'the intermediate degrees [.] between the positive and the negative poles' (Halliday 1994:88) of statements. Modal expressions may weaken or strengthen the content of a statement in four different respects: *probability* refers to a scale between the poles of *certainty* and *uncertainty*; *usuality* allows us to scale a message between the two poles of '*always*' and '*never*'; *obligation* informs us about the author's stance toward the '*allowdness*' of the content of his message; and *inclination* indicates to which degree the author is *willing* to do something.

In academic genres, indications of probability (or 'academic hedges') are quite common. Academic hedges comprise expressions like 'normally, usually' and so on. They are a sign of detachment, that is an interest in abstract ideas, and the modalization of content (Halliday 1994). Chafe and Danielewics (1987:109) 'have found that academic writers are particularly fond of expressions which indicate that things happen, in general . . . but not necessarily always'. As in the case of intertextuality above, in our sample texts, we find this kind of modal expressions more frequently in text 1 than in text 2. Text 1 contains some modal verbs and particles which limit the certainty of the ideational content of the writer's statement (*Galizan could be considered a dialect of *Spanish**; *We may say . . . native Galizan . . . will presumably continue*; *the current official attempt . . . may have serious negative implications*; *anything that passes as Spanish may also pass as 'Galician'*) whereas text 2 contains only one instance of an academic hedge (*Maybe subjective probability theory . . .*). Here again we find that the LINGUIST list posting corresponds closer to the conventional academic genres than the ETHNO posting which again is closer to the 'conversation' pole of communication if investigated systematically (Gruber 1997a, 2000a.).

In both sample texts, however, we find interpersonal elements hardly ever found in academic prose, namely the expression of *personal beliefs* and of *explicit evaluations*. As with academic hedges through which the validity of claims is limited in a general and/or abstract way, in 'personal beliefs', writers explicitly express that they themselves challenge the unrestricted validity of their claims, but in a much more personalized way: '*I personally think*' (text 1); '*I don't know what's there relevant to this*' (text 2). These personalized modalizations are a further indications for the above-stated assumption that scholarly email postings combine features of academic genres with features of everyday spoken genres. The use of explicit evaluations is a case in point. Especially in text 1, we find instances of explicit author's evaluations of the content of his message:

> The regularized, formal variety spread through the spoken media (particularly television) is, *curiously enough* . . .; and But, *paradoxically enough*, it is easier to air out one's disobedient views about Galizan in an international forum like LINGUIST than in Galiza itself.

These expressions of 'social esteem' (Martin 2000) are highly unusual in traditional academic genres and support the view that scholarly email postings represent a hybrid genre which combines characteristics of various other genres.

Another interpersonal characteristic of scholarly email postings is the rather high frequency of *first person singular pronouns*. Whereas authors of traditional academic prose try to use a rather impersonal rhetoric (Nystrand 1987; Bazerman 1988; Myers 1990) through which personal beliefs, stances and so on are veiled, the authors in both our sample texts 'intrude' into their postings in a personal way: '*I personally think*' (text 1); '*I don't know what's there relevant to this*' (text 2). This feature again places the texts closer to the 'spoken' pole of the 'spoken–written' continuum and indicates a higher personal involvement of authors than in traditional academic prose.

A last interpersonal characteristic of our sample texts (and of scholarly email postings in general) is the frequent use of *contractions* like '*I don't know what's there relevant to this*' (text 2); '*that doesn't mean . . .*' (text 2); '*there's lot's [sic] of interesting stuff . . .*' (text 2); '*there's no viable linguistic or sociolinguistic space . . .*' (text 1). Contractions are not only a characteristic of spoken language, they also indicate involvement and frequent contact between participants (Martin 1992:531f.).

In a further attempt to specify the generic properties of scholarly email postings, we will investigate aspects of the *logical (meta-) function* of our sample texts (Halliday 1994; Thompson 1996). '[T]he logical metafunction relates to the connections between the messages, and to the ways in which we signal these connections' (Thompson 1996: p. 35). Here we are concerned with the *kinds of connections* (conjunctions) between clauses we find on our texts, how they are realized (as *conjunctions, circumstantial adjuncts, verbs or nouns*; see Martin 1992) and which kind of clause combining prevails (*coordination vs. subordination*). In both sample texts, we find more coordinated than subordinated clauses and clause combinations are in most cases signalled by conjunctions (like '*and*', '*but*' and so on). Both results are somewhat atypical for written academic prose, in which subordinated clause complexes (that is the typical 'hard-to-understand' sentences) prevail and in which the kind of clause connections is typically realized by circumstantial adjuncts ('as a result A is B'), verbs ('A results in B') or nouns ('the result of A is B'). This result again places our sample texts closer to everyday spoken language than to written academic prose.

To sum up our pilot study, the linguistic features we found as typical of scholarly email postings are the following:

- ▪ Intertextual relations:
  - – direct quotation vs.
  - – indirect reference
- ▪ Interpersonal characteristics:
  - – person reference
  - – use of modal expressions
  - – expression of personal beliefs

- use of explicit evaluations
- occurrence of first person singular pronouns
▧ Clause combinations:
- coordination of clauses
- use of conjunctions to express relation between clauses

The results of our sample analysis show that scholarly email postings show characteristics of traditional academic prose, but also display features of oral genres of everyday conversations. Furthermore, we saw how technological features (software affordances) are used to realize 'traditional' characteristics of academic prose in a new form of communication. Thus, our analysis suggests that scholarly email postings are a hybrid genre in which technological possibilities of new forms of communication interact with genre knowledge and communicative aims of users. Furthermore, the results seem to indicate that the two discourse communities under consideration developed slightly differing subgenres which reflect differing communicative aims: On the LINGUIST list, contributors are oriented not only towards their immediate fellow discussants but also towards others who might not have followed the whole discussion and might want to find previous postings. In contrast, ETHNO discussants exhibit a stronger in-group perspective and seem to gear their contributions mainly to their immediate fellow discussants and thus indirectly exclude others from the discussion.

Of course, in a real-world study, the results of our mini-project would have to be verified by analyzing a representative sample of email texts. As was mentioned above at the beginning of the section 'Compiling a corpus of CMC texts', this is technically no problem as CMC is machine-readable and easily storable and retrievable. The results we found here, however, are findings corroborated by a wealth of studies on email communication (Eklundh 1986; Uhlirova 1994; DuBartell 1995; Collot and Bellmore 1996; Yates 1996; Herring 1996b; Gruber 1998a; Gruber 2000b).

Further research topics and questions for a study of email list communication practices include:[8]

▧ practices of topic initiation and of topic continuation;
▧ exchange structures in email discussions;
▧ 'flaming' and conflict management;
▧ implicit and explicit norms of communication (that is analysis of discussions of norm violations).

A wide range of interesting, new research areas opens up if we look at the linguistic diversity of internet communication and the way in which language choices, technical affordances of the new media and issues of identity construction and group constitution are intertwined (see the contributions in Danet and Herring 2007).

Summary

Forms of communication in the new media provide rich data for social science research projects. They allow insights into:

- the appropriation of new means of communication by users;
- the emergence of new genres as combinations of existing generic conventions, new technological means of communication and new communicative goals of users; and
- the formation and maintenance of (discourse) communities through new ways of communication.

At the outset of a research project, it is useful to first identify the communicative form at the centre of investigation alongside a number of technological and situational factors. When compiling a set of CMC texts for further investigation, ethical considerations about the use of data and privacy issues have to be observed in the same way as when dealing with 'traditional' discourse data.

Once the relevant situational factors have been identified and the ethical issues have been resolved, it is advisable to start a project with the sample analysis of a few carefully selected texts. Textual analysis proceeds usually from the macro- to the microtextual level. First you identify overall structural properties of your sample texts (and the variation of these structures) and then you focus on properties of the texts on the ideational, interpersonal and logical planes of language. The analysis of the ideational plane of your texts allows insights into the topics relevant for the persons whose interactions you investigate and how they talk about these topics (in terms of lexical choices, stylistics and regional variants and so on). Investigation of the interpersonal plane concentrates on forms of address, the use of modality, kinds of evaluations and different forms of speech acts. The results of this investigation show you which kinds of relationships are established and maintained between participants by the texts. The texts' properties on the logical plane show you how text-producers combine single ideas they express in their texts, that is whether they argue, narrate, describe and so on A further step of investigation then leads you to analyze the intertextual relationships between single texts. Apart from formal and technologically enabled properties of intertextuality, this allows you insights into the evolution and change of group structures. Taken together, the results of the investigation of all these aspects allow you to specify which genre (or genre-mix) the texts you analyzed realize.

In a final step of your project, you will try to substantiate the results of the qualitative analysis of some selected texts by investigating the whole corpus of texts you compiled. This will show you the generalizability of your results and will correct your interpretations.

Notes

1. Before going into further detail, a short definition of two basic terms is necessary: Although a core feature of many communicative forms in the new media is their multimodality (that is the possible integration of written and spoken language, sounds, pictures, and even video clips into one communicative product) I use the term 'text' to refer to a single functional communicative unit (in the sense of Beaugrande and Dressler 1981) even if this text contains non-linguistic elements and exists only in digital form. I use the term 'document' to refer to written (printed) records of digital texts and/or interactions. In this terminology, an email message is a 'text' and if it is printed out then this printout is the 'document' of this email. On the other hand, in IRC a participant's move is a single 'text', but the printout of the entire chat interaction is the 'document' of this interaction (which consists of a multitude of textual units).

2. Herring (2007) calls these forms of communication 'technological modes' of CMC.

3. Although Herring's (2007) 'faceted classification scheme' for CMC data is in some respects similar to the one presented here, the two schemes are not interchangeable, as Herring abandons the concept of 'genre' and uses instead a broad set of 'situation factor' dimensions in her scheme. This is a conception with which I disagree for theoretical reasons.

4. As regards hypertexts, the sender (author) of a hypertext is not necessarily a single person but may also be an institution or a web design team. But even in these cases different aspects of text production are performed by single specialists who cooperate to produce a hypertext which is intended to be viewed as a communicative product of one single source.

5. This characterization needs a qualification: of course, complex websites may also contain interactive elements like email or chat clients. But the interactivity these elements provide consists not of hypertext features but of features of email or chat.

6. Both lists provide new subscribers with a 'statement of purpose' in which the respective communicative aims of the lists are formulated: *Linguist List:* '[T]he goals of the list: to provide a forum for the discussion of those issues which interest professional linguists. It is most emphatically our intent that the list not acquire an ideological or theoretical bent of any kind whatsoever.' (Thursday 13 December 1990), Anthony Aristar: University of Western Australia, a_aristar@fennel.cc.uwa.oz.au, 'ANNOUNCING THE FORMATION OF LINGUIST'). *Ethno List:* 'You may use this hotline to discuss issues, share ideas and news items, ask questions, or ask for resources. Any contribution is welcome provided it is consistent with the professional focus of the hotline and with CIOS guidelines for hotline contributions (sent once to all new subscribers)' (Comserve@cios.org, 'Your request to join the Ethno hotline').

9. For other possible strategies of data collection in CMC research (and a discussion of their advantages and disadvantages) see Herring (2004:11f.).

10. See also Herring (2004) for an exhaustive list of possible research topics in CMDA.

Key readings

Crystal, D. *Language and the Internet*, 2nd edn (Cambridge: Cambridge University Press, 2006).

Herring, S.C. 'Computer-Mediated Discourse Analysis: An Approach to Researching Online Behavior', in S.A. Barab, R. Kling, and J.H. Gray (eds) *Designing for Virtual Communities in the Service of Learning* (New York: Cambridge University Press, 2004), pp. 338–76.

Herring, S.C. 'Computer-Mediated Communication on the Internet', *Annual Review of Information Science and Technology* 36 (2002), 109–68.

References

Bazerman, C. *Shaping Written Knowledge: The Genre and Activity of the Experimental Article in Science* (Madison: University of Wisconsin Press, 1988).

Bolter, J.D., 'Das Internet in der Geschichte der Technologie des Schreibens', in S. Münker and A. Roesler (eds) *Mythos Internet* (Frankfurt am Main: Suhrkamp, 1997), pp. 37–56.

Chafe, W., and Danielewicz, J. 'Properties of Spoken and Written Language', in R. Horowitz and J. Samuels (eds) *Comprehending Oral and Written Language* (San Diego, CA: Academic Press, 1987), pp. 83–113.

Collot, M. and Bellmore, N. 'Electronic Language: A New Variety of English', in S. Herring (ed.) *Computer-Mediated Communication: Linguistic, Social and Cross-Cultural Perspectives. Pragmatics and Beyond* series (Amsterdam: Benjamins, 1996), pp.13–29.

Danet, B., and Herring, S. (eds) *The Multilingual Internet: Language, Culture, and Communication Online* (New York: Oxford University Press, 2007).

de Beaugrande, R. and Dressler, W.U. *Einführung in die Textlinguistik* (Tübingen: Niemeyer 1981).

DuBartell, D. 'Discourse Features of Computer-Mediated Communication: "Spoken like" and "Written like"', in B. Warvik, S.-K. Tanskanen and R. Hiltunen (eds) *Organization in Discourse: Proceedings from the Turku Conference* (University of Turku, 1995), pp. 231–41.

Eklundh, K.S. 'Dialogue Processes in Computer Mediated Communication', *Linköping Studies in Arts* and *Science* 6, 1986.

Erickson, T. 'Persistent Conversation: An Introduction', *Journal of Computer Mediated Communication* 4 (from http:/jcmc.indiana.edu, retrieved 19 November 2004) (1999).

Fairclough, N. *Discourse and Social Change* (Cambridge: Polity, 1992).

Gregory, M. and S. Carroll. *Language and Situation: Language Varieties and Their Social Contexts* (London: Routledge & Kegan Paul, 1978).

Gruber, H. 'E-mail Discussion Lists: 'A New Genre of Scholarly Communication?', *Wiener Linguistische Gazette* 60/61 (1997a), 24-43.

Gruber, H. 'Thematische Progression in Internet Diskussionslisten', in R. Weingarten (ed.) *Sprachwandel durch den Computer* (Opladen: Westdeutscher Verlag, 1997b), pp. 70–93.

Gruber, H. 'Computer-Mediated Communication and Scholarly Discourse: Forms of Topic-Initiation and Thematic Development', *Pragmatics* 8(1) (1998a), pp. 21–47.

Gruber, H. 'Thematische und interdiskursive Aspekte von Beiträgen zu wissenschaftlichen e-mail Diskussionen', *Mitteilungen des deutschen Germanistenverbandes* 45(3) (special issue, 'Germanistik & Internet', ed. E. Hentschel) (1998b), 213–36.

Gruber, H. 'Scholarly E-mail Discussion List Posting: A Single New Genre of Academic Communication?' in L. Pemberton and S. Shurville (eds) *Words on the Web. Computer Mediated Communication* (Exeter: Intellect, 2000a), pp. 36–44.

Gruber, H. 'Theme and Intertextuality in Scholarly E-mail Messages', *Functions of Language* 7(1) (2000b), 79–115.

Gruber, H. 'Specific Genre Features of New Mass Media', in R. Wodak and V. Koller (eds) *Handbook of Communication in the Public Sphere* (Berlin: Mouton de Gruyter, 2008), pp. 363–81.

Halliday, M.A.K. *An Introduction to Functional Grammar*, 2nd edn (London: Arnold, 1994).

Herring, S.C. 'Linguistics and Critical Analysis of Computer-Mediated Communication: Some Ethical and Scholarly Considerations', *The Information Society* (12)(2) (special issue on 'The Ethics of Fair Practices for Collecting Social Science Data in Cyberspace') (1995), 153–68.

Herring, S.C. 'Posting in a Different Voice: Gender and Ethics in CMC', in C. Ess (ed.) *Philosophical Perspectives on Computer-Mediated Communication* (New York: State University of New York Press, 1996a), pp. 115–47.

Herring, S.C. 'Two Variants of an Electronic Message Schema', in S.C. Herring (ed.) *Computer-Mediated Communication: Linguistic, Social and Cross-Cultural Perspectives* (Amsterdam: Benjamins, 1996b), pp. 81–108

Herring, S.C. (ed.). *Computer-Mediated Communication: Linguistic, Social and Cross-Cultural Perspectives. Pragmatics and Beyond* series (Amsterdam: Benjamins, 1996c).

Herring, S.C. 'Computer-Mediated Communication on the Internet', *Annual Review of Information Science and Technology* 36 (2002), 109–68.

Herring, S.C. 'Computer-Mediated Discourse Analysis: An approach to Researching Online Behaviour', in S.A. Barab, R. Kling, and J.H. Gray (eds) *Designing for Virtual Communities in the Service of Learning* (Cambridge: Cambridge University Press, 2004), pp. 338–76.

Herring, S.C. 'A Faceted Classification Scheme for Computer-mediated Discourse', *Language@Internet*. http://www.languageatinternet.de/articles/761 (retrieved 11 September 2007)

Holly, W. 'Zur Rolle von Sprache in Medien. Semiotische und kommunikationsstrukturelle Grundlagen', *Muttersprache* 107 (1997), pp. 64–75.

Koch, P. and W. Österreicher. 'Schriftlichkeit und Sprache', in H. Günther and O. Ludwig (eds) *Schrift und Schriftlichkeit: ein interdisziplinäres Handbuch internationaler Forschung* (Berlin: de Gruyter, 1994), pp. 587–604

Lea, M., O'Shea, T., Fung, P. and Spears, R. '"Flaming" in Computer-Mediated Communication', in M. Lea (ed.) *Contexts of Computer Mediated Communication* (Hemel Hempstead: Harvester Wheatsheaf, 1992), pp. 89–113.

Martin, J.R. *English Text: Systems and Structure* (Amsterdam: Benjamins, 1992).

Martin, J.R. 'Beyond Exchange: APPRAISAL Systems in English', in S. Hunston and G. Thompson (eds) *Evaluation in Text: Authorial Stance and the Construction of Discourse* (Oxford: Oxford University Press, 2000), pp 142–76.

Münker, S. and Roesler, A. 'Vorwort', in S. Münker and A. Roesler (eds) *Mythos Internet* (Frankfurt am Main: Suhrkamp, 1997), pp. 7–15.

Myers, G. *Writing Biology: Texts and the Social Construction of Scientific Knowledge* (Madison, WI: University of Wisconsin Press, 1990).

Nystrand, M. *What Writers Know: The Language, Process, and Structures of Written Discourse* (Orlando, FL: Academic Press, 1987).

Swales, J. *Genre Analysis* (Cambridge: Cambridge University Press, 1990).

Thompson, G. *Introducing Functional Grammar* (London: Arnold, 1996).

Uhlirova, L. 'E-Mail as a New Subvariety of Medium and its Effects upon the Message', in S. Čmerjrkova and F. Stich (eds) *The Syntax of Sentence and Text (Festschrift for F. Danes)* (Amsterdam: Benjamins, 1994) pp. 273–282.

Yates, S. 'Oral and Written Linguistic Aspects of Computer Conferencing: A Corpus Based Study', in S.C. Herring (ed.) *Computer Mediated Communication* (Amsterdam: Benjamins, 1996), pp. 29–46.

Analyzing TV Documentaries

Alexander Pollak

4

Introduction

In the past decades, television has gained a continually increasing importance as one of the principal media through which people are informed about the present state of the world as well as about historical developments. In this context, the format of the television documentary has inherited a very important role as a powerful means through which to convey information and analysis. Because documentaries claim some measure of truth and credibility, they play a significant part in the production and reproduction of societal images and in the formation, affirmation or contestation of world views and perceptions among viewers. This explains the relevance within the social sciences of the analysis of documentaries as *documents*, that is, as meaningful cultural productions. Treating documentaries as documents that reflect their time and also as representations of particular contexts of production, can contribute to the understanding of past and present developments and societal forms of expression.

Defining documentaries

Before approaching the question of how to analyze television documentaries, we need to clarify what we mean by 'documentaries'. While at first glance it seems evident that there must be a significant difference between documentary films and fiction films, it is actually difficult to specify this difference and to draw a clear line between non-fiction and fiction genres.

In fact, establishing a fixed set of formal criteria that sets documentaries apart from other film genres proves to be an impossible task. This may be surprising, as one could establish a long list of what one would consider to be *typical* features of documentary films as opposed to fiction genres. The problematic aspect about such presumed typical features of documentaries however is that they can neither be generalized for every documentary, nor be excluded from other film genres (Nichols 2001:xi). Bill Nichols, in his introductory book on documentaries, writes:

> Documentaries adopt no fixed inventory of techniques, address no one set of issues, display no single set of forms or styles. Not all documentaries exhibit a single set of shared characteristics. Documentary film practice is an arena in which things change. (Nichols 2001:21)

Like fiction genres, documentaries may follow a rigid script, incorporate professional actors, use sound to dramatize shots or scenes or have a protagonist the story focuses on. On the other hand, fiction films may use original footage, may be guided by the voice of a commentator, may incorporate interviews and may lack a central protagonist.

Documentaries distinguish themselves from other genres through a quite definite claim to truth and factuality. In other words, in order to be able to differentiate, for analytical purposes, between documentaries and other genres, we need to turn away from the technical or content-related features of filmic representations and focus instead on their context of production and broadcasting.

Following this premise, we regard a film as a documentary when there is *the explicit or implicit claim by its producers and/or by the company that broadcasts it, that it is a documentary.*

At this point, it is important to emphasize that this definition does not mean that technical and stylistic features are of no relevance at all for the documentary genre. To the contrary, such features are of high significance in order for filmic representations to function as documentaries, and to satisfy the expectations of the audience. It is a central element of documentaries that they strive to confirm their claim of authenticity and factuality by employing particular filmic tools. These will be discussed below.

The powerfulness of documentaries

As pointed out above, the powerfulness of a documentary lies in the expectations of its audience. Since expectations guide perceptions, if audience members expect to learn something about the world by watching a TV programme, they become susceptible to the persuasive aesthetic of the documentary, and are likely to incorporate the documentary's content and images into their own world views.

However, the role of documentaries in our society, and the attitude of the audience towards them, is not free of conflicts and contradictions. On the one hand, it seems that in the past decades there has been a general loss of faith in the reliability and truthfulness of images, accompanied by an increased sensitivity towards the manifold interests that guide the production of documentary films. People are aware today of a history of manipulative images, as well as of the technological possibilities available in creating and generating images in the digital age. On the other hand, cameras have, to a certain extent, preserved their reputation as unerring eyes and the moving image can still be regarded as one of the strongest and most powerful means of communication for establishing seemingly authentic impressions of realities (Deacon et al. 1999:186). In many cases, for example when viewing historical documentaries, these films are the only sources that do not only create verbal images of past realities, but also show *real* images in the form of either original footage or digital simulations.

Types of documentaries

On the basis of our definition, the term *documentary* includes a range of different subgenres. Films categorized as documentaries can differ in their aesthetic, in their reference to either the past or the present and in the way they observe the world or, additionally, interact with it. Moreover, there may be differences in the usage and structuring of different kinds of footage, in focusing on the life and fate of individuals or on larger social and historical contexts, in their use or non-use of actors and sets, in their use of voice-over and music, and not least, documentaries differ in the way they disclose or conceal their constructed characters.

Closely related to documentary genres are so-called docudramas and reality shows. Docudramas, for example Steven Spielberg's *Schindler's List*, are defined by their claimed reliance on historical persons and events. Reality shows are formats in which cameras observe people either in their natural environment or in specifically constructed settings. Such reality formats support their authenticity claim by not using professional actors or firm scripts.

Each documentary genre raises different questions as to its societal significance, technical construction and ideological underpinning, and thus calls for different tools for analysis. The aim of this chapter is therefore to present and discuss a broad range of methodological tools from which the researcher can select the appropriate ones, and adapt them to her or his specific needs.

Preconditions for the analysis of documentaries

Much like all other forms of communication, documentaries also do not represent an objective approach towards reality, or rather towards the numberless realities that represent our world. Particularly for this reason, documentaries apply different tools in order to construct their quasi-authenticity, competence and trustworthiness. At the same time, most documentaries do not discuss their sources and intents.

Doing an analysis of documentaries therefore means adopting, to a certain extent, a constructivist view regarding documentaries as the result of numerous processes of selection and intervention. Documentaries create their own realities and it is part of the analytical endeavour to describe and contextualize these realities.

Basic premises for the study of documentaries are therefore curiosity and a certain degree of suspiciousness, which is fuelled by the awareness of the contradiction between the expectations for objectivity raised by documentaries and their actual constructedness. Documentaries are documents of their time and their context of production; their analysis may therefore contribute to explaining the state and development of societies.

Steps towards a meaningful analysis of television documentaries

Asking relevant questions

As is the case in all social scientific analysis, research questions and research hypotheses are paramount. Specifying research questions and disclosing underlying assumptions not only means identifying and defining the information we are looking for, but also explaining and justifying the perspective of the analysis.

While most research studies start with an explanation of how certain questions will be answered, a proper analysis should begin by making transparent how the research questions themselves were generated. Was it the thematic frame, the technical means or the aesthetics of one or more documentaries that has triggered our attention? Was the context of production the decisive factor? Or is it our task to test a pre-existing theory on documentaries through an empirical study?

Depending on our research motivation and interest, an indefinite number of questions can be asked with regard to the content, technical elaboration and circumstances of production of documentaries. Questions related to the content of documentaries could, for example, be:

- Which perspectives does the documentary favour and which does it minimize or exclude?
- What values and ideologies are incorporated into the content?
- How are social actors discursively represented?

Examples for questions related to the making of documentaries could be:

- How do the form, organization and content of a film construe meaning(s)?
- What means does the documentary use to judge events?
- How does it establish authority?

In addition, it is also important to ask questions related to a documentary's context of production:

▓ Which persons or institutions are directly responsible for or have indirectly influenced the production of a documentary?

▓ Is there a history of filmmaking, of forms of representations or of historical debates and events significant to the production of a certain documentary?

▓ What guides the expectations of the audience?

For some of the above research questions and approaches, it is in fact not the question itself that constitutes the vantage point for a study, but rather a certain sample of films, which has sparked curiosity and has caused us to reflect on possible ways to broaden our spectrum of knowledge.

Selecting an appropriate sample

Irrespective of whether a certain sample constitutes the vantage point for an analysis or whether the research question guides the selection of a sample, it is crucial to define the quality and quantity of the film data that best serve our research goals. Therefore, we need to define the minimum quantity of film data necessary in order to get valid and unbiased results, as well as the maximum quantity of film data that can be analyzed within a given period of time.

EXAMPLE 3.3

As an example, we will refer in this chapter to an interdisciplinary project on the politics of memory in Germany and Austria.[1] My part in the project was, besides examining images of history in print media, to conduct a study on the representation of World War II in German and Austrian documentary films. In order to limit the sample to a realistic, that is manageable, number of documentaries, I decided to focus on one major event only, the Battle of Stalingrad, in which German troops were defeated by the Soviet army. I chose six Austrian and two German documentaries, as well as one British–German documentary as objects of analysis and selected passages with an explicit reference to the role of the German Wehrmacht and its soldiers in the war for in-depth analysis (Pollak 2003a:192).

When regarding the maximum quantity of film data manageable, researchers need to be aware of the fact that film analysis can be a very time-consuming endeavour. Investigating verbal, visual and sound elements, and their interaction, leads to a high complexity for the transcription and analysis of data.

The validity of the film data is entirely dependent on whom or what the actual sample of documentaries represents. A sample can only develop explanatory power if it can be related in a meaningful way to its context of production (see the next section).

Choosing an adequate methodology

There may be cases where applying a certain methodology constitutes the main task of a research study and thus precedes and guides the definition of the research question and sample. Usually, however, the selection of an appropriate methodology is the third step in the process of setting up a research design. We need to find a way to describe, structure and process our data so that it corresponds with the research question.

The process of describing and structuring the film data requires defining an appropriate categorization system, which distinguishes between relevant and irrelevant elements of the documentary and guides the arrangement of the relevant elements.

Comment

In my work on Stalingrad documentaries, the main categories related to (1) the representation of German and Soviet soldiers; (2) the representation of the German and Soviet armies, and (3) the representation of the civilian population and of war atrocities, respectively. Of further importance was addressing and contextualizing the broader context of the war. Finally, national references in the Austrian documentaries were studied. This involved examining whether the role of Austrians in the Battle of Stalingrad was particularly emphasized (Pollak 2003a:192).

Categories need to be distinct and meaningful with regard to the overall research purpose and the further processing of the data. The researcher has to decide on qualifying criteria for each category, in other words, indicators need to be established, signifying which units of the sample fall within the remit of a category.

Comment

As we discuss in greater detail below, in many historical documentaries the content of images cannot be established with certainty. This is particularly true for original footage. Therefore, I had to rely in the analysis of the Stalingrad documentaries on the text of the commentator as the main indicator for the analytical relevance of shots, scenes and sequences.

In order to process the categorized data, we need to select and apply the appropriate analytical tools. It is necessary to decide whether a quantitative or a qualitative approach suits our research task best, or whether a combination of both is necessary, and we have to select the concrete tools that serve our needs best.

Quantitative analysis

In documentary analysis, a quantitative approach would entail counting certain elements within documentary films. Depending on the research question it may be useful to count the number of minutes certain topics are discussed, the number of overall minutes social actors are present, the quantity and duration of direct or indirect quotations, the number of positive, neutral or negative reference to persons or topics and so on.

However, the counting of certain elements of documentaries should never be an end in itself; it always needs to be clear why something is being counted. In addition, it needs to be clarified what the resulting figures are relating to. The latter operation is of utmost importance. Figures do not speak for themselves; other figures are required which these can be compared with. Counting can be made meaningful through, for example, diachronic comparison, cross-country comparison, comparison between different producers or broadcasting companies, or a comparison of the prominence of different items within a film.

The main weakness of purely quantitative approaches lies in the fact that numerical data alone can only partly contribute to a substantial analysis of films. Numerical data needs explanation, that is, it is necessary to relate it to our social world in order to attach it with meaning. It is only when qualitative analysis comes into play that concrete links between constitutive film elements, their context of production and underlying ideological concepts can be established.

Qualitative analysis

There are numerous qualitative approaches for the analysis of communication content and techniques. Many of them are discussed in other chapters of this volume; I will therefore focus on approaches that go beyond the analysis of verbal texts.

It is precisely because documentaries unify multiple means of communication that their qualitative analysis needs a high level of transparency and further explanation, as well as a self-critical view on the part of the researcher. Each communication dimension adds to the complexity of the meaning-making process of documentary films, as well as to the scope of interpretation.

The analysis of the verbal representation of social actors needs to be complemented by the analysis of their visual representation and by examining the sound bites that accompany their appearance. The analysis of verbal argumentation needs to be accompanied by the analysis of causal chains represented through images and through the gestures of social actors, as well as by the analysis of sound elements. As with written texts, we can analyze the thematic structure of documentary films, but in addition to this, the 'rhythm' of the film, the succession of different shots, footage and sound elements also need to be considered. In complement to a functional analysis of elements of verbal texts, the function of visual elements and means can also be analyzed, and the same is true for the analysis of intertextuality.

Analyzing verbal and multimodal aspects of documentaries

In the following, we shall focus on the analytic dimensions and approaches that go beyond the mere analysis of verbal text and focus on multimodal aspects of documentaries.

Visual semiotics

Visual semiotics – in the sense understood here – can be described as the attempt to elaborate something such as a *visual syntax*, in analogy to, and at the same time different from, the verbal syntax. According to Kress and Van Leeuwen, the relation between visual and linguistic structures is of a rather general nature:

> Visual structures realize meanings as linguistic structures do also and thereby point to different interpretations of experience and different forms of social interaction. The meanings which can be realized in language and in visual communication overlap in part, that is, some things can be expressed both visually and verbally; and in part they diverge – some things can be 'said' only visually, others only verbally. (Kress and Van Leeuwen 1996:2)

Hence, Kress and Van Leeuwen raise neither the claim that verbal and visual communication cover the same areas of creating meaning, nor the claim that they use the same mechanisms of meaning construction. Both communication forms have in common that they are guided by systems of rules and conventions. We elaborate on rules and conventions of visual meaning-making further below.

Of central importance for visual semiotics are two questions: the question of representation – what do images represent and how? – and the question of the relationship between the represented objects and our social world – what ideas and values do people, places and things represented in images stand for? (See Van Leeuwen 2001:92.) These two questions correspond with a key idea developed by Roland Barthes, namely the layering of meaning, with denotation – what is represented? – as the first layer and connotation – what is the meaning of the represented? – as the second layer (see Van Leeuwen 2001:94)

Comment

In the Stalingrad documentaries, I came across photographic images and original footage that were consistently repeated throughout and across documentaries. The footage showed snowstorms, bodies in the snow, hungry and cold Wehrmacht soldiers and columns of prisoners captured by the Soviet army. These images have served to implant a very specific event, 'Stalingrad', in the visual memory of media-consumers. The advance of the Wehrmacht troops towards Stalingrad and the context of the National Socialist war of annihilation were screened out, while the fate of individual Wehrmacht soldiers was foregrounded. The second – connotative – layer of meaning of these iconographic images therefore related to conveying an image of victimhood and innocence with regard to the masses of German soldiers in World War II (Pollak 2003a:219).

Representation

In their work on the representational meaning of images, Kress and Van Leeuwen (1996) distinguish between two different forms of image structures: conceptual structures and narrative structures. While in the case of conceptual structures things are represented in a non-connected (and non-narrative) form, narrative image structures are based on the connection of visual elements through vectors:

When participants are connected through a vector, they are represented as doing something to or for each other. From here on we will call such vectorial patterns narrative and contrast them to conceptual patterns. Where conceptual patterns represent participants in terms of their class, structure or meaning, in other words, in terms of their generalized and more or less stable and timeless essence, narrative patterns serve to present unfolding actions and events, processes of change, transitory spatial arrangements. (Kress and Van Leeuwen 1996:56)

The concept of vectors with regard to images corresponds to the concept of transitivity in verbal texts. The latter concept has particular importance in so-called systemic functional linguistics (SFL), a linguistic approach that regards language as a network of intertwined options, with each option standing for a different meaning construction. SFL is based on the assumption that there are three meta-functions of language (use): (1) an ideational, (2) an interpersonal and (3) a textual metafunction. The ideational metafunction of language refers to the linguistic representation of experiences, perceptions and contents of consciousness. The interpersonal metafunction refers to the function of language as a means to establish and negotiate a relationship between text-producer and text-recipient. The textual metafunction refers to the structure and inner organization of texts as fundamental for any transfer of meaning (Halliday 1994). Systemic functional linguistics recognizes two uses of the term *transitivity*: on the one hand the term describes a grammatical system which construes the world of experiences through a typology of different forms of processes; on the other hand 'transitivity' stands for a major principle of the ideational metafunction, a principle that can in simple words be expressed through the question, 'Who does what to whom?' It is the latter use of transitivity that is of interest here. The question of who does what to whom sheds light on the question of agency constructions, and thus on the activation or passivization of social actors as well as on the construction of relationships of impact between active and passive social actors.

Comment

In the study on Stalingrad documentaries, the construction of the armies and their soldiers as either active or passive actors in the war constituted an important element of the overall constructed image of World War II in these films. In the context of the Stalingrad documentaries, 'active' representation meant that on either the visual or the verbal level somebody is shown as a participant in an activity that has a certain impact on something or somebody. In this sense, 'passive' representation means that the respective actor either is not related to any such activity or else plays the passive part, that is the one to whom something is being done in this activity. Viewing images from a more abstract level, the acting on something or on somebody is symbolized through 'vectors', that is through connecting lines like an arm, the barrel of a gun, the trajectory of a missile and so on (Pollak 2003a:219).

What is problematic about the concept of narrative structures displayed through vectors as developed by Kress and Van Leeuwen is that it provides much room for interpretation as to what could be regarded as the vector (or connector). Considering that it is already difficult to interpret in a reliable way the presence and function of connecting lines and bodies in photos, such an interpretation seems even more difficult for moving visual elements. However, on a superficial level it is much easier to interpret who approaches whom and what is pointing where for moving images, since one can focus on those elements that move towards or away from each other and disregard elements that show no movement at all. Therefore, owing to the problematic lack of reliability in vectorial analysis, it may make sense to limit such an analysis to on the one hand moving parts of the scene and on the other hand verbal elements of filmic representations, and to then analyze the interrelationship between visual and verbal transitivity.

Modality

One important criterion in everyday communication is the weight attached to a particular utterance. What is in linguistic terms the *modality system* and marked by modal markers such as 'may' or 'might' can also be transferred to nonverbal semiotic phenomena. Hodge and Kress (1988) distinguish in this context between 'realistic' and 'non-realistic' forms of representation. Thus, verbal or (audio-)visual modality markers have a guiding function for the receivers' attribution of realistic value to a representation. Kress and Van

Leeuwen list eight different modality markers for non-moving visual representations: (1) colour saturation (a scale running from full colour saturation to
the absence of colour); (2) colour differentiation; (3) colour modulation; (4)
contextualization (a scale running from the absence of background to the most
fully articulated and detailed background); (5) representation (a scale running
from maximum abstraction to maximum representation of pictorial details);
(6) depth (a scale running from the absence of depth to a maximally deep perspective); (7) illumination (a scale running from the fullest representation of
the play of light and shade to its absence); and (8) brightness (Kress and Van
Leeuwen 1996:165). For filmic representations one could add further modality markers, like the story line, the behaviour of social actors, the voice of the
commentator, or the music or sound that accompanies the images. For documentary films, however, it is less the question of how realistic they are that is
of importance, but rather the question of marking authenticity and credibility.
Documentary films are per se a *realistic* genre; what they need to prove are the
accuracy and validity of their perspective on social actors and events.

Composition

Of additional essence for the analysis of films is what Kress and Van Leeuwen
call the compositional structure of images. Kress and Van Leeuwen identify
three interrelated systems, working together in the construction of representational and interactive meanings of images: (1) information value, (2) salience
and (3) framing (Kress and Van Leeuwen 1996:183).

According to Kress and Van Leeuwen, an image consists of various zones
(left and right, top and bottom, centre and margin) of relevance for the *informational value* attached to elements of the image placed in these zones, as well
as for the interrelation of elements. The concept of *salience* addresses the fact
that image (or film) elements attract the viewer's attention to different degrees,
depending on their placement, their size, their colour, their sharpness, the way
they move, the sound that accompanies them and so on. Finally, one should
also observe the presence or absence of framing devices contained in images.
Such devices may work as connectors or disconnectors of image elements
(ibid.:183).

Conventionalized meanings of technical elements of filming

Throughout history, filmic representations have always made use of and
referred to meaning conventions associated with certain forms of using cameras and other technical devices. Spaces and angles of camera shots play as
much a role in filmmaking as image composition, colour, lighting and sound.

The closer a shot focuses on social actors, the more intimate the audience's
relationship to this person becomes and the stronger positive or negative emotions associated with the represented subject become. At their extreme, close-
ups show only small parts of the body of a person or even only fractions of a

face. On the other hand, medium shots show at least the face and shoulders of persons, and long shots reveal larger situational contexts or even entire landscapes with or without humans. While shots from above are associated with power over the people or objects shown, shots from below are related to a feeling of subordination.

It is also common sense that black-and-white film material is associated with historical events and the *authentic* representation of sceneries, while computer-generated animations epitomize constructedness and the lack of seemingly authentic evidence. Moreover, illumination and shadows have a major impact on making a person appear trustworthy or rather dubious and can make a setting looking peaceful or potentially threatening.

Despite the many conventions that guide filmmaking and thus film analysis, the researcher needs to be aware of the fact that many forms of representation are open to more than one way of interpretation. Therefore, each analysis should carefully describe relevant elements of technical film realization and discuss possible meanings and ambiguities.

Connection between image and speaker content

In many TV documentaries, particularly in relation to historical events, it is a common approach to show original or contemporary footage with a background voice that describes, explains and discusses persons, settings or events. For the analysis of documentaries it is therefore of utmost importance to study the relationship between the images shown and the content the commentator's voice refers to. Do the images guide the speaker content or do the speaker's comments define the images? Are images presented as evidence, as illustration or as means to produce certain sentiments? And is there a close connection between images and speaker content or only a loose one?

Remarkably, in documentary films, it is precisely the seemingly most 'authentic' form of film material – namely original footage – that is in many cases the one most loosely connected to the speaker content. There are many examples of documentaries where original footage neither provides evidence for what the commentator says nor serves as an illustration of how things happened. Rather, its function is to provide a feeling of authenticity and of being able to put oneself into times and places represented. In addition, there are cases where film material shows a very low level of stringency in terms of attempting to convey a firm scope of meaning.

EXAMPLE

In this context, in April 2000 I conducted an experiment with a group of university students, whom I confronted with original footage from one of the documentaries about the Battle of Stalingrad. I presented the footage without the voice of the commentator and asked the students to provide their opinion on the context and meaning of the images. The range of associations attached to the images was striking. Students referred to the documentary extracts as representing World War I, World War II, Pearl Harbor or even the 1991 Gulf War. And even for those who associated the images with World War II, it was unclear whether the persons represented in the images were German POWs, Soviet POWs or Jewish prisoners in concentration camps.

Main actors in television documentaries

Documentaries should be described not only in terms of how social actors are represented in them, but also in terms of the role different actors take in the construction of the documentary. We have already mentioned that in many documentaries, commentators take on an important role. Here we can distinguish between commentators who remain invisible and commentators who become visible elements within the films and recognizable as individuals. While commentators guide through film sequences, it is the function of moderators to guide through an entire film. Moderators are responsible for explaining and justifying the significance and meaning of the documentary and for setting contexts that influence the perception of the viewers. Another important function of social actors in documentaries is that of experts or witnesses. Experts are usually presented as persons with a specific knowledge in one of the fields addressed in the documentary. Because they are presented in a personalized way, their voice does not necessarily have to have more authority than the voice of an invisible and anonymous commentator who provides information in a 'god-like' manner.

The function of witnesses is to provide evidence for events and to fill them with life. A witness can be defined as a person who has been on the site of an event or who has been personally affected by an incident. Sometimes the function of witnesses is also extended to persons who know somebody who have seen or experienced events. A documentary based mainly on presenting biographical accounts and interviewing witnesses may have the effect of decontextualizing and depoliticizing events, that is of reducing them to personal experiences and feelings.

Comment

A significant proportion of the content of the selected Stalingrad documentaries consisted of depictions of the fortunes of individual soldiers. This occurred in the form of re-narrations or interviews with witnesses, in which those involved were able to speak for themselves. These narratives presented, for the most part, only a very restricted view of the day-to-day events of war, omitting any reference to the 'war-of-annihilation', and thereby contributing significantly to the image of the 'untainted Wehrmacht' (see Pollak 2003a:219, 2003b:156).

Levels of analysis and selection of a transcription method

Levels of analysis

In his work on analyzing film and television, Rick Iedema (2001) distinguishes between six levels of analysis (see Table 4.1). According to Iedema, the lowest level of analysis is constituted by so-called frames (Iedema 2001:188). A frame is defined as a still taken from a shot. Studying frames therefore means to transform moving images into stills in order to realize and analyze details of actors, objects and the setting of a documentary. The next analytical level is marked by shots, which are uncut takings by a camera. Usually, in film analysis, shots are seen as the lowest or most narrow filmic level or, corresponding to the approach of Kress and Van Leeuwen, shots could be viewed as a strong framing device, connecting film elements (see the sample transcript in Table 4.2). At the third level of Iedema's hierarchy are scenes. Scenes include more than one shot and are defined by a continuity of time and space, that is, there is no occurrence of time steps or significant changes of places included. A scene can include shots from different cameras and angles and there are examples of films that consist mainly of only one scene, like for example Sidney Lumet's *12 Angry Men*.

Each level further up in the hierarchy offers a larger space for interpreting the boundaries of the respective filmic level. Sequences are defined by Iedema as a succession of scenes that display thematic continuity. Here, boundaries are already far less clear than for scenes or shots. This is even truer for so-called

Table 4.1 Six levels of telefilm analysis. *Source*: Iedema (2001:188f.)

Level	Description
1 Frame	A frame is a salient still taken from shot.
2 Shot	A shot is constituted of the salient camera position(s) which make up a scene.
3 Scene	In a scene the camera remains in one time-space.
4 Sequence	In a sequence the camera moves with specific character(s) or subtopic across time-spaces.
5 Generic stage	Roughly, stages are beginnings, middles, and endings; Each genre has a specific set of stages: – narratives tend to have an orientation, a complication, a resolution, and a coda; – factual or expository genres may have an introduction, a set of arguments or facts, and a conclusion, or an introduction and a series of facts or procedures.
6 Work as a whole	Depending on the nature of the lower levels, the work will be more or less classifiable as a particular genre; the primary distinction is between fictional or 'narrative' and 'factual'.

Table 4.2 Excerpt from a documentary transcript

Shot	Visual content	Sound	Commentator's voice
1	Medium shot (MS) of Walter Pissecker (commentator),	No background sound	Walter Pissecker:
	Tank in the background (close shot);		'Good evening Ladies and Gentlemen.
	Location of the shot unknown;		It is not a round anniversary, but today forty-eight years have passed since Adolf Hitler came to power in Germany.
	Insert: "Walter Pissecker'		
	Pissecker holds a microphone in his right hand and looks into the camera.		Exactly ten years later, thirty-eight years ago, was the turning point for the beginning of the end of his regime, the defeat at Stalingrad. On this day, the majority of the troops capitulated and became prisoners. The end of the sixth army was near.
	While Pissecker is speaking, the camera gradually zooms in.		
	Close shot (CS) of Walter Pissecker. He fetches a piece of paper from his coat and starts reading from it.		The German army report reported on this day: 'The initial airborne supply as well as successful morale spirits among the troops.'
	WP looks into the camera again and sums up.		Nothing new in the east. thirty-eight years ago.'
2	Title insert 'Der 30. Jänner 1943 in Stalingrad' (30 January 1943 in Stalingrad)	Background sound: dark monotonic sound (of the engines of aeroplanes).	Invisible commentator: 'The processes that led to 30 January
3	Long shot (aerial photo) of three small aeroplanes (flying from the right side of the screen to the left side of it)	Background sound: dark monotonic sound (of the engines of aeroplanes).	1943 in Stalingrad have already so many times been . . .'

generic stages, which mark, according to Iedema, major shifts in the characters and the narrative style of films, or there may also be a significant change in the use of cameras and sound. Stages can be defined in a narratological sense as marking the beginning, the middle part(s) and the end of a film or they can be defined as subgenres that make up the overall genre a film is associated with (Iedema 2001:188).

The highest filmic level in Iedema's ranking is the work as a whole, which may suggest a certain classification of the film. Nevertheless, as was discussed above, our approach towards classifying a film is not based on the film itself, but on the claims attached to it by its producers and broadcasters (Iedema 2001:188).

Selection of the transcription method

Essential for implementing a qualitative approach is the method of transcription we use in order to make the film data effectively useable for analysis. Depending on our research question, the respective sample and the chosen method of analysis, we have to decide on the following:

- Which filmic modes shall be included in the transcription process? – For some research questions it may be enough to mainly transcribe visual elements or to mainly refer to verbal or sound elements.
- How detailed shall the transcription be?
  - What shall be the smallest unit of transcribing visual elements?
  - Shall the transcription of verbal elements include intonation, pauses, dialects and so on?
- How can the effects that the different modes have on each other, and on the representation as a whole, be made accessible to us as researchers?

Since the overall meaning of a film, or its parts, can be fully gathered only by considering all its modes, we should in general aim for a comprehensive transcription of films or of its parts that we have decided are relevant for the purpose of our analysis. In terms of the degree of detail of the transcription, there can be no general recommendation, except to not transcribe in more detail than necessary in order to answer the research question. The smallest unit of transcribing visual elements is usually either the frame or the shot. While the frame excludes spoken texts and sound elements – a still has no underlying sound – the shot is the smallest unit that incorporates all filmic modes.

For the analysis of history documentaries, I used the following template:

Including necessary context information

In order to be able to establish the broader meaning of a documentary we need information that connects it to other filmic representations as well as to the extrafilmic world. In their approach of critical discourse analysis, Ruth Wodak and Martin Reisigl distinguish between four levels of context: (1) the (inner-)textual context or co-text; (2) the intertextual context; (3) the institutional context; and (4) the socio-political context (see Reisigl and Wodak 2001:41). Correspondingly, for film analysis, we could distinguish between (1) the context produced by the filmic representation itself or elements of it; (2) intertextuality in the sense of reference to other films and use of different sources of film material; (3) the institutional context of film production and film broadcasting, and (4) the historical and political context that shaped institutions, debates and forms of representation.

The first context layer regards the relationship between different elements of a documentary and has already been discussed above. When examining the question of intertextuality, it is important to gather as much information as possible on the sources that the documentary is based on, in order to relate it to other filmic or non-filmic representations and in order to have a better understanding of which sources are prioritized and which are emphasized less, or even excluded. Studying the institutional context includes posing the question of who the persons and organizations involved in producing a documentary are. In addition, it may make sense to study the structures and mechanisms behind launching a film as well as the context of its reception, that is, which population groups have been able to watch this documentary. Finally, it is important to relate questions regarding the first three contextual layers to a broader history of events, debates and societal structures related to the documentary's subject.

The final step in conducting a meaningful analysis of television documentaries is to ensure that gathered information can be contextualized and related to all other information available in a logical and transparent way. This step is crucial for all research work and includes the following:

- the researcher should clarify her or his interest, position and perspective vis-à-vis the research question and the material;
- all analytical steps should be constantly questioned, reviewed and, if necessary, adapted to changing circumstances;
- all analytical procedures as well as all included context information should be carefully listed.

In a certain sense one could say that the analysis of documentaries is somewhat similar to making a documentary about a documentary; it becomes clear that one cannot and should not deny the authorship of an analysis, that is the interpreter's bias. However, we should develop a research design that minimizes the bias and keeps the analysis as transparent as possible. Part of the transparency paradigm is to also highlight the limitations of a study or of an approach. I will therefore conclude this chapter by highlighting some of the limitations of film analysis in general and of the analysis of documentary films in particular.

As we have referred to the constructedness of documentaries, we should also refer to the fact that the analysis of documentaries is based on numerous processes of selection, description and interpretation. When working with visual material, one needs to be aware that images usually open up even more interpretive space than texts already do. It may therefore make sense to see film analysis as something that should preferably be done by a group of people who can discuss different impressions and views. In addition, the richness of images may lead to over-interpreting their meaning in the sense that elements that are marginal for the film are strongly emphasized and highlighted in the analysis. Finally, one should not expect that an analysis of documentaries could provide any certainty about the 'true' intentions of the filmmaker. The purpose of an analysis should rather be to discuss the actual means and perspectives of a film product, its historical and institutional roots and its potential political and societal impact.

Note

1. The project 'How History is Made: Constructing Memories of the Wehrmacht and the Second World War' was funded by the Wittgenstein prize of the Austrian Science Fund and headed by Prof. Ruth Wodak (URL: www.oeaw.ac.at/wittgenstein). The work on the project was conducted between October 1999 and October 2002 and was concerned with questions of collective and individual memory relating to the role of the Wehrmacht and its members during the World War II. It included the analysis of various data sets from important social fields (including media, schoolbooks, interviews, films, questionnaires, documentary films and political discourses), in order to track the transformation and development of arguments and topics across the decades and in different public spheres. (See Heer *et al.* 2003, 2008.)

Key readings

Kress, G. and Van Leeuwen, T. (eds) *Reading Images* (London: Routledge, 1996).
Nichols, B. *Introduction to Documentary* (Bloomington: Indiana University Press, 2001).
Van Leeuwen, T. and Jewitt, C. (eds) *The Handbook of Visual Analysis* (London: Sage, 2001).

References

Caldas-Coulthard, C.and Coulthard, M. (eds) *Texts and Practices* (New York: Routledge, 1995).
Deacon, D., Pickering, M., Golding, P. and Murdock, G. (eds) *Researching Communications: A Practical Guide to Methods in Media and Cultural Analysis* (London: Sage 1999).

Halliday, M.A. K. *An Introduction to Functional Grammar* (Auckland: Arnold, 1994).

Heer, H., Manoschek, W., Pollak, A. and Wodak, R. (eds) *Wie Geschichte gemacht wird? Zur Konstruktion von Erinnerungen an Wehrmacht und Zweiten Weltkrieg* (Vienna: Czernin Verlag, 2003).

Heer, H., Manoschek, W., Pollak, A. and Wodak, R. (eds) *The Discursive Construction of History: Remembering the Wehrmacht's War of Annihilation* (Basingstoke: Palgrave Macmillan, 2008).

Hodge, R. and Kress., G. *Social Semiotics* (Cambridge: Polity, 1988).

Kress, G., and Van Leeuwen, T. (eds) 1996, *Reading Images* (London: Routledge, 1996).

Iedema, R. 'Analysing Film and Television: A Social Semiotic Account of Hospital: An Unhealthy Business', in T. Van Leeuwen and C. Jewitt (eds) *The Handbook of Visual Analysis* (London: Sage, 2001), pp. 183–206.

Nichols, B. *Introduction to Documentary* (Bloomington: Indiana University Press, 2001).

Pollak, A. 'Was vom Zweiten Weltkrieg übrig blieb [What Remains of the Second World War]', in H. Heer, W. Manoschek, A. Pollak and R. Wodak (eds) *Wie Geschichte gemacht wird. Zur Konstruktion von Erinnerungen an Wehrmacht und Zweiten Weltkrieg* (Wien: Czernin Verlag, 2003a), pp. 192–224.

Pollak, A. 'Das Geschichtsbild der "sauberen Wehrmacht" [The myth of the "untainted Wehrmacht"]', in Heer, H., W. Manoschek, A. Pollak, R. Wodak (eds) *Wie Geschichte gemacht wird. Zur Konstruktion von Erinnerungen an Wehrmacht und Zweiten Weltkrieg* (Wien: Czernin Verlag, 2003b), pp. 145–70.

Reisigl, M. and R. Wodak *Discourse and Discrimination: Rhetorics of Racism and Antisemitism* (London: Routledge, 2001).

Van Leeuwen, T. 'Semiotics and Iconography', in T. Van Leeuwen and C. Jewitt (eds) *The Handbook of Visual Analysis* (London: Sage, 2001), pp. 92–118.

Analyzing Political Rhetoric

Martin Reisigl

Introduction

For a long time, the analysis of political rhetoric has merely been carried out as a side job both on the part of political scientists interested in issues of language and on the part of linguists or rhetoricians interested in political issues. Consequently, respective studies in linguistics or rhetoric and political science have frequently been amateurish with respect to their development and use of theory, methods and methodology. In this chapter, I attempt to show that a remedy for the many shortcomings in this area can be found in a transdisciplinary, *politolinguistic* approach that brings together and connects rhetoric, critical discourse analysis and concepts in political science.

What is political rhetoric?

The analysis of political rhetoric first poses the question of what *political rhetoric* means. This question can be answered in two steps: by clarifying first the notion of 'rhetoric' and second that of 'the political'.

Rhetoric denotes both the *ars bene dicendi et scribendi* (that is the practical art of speaking and writing well in public spheres through the use of various communicative genres) and the theory about eloquence. Thus, rhetoric ought not to be simply connected with the use of flowery figurative speech, that is speech that is merely *ornatus*. Rather, the qualification of *bene* (good) is conceived in a much wider sense that goes far beyond the question of poetic aestheticism or ornamental language. In addition, normative criteria of rhetorical assessment also relate to principles such as clarity and understandability (*perspicuitas*), grammatical correctness (*puritas*), evidence or vividness (*evidentia*), and adequacy (*aptum*) with respect to the speaker or writer, the hearer or reader, the situation and the topic (see Plett 2001:27–32). Generally though, effectiveness or efficiency is most central to the question of rhetorical *goodness*. In this respect, rhetoric can be characterized as the practical science and art of effective or efficient speaking and writing in public. It is the science and art of persuasive language use; the three crucial objectives of such persuasion are *logos*, *ethos* and *pathos* (see Plett 2001:2–4).

Whereas persuasion connected with *logos* consists of bringing about a rational conviction by sound argumentation (*probare*), factual information (*docere*) and reasonable admonition or exhortation (*monere*), types of persuasion related with *ethos* and *pathos* are linked with reaching consent through forms of non-argumentative *linguistic force*, such as emotionalization, suggestion, demagogy, propaganda and the use of threats (manipulative persuasion). The goal of *ethos* is to create a gentle and constant attitude or emotion as part of the hearers' and readers' habitus by advertising (*conciliare*), or through aesthetic pleasure and entertainment (*delectare*). Rhetorical *pathos*, instead, aims at rousing momentarily violent, fierce and intense emotions through rhetorical instigation (*movere*).

All these purposes can be found in contemporary political rhetoric. They are identified with terms such as political education (*docere*), political control (*monere*), political deliberation (*logos*), political justification or legitimization (*probare*), political advertising (*conciliare*), politainment (*delectare*) and political incitement (*movere*).

Following the above explication of rhetoric, we can conclude that *rhetorical analysis* means to analyze the employment and effects of linguistic (including *nonverbal*) and other semiotic means of persuasion in rhetorical terms.

The second step in answering the question of what political rhetoric denotes consists of explaining the meaning of *political*. The most simple explanation states that everything politicians do in pursuance of their profession can be ascribed the attribute of being political. Such a conception of the political implies that political rhetoric is rhetoric produced by politicians. This understanding neglects the fact that political matters enter the life of everyone, that non-politicians also produce political rhetoric in *private* contexts, and that – as has particularly been shown by feminist critique – a rigid binary opposition of the private and the public-political sphere is untenable. Thus, we have to keep a broader understanding of the political in mind. However, in the given context, we can just focus on prototypical political rhetoric, that is rhetoric employed by politicians. For this chapter's purpose, the analysis of political rhetoric will therefore be conceived of as an *analysis of the use of rhetorical means of persuasion by professional politicians*.

The politolinguistic approach

Politolinguistics assumes a transdisciplinary perspective. It combines rhetoric, political science and linguistics (especially critical discourse analysis – see Reisigl and Wodak 2001; Reisigl 2003). Politolinguistics theoretically differentiates among *three different dimensions of the political*: polity, policy and politics (Meyer 2000:52–99).

The dimension of *polity* constitutes the formal and structural framework as being the basis of political action. Polity manifests itself in basic political norms, principles, rules and values of a political culture, as well as in the legal procedures and political institutions of a political system designated to found political order. Political rhetoric associated with this dimension is carefully and deliberately formulated. Thus it usually takes a significant amount of time to produce it. As it is generally consensus-oriented, it is often the result of political compromises not prepared by single authors, but by various authors with frequently differing political affiliations. Prototypically, its objectives are *logos* and *ethos*, particularly political legitimization, control and education as well as political identity promotion.

Political action concerns the dimensions both of policy and of politics. Policy involves the content-related dimension of political action that aims at shaping the various political areas and is performed primarily by members of the government and civil servants of respective political institutions (ministries). Policy manifests itself in areas such as domestic affairs, foreign policy, economic policy, social policy and so on. It relates to the planning and articulation of governmental tasks and programmes. Policy rhetoric is frequently bureaucratic (for example administrative decisions) and often programmatic (for example inaugural addresses). Its main goals are political justification (*probare*), political instruction (*docere*) and winning political allies (for example coalition partners) over to one's side (*conciliare*).

Processes regarding the articulation of political interests and positions of dissent or consent are labelled as *politics*. This political dimension concerns conflicts among *single* or *collective* political actors. The crucial aims of political actors doing politics are to assert themselves against opponents, to gain followers, and to persuade addressees to adopt a promoted political opinion. Speaking in rhetorical terms, *conciliare* (in the sense of gaining party affiliation) and *movere* (in the sense of rapid political mobilization) are at the centre of political goals. Political rhetoric strongly related to this dimension is prototypically performed in election campaigns. In a broader sense, every genre of political rhetoric has the goal of advertising political position and maintaining power.

Politolinguistics – as I understand it – works with a second distinction organized around the functional concept of the *field of political action*. Following Girnth and Bourdieu (see Girnth 1996), I comprehend fields of action as 'places of social forms of practice' (Bourdieu 1991:74) or as 'frameworks of social interaction' (Reisigl 2003:148). Various institutionalized purposes of discursive practices are pursued and realized in these fields. According to these purposes, we can differentiate among at least eight political fields:

1. law-making procedure (for example relating to the manufacturing or amendment of specific acts),
2. formation of public attitudes, opinions and will (for example relating to confrontations of political opponents in TV discussions),

3. party-internal formation of attitudes, opinions and will (for example relating to party conventions),
4. inter-party formation of attitudes, opinions and will (for example relating to coalition talks),
5. organization of international and (especially) interstate relations (for example relating to negotiations of state treaties),
6. political advertising (for example relating to election campaigns),
7. political administration (for example relating to the implementation of specific acts by civil servants),
8. political control (for example relating to petitions for a referendum).

Political discourses[1] connect with these fields of political action in such a way that a 'political discourse' about a specific topic can have its origin within one of the fields and advance within other fields. Consequently, discourses can *traverse* different fields. Discourses are defined as thematically connected and problem-related semiotic (for example oral or written) occurrences that relate to specific semiotic types, which serve particular political functions (see Reisigl and Wodak 2001:36–7; Reisigl 2003:128–42; Reisigl 2008; also Chapter 1 by Wodak in this volume).

A selection of analytical categories

The politolinguistic approach is more function- and persuasion-oriented than other attempts to analyze political rhetoric. It establishes a transdisciplinary conjunction of disciplines and integrates argumentation theory as well as other components of rhetoric. However, the choice of categories for politolinguistic analysis depends always on the concrete research topic and the specific data to be analyzed. In several studies on political discourses (for example Reisigl and Wodak 2001; Reisigl 2003), a group of adaptable questions and related categories has proven to be useful heuristic devices for analysis of political *realities*. Especially national(ist), racist, anti-Semitic, sexist and populist rhetoric can be analyzed by systematically answering the following five questions:

1. How are social actors – either individual persons or groups – linguistically constructed by being named (nomination)?
2. What positive or negative traits, qualities and features are attributed to the linguistically constructed social actors (predication)?
3. Through what arguments and argumentation schemes do specific persons or social groups try to justify or delegitimize claims containing specific nominations and predications (for example claims of discrimination of others)?
4. From what perspective or point of view are these nominations, predications and argumentations expressed (perspectivation)?

5. Are the respective utterances (nominations, predications, argumentations) articulated overtly, are they intensified or are they mitigated (mitigation versus intensification)?

In this chapter, I illustrate a few analytical categories, focusing on the example of rightist populist rhetoric in Austria. The critical analysis will concentrate particularly on (1) (rightist) populist nomination; (2) (rightist) populist predication; (3) (rightist) populist argumentation; and (4) (rightist) populist perspectivation.

How to conduct a politolinguistic analysis of political rhetoric – a theoretical outline of the research practice

Students attending introductory courses on discourse analysis or reading discourse-analytical textbooks, such as this one, may hope to equip themselves with a defined analytical toolbox they can easily apply. However, there is no simple recipe of how to conduct a politolinguistic analysis on political rhetoric: discourse analysis cannot be applied mechanically and automatically, since every good analysis is based on accurate interpretation and scientific creativity, and requires previous theoretical and practical knowledge, which cannot be taught in a single chapter of a textbook. This also holds true for quantitative analyzes, which rely always on the previous theoretical definition of qualitative categories, which are to be measured (by counting).

Thus, the following clear-cut sequence of eight stages and steps in research practice merely forms an idealized outline with the purpose of offering a short orientation:

1. The starting-point of the research is the awareness of a social and political problem that possesses linguistic aspects. The first step consists of consulting previous knowledge about the problem.
2. The second step is the triangulatory collection and 'creation' of discursive data for analysis (by means of observation, audiovisual registration and so on), tied to the research on, and gathering of, contextual information (by research in archives, by source research, and so on). Data collection focuses on the selection of specific discourses, of discursive macrotopics, of specific fields of political action, of specific semiotic media, of specific genres, of specific political actors, of specific areas of communication or 'speech communities', and of a specific period of time.
3. The third phase comprises the preparation and selection of data for the specific analyzes. The principal tasks to be completed in this phase are to examine the data and to further sort it. If required by the research question, oral data has to be transcribed.

4. The fourth step is dedicated to the specification of the research question and the formulation of hypotheses on the basis of a rapid checking of the data or a part of it.

5. A qualitative pilot analysis may follow as the fifth research step. The pilot analysis aims to adjust the analytical instruments and to further spell out the research question in detail.

6. The research proceeds with detailed case-studies which are chiefly qualitative, but can partly also be quantitative. This stage operates on the macro-, meso- and microlevels of linguistic analysis as well as on the level of context. This step leads to an overall interpretation of the results of analysis and takes into account the social, historical and political context of the analyzed discursive data (see the section 'Context' in Chapter 1).

7. The formulation of a critique that seeks to reveal problematic discursive strategies, to solve specific problems of (institutional) communication, or to improve communication and can follow the analytical steps outlined above. The 'critique' relies on ethical principles such as democratic norms and human rights. It points to opaque, contradictory and manipulative relations among power, language and social structures and commits itself to cognitive and political emancipation (and improvement of communication).

8. The application of the detailed analytical results on the basis of accurate critique can be seen as the last stage of research. This application may consist on the one hand of the publication of a book and various journal articles, and, on the other hand, of widely accessible written recommendations and newspaper commentaries, training seminars, further education courses, didactic expositions and radio transmissions (see Reisigl 2007).

It is impossible to discuss and illustrate each research stage comprehensively within the given framework. In the following, I will focus on one single example.

Doing politolinguistic analysis – an example

Activation and consultation of preceding theoretical knowledge about the problem in question (Step One)

At the beginning of politolinguistic research lies the analyst's interest in a political problem with a linguistic or discursive aspect. Focusing on the example of rightist populist rhetoric in Austria, the issue to be investigated may read: *Is right-wing populist rhetoric dangerous for Austrian democracy or can it be so?* Being aware of this issue, researchers will try to gain access to prior studies on the problem in question by studying relevant literature.[2] By doing so, the issue in question can be approached step by step. At first, a theoretical *tour d'horizon* allows researchers to outline the above-mentioned research question through differentiating questions, such as: (a) What does the respective literature incorporate under the term *populism*? (b) What is *right-wing populism* according to the relevant literature? (c) What can – according to the relevant literature – be stated about populist rhetoric? (d) What does the relevant literature tell us about the relationship between (right-wing) populism and democracy?

A critical consultation of selected social-scientist literature about populism leads to the following answers to these four questions:

(a) There is no concept of populism on which all social scientists unanimously agree. Nohlen (1998:514f.) distinguishes among three different meanings of 'populism': (1) populism as a *politics which is judged either negatively or positively*; (2) populism as a *social-political movement* that concentrates on masses of people on the one side (*national populism*) and on single politicians as leaders on the other side; (3) populism as a *political strategy of mobilization and unification*. Taguieff (2003:101–9) captures six different conceptualizations: (1) populism as *a movement or as a type of political mobilization*; (2) populism as *an authoritarian or semi-plebiscitary regime* with a charismatic leader at the top; (3) populism as *an ideology or a doctrine*; (4) populism as *an attitude*; (5) populism as *a rhetoric, a specific form of communication or 'polemism'*; (6) populism as *a form of provisional or temporary legitimization in post-dictatorial and post-totalitarian times*.

On the basis of a cursory knowledge of some discursive data and a careful comparison of the different theoretical concepts, I personally came to the following theoretical conclusion: Populism does not constitute an ideology in the classical sense. It consists of a *syncretic combination of heterogeneous and theoretically inconsistent elements*. It *relates to political representation* (see Arditi 2005:78–97) and is a *political style in the sense of a complex syndrome and functional way of political expression or articulation* (see Wiles 1969; Altermatt 1996:193; Laclau 2005:34 and 44ff.).

(b) Most of social science literature on *populism* concerns itself with *right-wing populism*. Scholars sometimes oppose this concept to the notion of *left-wing populism*. We learn from relevant literature that the distinction between the two populisms is – first of all – a content-related one and that the differentiation is not always easy to draw, since the categories of *left* and *right* are nowadays less clear-cut than they have been in the past. Political developments during past decades have led to the formation of new political movements and parties such as ecological, regional, ethnic and minority-oriented ones, which – much like large *people's parties* that assemble politically heterogeneous followers – do not fit comfortably into traditional left-versus-right schemes. Nevertheless, we can state: Right-wing populism and left-wing populism have many features of style, form and media in common. They show content-related differences, among others, with respect to their attitude towards National

Socialism, fascism, racism, anti-Semitism, xenophobia as well as the welfare state, and with respect to their understanding of social policy, migration policy and security policy. An important conceptual differentiation that traverses the above-mentioned opposition is the distinction between oppositional populism (for example the FPÖ's oppositional populism before February 2000) and governmental populism (for example the FPÖ's governing populism from February 2000 until January 2007).[3]

(c) There has been little discourse-analytical work on *(right-wing) populist rhetoric* until now (see Wodak and Pelinka, 2002). The core of all populism is *a generalized claim of representation*. This claim is often discursively realized by the *linguistic reference to the imagined community of 'the people'* (see Walton 1999; Kienpointner 2002; Reisigl 2002: 186ff.; Taguieff 2003:19; see also below). *People* (in German: *Volk*) is a highly ambiguous category which can rhetorically be analyzed as a synecdoche (see Mény and Surel 2004:171), that is a rhetorical trope constituted by a whole or more standing for a part or less (this is the case in the present context), or vice versa. Three synecdochic meanings of the collective *the people* can be ascribed to different forms of populism: (1) *the people as nation* (in a culturalist sense) is especially linked with right-wing populism and national populism; (2) *the people as class* (in a socio-economic sense) is especially linked with left-wing populism; (3) *the people as political sovereign* is especially linked with a type of populism most likely to be compatible with democracy (Mény and Surel 2004:172–96). Also, most of populist rhetoric has *pathos* (that is political mobilization by stirring up emotions, frequently irrational ones) as its rhetorical main goal.

(d) The examination of relevant literature (see, for instance, Panizza 2005) illustrates that the relationship between right-wing populism and democracy is a dynamic, variable and conflicting one. Populism can endanger democracy (especially if authoritarianism, racism, anti-Semitism and *xenophobia* are involved). Sometimes, however, it expresses a crisis of democratic representation and justly criticizes undemocratic political representation and political corruption.

Gathering discursive data and research on the context (Step Two)

Depending on the research question, on the pragmatic conditions of research, that is resources of time, money and personnel, as well as the context of utilization (for example research for a university seminar, for a PhD, on behalf of an official institution and so on), researchers choose a (more or less) triangulatory approach in order to gather data. Triangulation with respect to data means to collect a variety of empirical data (that is texts of possibly different genres relating to the same general theme), as well as background information with the help of a multiplicity of elicitation methods (for example observation, audiovisual data, interview, research in archives, recording and so on).

With respect to the research question delineated in Step One, (*Is right-wing populist rhetoric dangerous for Austrian democracy or can it be so?*), data collection and context exploration may combine the subsequent criteria:

- *A specific period of time* related to *discursive events* connected with the rise and manifestation of right-wing populism of Austria including, among others, various regional, national and supra-national election campaigns in the last two decades; the FPÖ's so-called 'Austria First Petition' in 1992 and 1993[4] as well as additional right-wing populist petitions since then; the change of government in February 2000; the period during the so-called 'Sanctions of the EU-14 against Austria', that is the bilateral political measures against the FPÖ's participation in the coalition government, and so on.
- *Specific political actors* (for example politicians of the FPÖ and the BZÖ).
- *Specific discourses*, for example the discourse about the 'Austria First Petition' (see Reisigl and Wodak 2001:144–204), the discourse about the 'Sanctions of the EU-14 against Austria' (see Reisigl and Wodak 2002), or the discourse about Turkey's application for membership in the EU.
- *Specific fields of political action*, for example the fields of political control, of political advertising and of the formation of public attitudes, opinions and will.
- *Specific semiotic media* as well as *genres* relating to election and petition campaigns (slogans, election programmes, election speeches, TV interviews and TV debates, leaflets, newspaper articles, and so on).

In the present case, it is interesting to collect discourse data produced before and after the installation of the ÖVP–FPÖ coalition government in 2000, in order to be able to assess whether this change had an influence on rightist populist rhetoric and on the relationship between right-wing populism and democracy in Austria.

Preparation and selection of data (Step Three)

Usually, more data will be gathered at first than can be analyzed. Thus, *further restrictions* are necessary in order to attain a corpus which is manageable. Criteria such as representativity/typicality, (intertextual or interdiscursive) impact, salience, exceptionality (extreme cases), redundancy and originality of data with respect to the research question will help *to order and select concrete discourse fragments*.

Specification of the research question and formulation of hypotheses (Step Four)

The perfunctory overview of the corpus allows to *specify the research question* and to elaborate some *hypotheses* connected with the issue in question. In our case, the research question can be spelled out in the following way:

▪ *If right-wing populist rhetoric is dangerous for Austrian democracy, it should be clarified (a) which concrete dangers for democracy it involves and (b) whether or not oppositional rightist populist rhetoric holds more risks for democracy than governmental rightist populist rhetoric.*

The question in (b) can be answered by comparing the situation in Austria before and after February 2000. Among the many potential hypotheses that help to approach the research question are:

▪ *Oppositional populism versus governmental (right-wing) populism*

The rhetoric of oppositional (right-wing) populism manifests itself in political discourses primarily situated in (1) the field of political advertising, (2) the field of political control and (3) the field of formation of public attitudes, opinions and will.

The rhetoric of governmental (right-wing) populism is articulated (1) in the field of the formation of public attitudes, opinions and will, and partly (2) in the field of inter-party formation of attitudes, opinions and will (for example national populism).

▪ *(Right-wing) populism and politics, polity and policy*

(Right-wing) populism involves, in the first place, the political dimension of politics, in the second place the dimension of polity, and only in the third place the dimension of policy.

▪ *(Right-wing) populist rhetoric and democracy*

(Right-wing) populist rhetoric endangers democracy, if it succeeds in implementing its authoritarian, racist, anti-Semitic and 'xenophobic' beliefs, either in the political dimension of politics or by influencing the government's policy.

(Right-wing) populist rhetoric fulfils a democratic controlling function, if it justly criticizes undemocratic political representation and political corruption.

Pilot analysis (Step Five)

On the basis of the results of the previous stages, a *qualitative pilot analysis* can follow as a next step. This initial analysis of a single text serves, among others, as a means of tuning analytical tools.

EXAMPLE 5.1

To briefly illustrate populist rhetoric in Austria, I take a representative example of oppositional rightist populism authored by the FPÖ-politician Heinz Christian Strache in October 2004. When the article was published in the daily *Die Presse*, Strache was leader of the Viennese FPÖ and regularly writing guest commentaries in this newspaper. One of the comments reads as shown in Table 5.1.

The right column of Table 5.1 summarizes the macro- and mesostructure[5] of the article. Strache's text belongs to the genre of the *newspaper article* and to the subgenre of the *commentary*: In contrast to rather fact-oriented subgenres, a comment is an opinion-oriented article with the rhetorical purpose of persuasion. This implies that the author attempts to justify his personal point(s) of view.

The external dispositional macrostructure of the article comprises five paragraphs, whereas *the topical and functional macrostructure* consists of three parts: an <u>introduction</u>, an <u>exemplification</u> and a <u>conclusion</u>.

The micro analysis of argumentation is roughly outlined in the right column. Strache oscillates between (more or less) plausible topoi and fallacious argumentation schemes.[6]

The first sentence has the character of a populist argumentation scheme that fallaciously relies on the authority of the anonymous *vox populi* (this fallacy is named as *argumentum ad verecundiam,* meaning the misplaced appeal to competent or unimpeachable authorities, instead of relevant arguments). It serves to support a second populist fallacy, which reads as follows: 'Since the politicians do what they want, they are very reluctant to let the citizen interfere.' This argumentation scheme is formulated with the help of two generalizing nominations ('the politicians' implying 'all politicians' and 'the citizen' implying 'all citizens'). It can be proven to be fallacious if we successfully refer to just one politician who acts in favour of some citizens. The subsequent argumentation scheme employed in the first paragraph relies on factual data (the Europe-wide trend of electoral refusals), but the direct causal connection between the politicians' alleged lack of consideration for the citizens and the citizens' political fatigue is not assured. Thus, we cannot easily decide whether this argumentation scheme is a plausible topos or a fallacy. Nevertheless, Strache linguistically

Table 5.1 Macro- and mesostructure of the example of Strache's newspaper comment

Example	Macro- and mesostructure
23 October 2004 – Opinion/Guest Comments	Date of publication and indication of newspaper section
Guest Comment: Those Up There . . .	Title including the naming of the subgenre
BY HEINZ-CHRISTIAN STRACHE	Identification of the author
Paragraph 1 Those up there do what they want anyway, one hears again and again. 'The politicians', who let themselves be elected every few years, are meant, though, otherwise, they are very reluctant to let the citizen interfere. It's a fact: 'Those up there' do what they want. No wonder that the political unwillingness increases. The Europe-wide trend in communal and regional elections is heading in the direction of 50 per cent refusing to participate in elections. In EU elections even two-thirds abstain from going to the polls. Democracy loses its citizens. Frustration remains.	*Section 1: Introduction to the political problem – Crisis of representation: lack of citizens' possibilities to participate politically and the consequence of citizens' political fatigue*
Paragraph 2 The actual case of Turkey: Geographically and culturally, its joining the EU would break up the European framework. The chapter of Europe would be closed, that of Eurasia would be opened.	Section 2: Exemplification of the problem – With the case of Turkey aspiring to join the EU
Paragraph 3 All opinion polls show: The Europeans don't want this. But now 'those up there' do not want to allow the people a say. The vote of the EU-citizens against Turkey becoming a member of the EU would be too strong. Therefore let's first negotiate between Brussels and Ankara. At this time the 'point of no return' is exceeded. The USA, EU lobbies and industrialists rejoice. A few will heavily profit from it, the great majority will foot the bill, Europe will be buried. 'Those down there' will – once more – be left over.	Exemplification with general reference to the EU

Table 5.1 *continued*

Example	Macro- and mesostructure
Paragraph 4 In our place, Schüssel and Häupl are 'those up there'. Schüssel already looks forward to the EU presidency of Austria and does not want 'any waves'. Häupl – utterly banally – aims at winning Turkish voters in Vienna.	Exemplification with specific reference to Austria
Paragraph 5 I understand why more and more people say: 'Go and take a running jump!' And the polls remain half-empty on election days. I am, by the way, one of those 'down there', and never want to belong to those 'up there'. I am convinced that we 'down here' can be ahead by a nose at the end of the day if we don't refuse.	*Section 3: Conclusion* –Political advertising (by application of the two populist principles of assuming a perspective of looking up from below and of suggesting that the writer 'is one of you and for you') and political mobilization (propagated as solution of the problem)
The author is leader of the Viennese FPÖ.	Characterization of the author's political role
The actual case of Turkey shows: No wonder political unwillingness increases.	Summarizing heading

reinforced his contention with the evidentializing formula 'It's a fact.' This discursive intensifying strategy[7] is questionable, because the certainty claimed by Strache is not given, all the less since Strache presumes to pass judgement on 'all politicians up there'.

The second paragraph centres on a topos or fallacy of threat. This argumentation scheme can be paraphrased as: 'If Turkey joined the EU, the European framework would geographically and culturally break up, and the chapter Europe would be closed.' The soundness of this argumentation scheme depends on additional arguments that back the scheme. Strache does not offer any backing. As a consequence, the validity of the scheme remains uncertain.

The third paragraphs starts with an *argumentum ad verecundiam*. Just one opinion poll carried out somewhere in the EU in which a majority of the respondents favour Turkey's joining of the EU suffices in order to discredit Strache's generalizing assertion about 'all opinion polls' as a fallacy. The fallacy is followed by four interconnected causal argumentation schemes used as arguments against Turkey's joining of the EU and – in part – as topoi or fallacies of threat. These arguments go: (1) If Turkey's joining of the EU was put to the vote, a strong majority of EU citizens would vote against Turkey's membership. (2) Since EU citizens would not accept Turkey as a member of the EU, the responsible EU politicians decide first to have negotiations between Brussels and Ankara (please note the generalizing reference through the use of the two city names). (3) If negotiations between Brussels and Ankara start, Turkey's membership in the EU will be unavoidable. (4) If Turkey joins the EU, the USA, EU lobbies and industrialists will be happy, a few will profit a lot, the great majority will foot the bill, Europe will be buried and 'those down there' will – once more – be left over. The validity of these four argumentation schemes – each of which can be questioned by a series of arguments – remains in doubt.

The fourth paragraph continues with two causal topoi employed as arguments for the claim that Austria's Chancellor Schüssel and Vienna's social-democratic Mayor Häupl follow their interests without consideration for the 'normal' Austrian citizens. The first argumentation scheme reads as follows: Since Chancellor Schüssel already looks forward to the first half of 2005, when he will increase his political importance because of Austria's EU-presidency, he does not want 'any waves' caused by a negative discussion or vote on Turkey. The second argumentation scheme goes: Since Vienna's Mayor Häupl aspires to win Turkish voters in Vienna, he does not want to anger Turkish voters by a negative discussion or vote on Turkey's application. Although Strache cannot know with certainty what the intentions and motives guiding Schüssel and Häupl are, the two conclusion rules could be plausible.

The fifth paragraph concludes with the attempt to politically advertise and mobilize. Strache resorts to two classical populist principles, which can be summarized as follows: Since I am also one of you, and standing down here for you, looking critically at those up there, I understand your political fatigue

Table 5.2 Nominations and predications in Strache's comment

Upholders of rightist populism and groups of friends			
I/ we		Not those up and out there – you, ours, those down there/here	
Nomination	Predication	Nomination	Predication
I	One of those down there/here		
	Never wanting to become one of those up there	The citizen/the citizens	Politically unwilling/ tired of policy and politics
	Understanding people tired of policy and politics		Frustrated by the politicians
	Convinced that we 'down here' can be ahead by a nose at the end of the day	The Europeans/ the EU-citizens	Not willing to accept Turkey as a member of the EU
		Two-thirds [of voters]	Abstaining from their political right to vote
		Europe	A closed chapter
		The people	Excluded from political participation by the politicians
		The great majority	Payers of the price
		Those down there ['those' = nomination, 'down there/ here' = predication]	The left over
In our place [German: 'bei uns']			
		Austria	Expecting to obtain EU-presidency
		More and more people	Saying 'Go and take a running jump!'
We down here ['we' = nomination, 'down here' = predication]			
	Potentially ahead by a nose at the end of the day		Potentially ahead by a nose at the end of the day
	Not refusing		

Groups of opponents/enemies			
Those up there (the powers that be)		Those out there	
Nomination	Predication	Nomination	Predication
Those up there/ 'those up there' ['those' = nomination, 'up there' = predication] = they	Without consideration for the citizen		
		Turkey	Willing to join the EU
			Geographical and cultural destroyer of the European framework
'the politicians'	Very reluctant to let the citizen interfere		
		Eurasia (in part outside)	An open chapter
Brussels (in part imagined as being outside)	Negotiator with Ankara	Ankara	Negotiator with Brussels
EU lobbies (maybe in part imagined as being outside)	Rejoicing profiteers	The U.S.A.	Rejoicing profiteers
Industrialists maybe in part (considered to be outside)	Rejoicing profiteers	Turkish voters in Vienna	Potentially voting for the social democrat and mayor Häupl
A few (maybe in part considered to be outside)	Heavy profiteers		
Schüssel	One of those up there Joyfully expecting Austria's EU-presidency Not wanting 'any waves' Schüssel and Häupl as those up there		
Häupl	One of those up there Targeting the Turkish voters in Vienna		
[you = politicians]	Invited to go and take a running jump		

and thus deserve your trust and support as voters. Strache's endeavour to mobilize politically builds on the following conclusion rule: If you don't abstain politically, but participate and sustain me, we can win through our stance of being against Turkey becoming an EU member state, and thereby resolve the problem of political fatigue. Strache seems not to know for sure whether his claim will really come true. Thus he mitigates his statement by the personalizing use of a verb of judgement ('I am convinced') and the modal verb 'can' instead of 'will'.

From a point of view of perspectivation, the last paragraph appears remarkable for two reasons. (1) The *worm's-eye view* typical for oppositional populist rhetoric raises the question of whether readers will actually take Strache's perspective to be convincing, because Strache is a member of a party that participates in the government, which oppositional populists usually attack as 'those up there'. (2) It is only in the last paragraph that the author explicitly introduces an I-perspective. He assumes this perspective three times in the main clauses, interpolating the vivid perspective of fictitious direct quotation. Then he changes to the addressee-including we-perspective, in order to establish a populist group identity of 'those down here' who should politically act against 'those up there' and 'those out there'.

With respect to the research question, we can conclude that Strache's argumentation in part plausibly touches actual problems of political representation. In this sense, his comment fulfils a political controlling function. But wherever his argumentation becomes fallacious and aims at stirring up irrational emotions of anxiety oriented against alleged internal and external political enemies, his rhetorical manoeuvre results in being a danger to democracy.

The pilot analysis that helps to establish the analytical categories and to detail the hypotheses cannot fully be displayed in the present context. Nevertheless, two points may be summarized here. A detailed analysis comes to the following overview of nominations and predications (see Table 5.2.).

Most of these nominations and predications are typical for populist rhetoric in Austria (see Step Six).

The contextual analysis of Strache's article, will, among other things, focus on the general alignment of the newspaper. It will reveal that *Die Presse* is a libertarian-conservative Austrian daily with a medium-sized circulation among the population. Intertextual research will reveal that, between March 2003 and February 2005, Strache published 26 guest commentaries in *Die Presse*, averaging at least one every month. A detailed qualitative case-study (Step Six) could extend the corpus to these 26 texts and investigate topical continuities as well as intertextual differences and changes. It could, for example, focus on asking in what way Strache introduces typical populist topics in his commentaries. This would illustrate that the Viennese FPÖ politician persistently appeals to the Austrians' fear of Turkey becoming an EU member state. Against the background of such an intertextual approach, one could decide to investigate (right-wing) populist rhetoric in the discourse on Turkey and the

EU or (right-wing) populist rhetoric in the discourse about the crisis of political representation in the EU.

The study should further consider the wider political and historical context i.e. observations such as the following ones:

■ Ad political context: A striking contradiction can be detected between Strache's rhetoric as an oppositional right-wing populist who criticizes the government and the fact that – at the time of writing the commentaries – Strache himself (though regionally) represents a party that is part of a coalition government. As the historical developments of 2005 show, this performative self-contradiction, violating both the principle of coalition discipline and of party cohesion, exacerbated the situation and finally led to the splitting of the FPÖ into two parties: Haider's BZÖ sought to remain part of the Austrian government and thus lost much political support in subsequent elections, and the FPÖ under the new leadership of Strache continued to hold the oppositional course and thus lost far fewer voters than expected. This suggests that right-wing populist rhetoric is more successful if articulated from an oppositional point of view.

■ Ad historical context: Discourse historical research on Austrian right-wing populist rhetoric reveals that Strache copies point by point the formerly successful FPÖ leader Haider during the 1980s and the 1990s. These commonalities include problematic dealings with right-wing extremism and National Socialism. The task of a discourse historical study is not only to observe such continuities and commonalities, but also to document changes and differences.

Detailed case-studies (Step Six)

The next step of research consists of *detailed case-studies on the macro-, meso- and microlevels of linguistic analysis, as well as on the level of context*. This step, which cannot be demonstrated in the present chapter, leads to an overall interpretation within the wider social, historical and political context.

An overall interpretation of some important results on the case-study on Austrian right-wing populism can be summarized as follows.

General characteristics of oppositional right-wing populism in Austria are:

1. a strong distrust of the 'establishment', 'the powers that be', especially of the government, professional politicians, bankers and the big business community;
2. an oversimplified picture of the society with rigid distinctions between friends and enemies and with regressive, anti-modernist and anti-welfare-state utopianism;
3. a strong tendency of personalism and personalization on the one hand; of collectivism and assimilatory identity politics on the other hand;

4.   agitation, irrationalism and anti-intellectualism;
5.   a seemingly radical-democratic or grass-roots-democratic attitude on the one hand; an anti-democratic, authoritarian, hierarchical and leader-oriented attitude on the other hand (Reisigl 2002:153–60; see also Ter Wal 2002; Wodak and Pelinka 2002).

The rightist governmental populism of the BZÖ and the former FPÖ has lost the first characteristic and transformed the fourth and fifth features more and more since 2000. Among the rhetorical principles of oppositional right-wing populists in Austria are:

1.   the subdivision of the world of social actors into friends and enemies by Manichean division and the rhetorical construction of internal and external scapegoats;
2.   the reduction of complexity by drastic and simplistic illustration and hypostatization,
3.   the principle of *not mincing one's words,*
4.   the insulting of the political opponent,
5.   the assumption of a *worm's-eye view* (a perspective of looking up from below),
6.   the suggestion that the speaking or writing ego *is one of yours and for you,*
7.   pathetic dramatization and emotionalization,
8.   insistent repetition,
9.   calculated ambivalence,
10.   the promise of salvation and liberation (Reisigl 2002:166–74).

Governing rightist populists can usually not rely on principles (3), (4), (5), (6) and (10) in the same manner as oppositional populists. Governing populists suffer from a crisis of credibility, of *ethos.* Their ruling policy contradicts former announcements and claims. The FPÖ lost votes in all regional and European elections, except for the election in Carinthia in 2004. This was attributed to not having kept election promises, unprofessional policy, high consumption of personnel (governmental FPÖ politicians had often to be replaced after a short period of time), being co-responsible for specific political measures, Haider's destructive unpredictability and so on. For the time being we can conclude that governing right-wing populism seems to be a medium-term phenomenon, whereas oppositional right-wing populism still remains a problem that should not be underestimated.

Three salient discursive features of right-wing populist rhetoric in Austria are as follows:

(I) Right-wing populist nomination
The oppositional right-wing populist world view knows four main groups of social actors (see Reinfeldt 2000). Accordingly, these populists resort to the subdivision by nomination presented in Table 5.3 (see Reisigl 2002:175–9).

Table 5.3 Oppositional right-wing populist nomination of main groups of social actors

Upholders of rightist populism and groups of friends		Groups of opponents/enemies	Not we / Those out there
I/we	Not those up and out there, you, ours Those down there/here	Those up there (the powers that be)	
The leaders and cadres as well as members of the populist movement, and so on	The potential voters, 'the little man', 'ordinary people', 'the man in the street', 'the people', and so on	The establishment: the government the professional politicians, the bureaucrats, the big business people, the legal establishment, the bankers, and so on.	The others: the aliens, the foreigners, the Jews, the minorities partially the EU, partially the USA, other cultures/cultural areas/civilizations, Islam, Turkey terrorism, and so on

If rightist populists come to power, the composition of the main groups of social actors changes in at least two respects: First, the government or at least parts of the establishment must be integrated into the we-group. Second, the loss of the previous enemy, of 'those up there', is compensated by attempts to find new scapegoats such as the political opposition ('those over there') as 'internal enemies' and 'external opponents', such as 'the EU', 'the USA', 'Turkey', 'terrorism', 'Islam' and 'alien civilizations, cultures or cultural areas'. In Austria, the attacks on the EU were must successful during the period of the sanctions of the EU-14 against Austria (Reisigl and Wodak 2002). However, since their participation in the government, Austrian right-wing populists have not been able to attack the EU as radically as before.

(II) Right-wing populist predication
Only one remarkable aspect of populist predications (for details see Reisigl 2002:180–5) will be stressed in the present context. Predication strategies formerly directed against the powers-that-be by oppositional right-wing populists (see Example 5.1) can become a boomerang after these enter government. This was the experience of the FPÖ, which after the governmental change in 2000 was criticized for broken promises, for programmatic contradictions, lack of governing competence and professionalism, incapacity to resolve party-internal conflicts (that is lack of party cohesion), nepotism, corruption, the waste of tax money, unpredictability and lack of credibility (Heinisch 2004:257).

(III) Right-wing populist argumentation
There are various argumentation schemes strategically employed by oppositional right-wing populists (Reisigl 2002:185–96). The topos of the people and *argumentum ad populum*, as well as the topos or fallacy of (the 'people's') democratic participation can be found at the centre of populist argumentation. The latter is a special case of the former argumentation scheme. Both schemes occur in Strache's commentary. Generally, they can be formalized as shown in Table 5.4

The Austrian example has demonstrated that governing right-wing populists cannot employ these as well as other populist argumentation schemes without the risk of losing their credibility. This example has further shown that populist schemes are sometimes utilized as plausible topoi, but more often realized as fallacies. In the latter case, they have to be criticized as endangering democracy.

Formulation of critique (Step Seven)

With respect to our example, the *careful formulation of a critique* aims to answer the research question by raising awareness of problematic discursive strategies, for example right-wing populist nominations and predications that are insulting and discriminating as well as fallacious right-wing populist argumentations. In a wider sense, a critique attempts to develop an accurate

Table 5.4 Two basic populist argumentation schemes

Name of topos	Name of fallacy	Paraphrase
Topos of the people	Argumentum ad populum (sometimes as argumentum ad verecundiam)	1. Version 1 (negative): If the people refuse a specific political action or decision, the action should not be performed/the decision should not be taken. 2. Version 2 (positive): If the people favour a specific political action or decision, the action should be performed/the decision should be taken.
Topos of (the 'people's') democratic participation	Fallacy of (the 'people's') democratic participation	Version 1: If a specific political decision, action or non-action concerns all citizens/the people, the citizens/the people should be asked for their opinion. Version 2: If I or we are in power, the people, 'the man on the street' will democratically participate in political decisions.

characterization of the most striking anti-democratic strategies and elements that can be found in the right-wing populist rhetoric of Austrian politicians. Additionally, it aims to identify populist strategies and elements with political controlling functions.

Application of analytical results (Step Eight)

The *social application of the analytical results* will build on the critique. In our case, the utilization may consist of offering politolinguistic tools that enable us to identify democratically dangerous right-wing populist rhetoric that infringes on principles of rational deliberation. Critical instruments and results of analysis can be disseminated with the help of scholarly publications, newspaper comments, recommendations, trainings, further-education courses, exhibitions, radio transmissions, parliamentary symposia and so on.

Concluding remarks

The present chapter has summarized how politolinguistics fruitfully integrates discourse-analytical, rhetorical and political-scientific concepts in order to analyze interdisciplinary topics such as populist rhetoric. This approach provides a more adequate analytical framework than mono-disciplinary approaches in political science and linguistics. The sequential presentation of the research practice was not designated to suggest that there exists one optimal recipe of how to do a politolinguistic analysis on political rhetoric. There is no analytical toolbox that can be applied to all research questions relating to political rhetoric. As in most cases of qualitative discourse analysis, politolinguistic categories of analysis have to be carefully adapted to each single issue in question, and the interpretations involved in all eight stages of research profit a lot from the creative application of prior researchers' knowledge. There are many ways of doing critical politolinguistics. I hope, nevertheless, that the present outline offers an accessible orientation that encourages future discourse-analytical research on political issues.

Notes

1. I consider *discourse* to be a multifaceted bundle of semiotic social practices that relate to a specific macrotopic and to the argumentation about validity claims such as truth and normative validity, and that – usually – involve various social actors who participate in the discourse and bring in different points of view (Reisigl 2003:92).
2. The selection of literature reflects individual research strategies, the researchers' knowledge of languages, pragmatic restrictions of resources such as time, money and personnel, the historical context, intellectual trends, and so on.
3. The Austrian Freedom Party (FPÖ) was founded in 1956. It quickly became an electoral home for many former Austrian Nazis. Thus, the FPÖ has never been a 'liberal' party in the European sense. In 1986 Jörg Haider was elected as leader of the party. Between 1986 and 1999 the party gained many votes, its share of the poll even rising to about 27 per cent in October 1999. Between February 2000 and April 2005 the FPÖ was part of a coalition government dominated by the Austrian People's Party (ÖVP) presided over by Chancellor Wolfgang Schüssel. In April 2005, after a series of electoral defeats, Haider split the party and founded the 'Alliance for the Future of Austria' (*Bündnis Zukunft Österreich*/BZÖ). While Haider's BZÖ continued to be part of the government until January 2007, the remaining FPÖ, led by Heinz-Christian Strache, became an opposition party in 2005.
4. The 'Austria First Petition' was an 'anti-foreigner' petition launched in January 1993 by the Austrian Freedom Party. It was signed by 417,278 Austrians, half the number expected by Jörg Haider, but nevertheless a high figure, although there was massive public protest against the petition, which had already started in 1992.
5. In the given context, mesostructural textual units relate to single paragraphs, whereas macrostructural units relate to sections (which usually include more than one paragraph).
6. A *topos* can be seen as plausible argumentation scheme. It functions as a link that leads from the premises to the conclusion of an argumentation. As such, it is not always explicitly verbalized, but can be paraphrased by formulations such as *if x*,

then y or *since x, therefore y*. A *fallacy* is an argumentation scheme that infringes rules of rational and plausible argumentation such as the freedom of speech, the obligation to give reasons, the correct reference to previous utterances by the antagonist, the obligation to *matter-of-factness*, the correct reference to implicit premises, the respect of shared starting-points, the use of plausible arguments and schemes of argumentation, logical validity, the acceptance of the discussion's results and the clarity of expression and correct interpretation (see van Eemeren and Grootendorst 1992:102–217). Technically speaking, fallacies can often be named in Latin as *argumentum ad x*. It is sometimes difficult, if not impossible, to concretely distinguish between a plausible argumentation scheme (topos) and its perverted pendant (fallacy).

7. Please note that the *argumentum ad verecundiam* can also be considered to be the realization of an intensification strategy.

Key readings

Reisigl, M. '"Dem Volk aufs Maul schauen, nach dem Mund reden und angst und bange machen" – Von populistischen Anrufungen, Anbiederungen und Agitationsweisen in der Sprache österreichischer PolitikerInnen', in W. Eismann (ed.) *Rechtspopulismus in Europa. Österreichische Krankheit oder europäische Normalität?* (Vienna: Cernin-Verlag, 2002), pp. 149–98.
Reisigl, M. 'The Dynamics of Right-Wing Populist Argumentation in Austria', in F.H. van Eeemeren *et al* (eds) *Proceedings of the Sixth International Conference on Argumentation, organized by the International Society for the Study of Argumentation at the University of Amsterdam, June 27–30, 2006* (Amsterdam: Sic Sat, 2007).
Reisigl, M. 'Rhetorical Tropes in Political Discourse', in K. Brown (ed.) *The Encyclopedia of Language and Linguistics*, vol. 10, 2nd edn (Oxford: Elsevier, 2006), pp. 596–605.
Ter Wal, J. 'Anti-Foreigner Campaigns in the Austrian Freedom Party and Italian Northern League: The Discursive Construction of Identity', in R. Wodak and A. Pelinka (eds) *The Haider Phenomenon in Austria* (New Brunswick: Transaction, 2002), pp 157–79.
Wodak, R. and Pelinka, A. (eds) *The Haider Phenomenon in Austria and Europe* (New Brunswick: Transaction, 2002).

References

Altermatt, U. *Das Fanal von Sarajewo. Ethnonationalismus in Europa* (Paderborn: Schöningh, 1996).
Arditi, B. 'Populism as an Internal Periphery of Democratic Politics', in F. Panizza (ed.) *Populism and the Mirror of Democracy* (London: Verso, 2005), pp. 72–98.
Bourdieu, P. *Sozialer Raum und 'Klassen'. Leçon sur la leçon. Zwei Vorlesungen* (Frankfurt am Main: Suhrkamp, 1991).
Girnth, H. 'Texte im politischen Diskurs. Ein Vorschlag zur diskursorientierten Beschreibung von Textsorten', *Muttersprache* 1 (1996), 66–80.

Heinisch, R. 'Die FPÖ – Ein Phänomen im internationalen Vergleich. Erfolg und Misserfolg des Identitären Rechtspopulismus', ÖZP 3 (2004), 247–61.

Kienpointner, M. 'Populistische Topik. Zu einigen rhetorischen Strategien Jörg Haiders', Rhetorik, 21 (2002), 119–40.

Laclau, E. 'Populism: What's in a Name?', in F. Panizza (ed.) Populism and the Mirror of Democracy (London: Verso, 2005), pp. 32–49.

Mény, Y. and Surel, Y. Populismo e democrazia (Bologna: Mulino, 2004).

Meyer, T. Was ist Politik? (Opladen: Leske & Budrich, 2000).

Nohlen, D. 'Populismus', in D. Nohlen, R.-O. Schultze and S.S. Schüttemeyer (eds) Lexikon der Politik, vol. 7: Politische Begriffe (Munich: Beck, 1998), pp. 514–15.

Panizza, F (ed.) Populism and the Mirror of Democracy (London: Verso, 2005).

Plett, H. Einführung in die rhetorische Textanalyse (Hamburg: Buske, 2001).

Reinfeldt, S. Nicht-wir und Die-da. Studien zum rechten Populismus (Vienna: Braumüller, 2000).

Reisigl, M. ' "Dem Volk aufs Maul schauen, nach dem Mund reden und angst und bange machen" – Von populistischen Anrufungen, Anbiederungen und Agitationsweisen in der Sprache österreichischer PolitikerInnen', in W. Eismann (ed.) Rechtspopulismus in Europa. Österreichische Krankheit oder europäische Normalität? (Vienna: Cernin-Verlag, 2002), pp. 149–98.

Reisigl, M. 'Wie man eine Nation herbeiredet. Eine diskursanalytische Untersuchung zur sprachlichen Konstruktion der österreichischen Nation und österreichischen Identität in politischen Fest- und Gedenkreden', PhD thesis, University of Vienna, 2004.

Reisigl, M. 'Rhetoric of political speeches', in R. Wodak and V. Koller (eds) Handbook of Applied Linguistics, vol. 4, Language and Communication in the Public Sphere (Berlin: Mouton de Gruyter, 2008), pp. 243–69.

Reisigl, M. and Wodak, R. Discourse and Discrimination: Rhetorics of Racism and Antisemitism (London: Routledge, 2001).

Reisigl, M. and Wodak, R. 'Nationalpopulistische Rhetorik – Einige diskursanalytische und argumentationstheoretische Überlegungen zur österreichischen Debatte über den "nationalen Schulterschluß" ', in A. Demirović and M. Bojadžijev (eds) Konjunkturen des Rassismus (Münster: Westfälisches Dampfboot, 2002), pp. 90–11.

Taguieff, P.-A. L'Illusione populista. Dall'Arcaico al mediatico (Milano: Mondatori, 2003 [2002]).

Ter Wal, J. 'Anti-Foreigner Campaigns in the Austrian Freedom Party and Italian Northern League: The Discursive Construction of Identity', in R.Wodak and A. Pelinka (eds) The Haider Phenomenon in Austria (New Brunswick: Transaction, 2002), pp. 157–79.

Van Eemeren, F.H. and Grootendorst, R. Argumentation, Communication, and Fallacies (Hillsdale, NJ: Erlbaum, 1992).

Walton, D.N. Appeal to Popular Opinion (University Park: Pennsylvania State University Press, 1999).

Wiles, P. Populism: A syndrome, Not a Doctrine, in I. Ghita and E. Gellner (eds) Populism: Its Meaning and Characteristics (London: Weidenfeld, 1969), pp. 166–79.

Wodak, R. and Pelinka, A. (eds) The Haider Phenomenon in Austria and Europe (New Brunswick: Transaction, 2002).

Analyzing Interaction in Broadcast Debates[1]

Greg Myers

Introduction

How does a voter get a sense of who the candidates are in an election, and what is at stake? Much of the information comes through TV spots, press ads, indirect mail, posters – media the campaigns pay for and control. Press coverage, which might seem more open, focuses on more or less predictable media events such as party conferences and photo opportunities created by the campaigns. Newspaper editorials, radio phone-ins, blogs, late-night comedians and informal conversation may tell a voter about the issues, but not about the candidates. Formal debates seem to promise an insight into what the candidates are like and how they think on their feet. Such debates play a relatively small part in campaigns in the United States, and no part at all in many other democratic countries (though see Schrott 1990; Galasiński 1998; Coleman 2000). But they are heavily studied by academics and professional politicians, perhaps because for better or worse they are the closest our heavily mediated systems get to an ideal of democracy as face-to-face encounter. In such an encounter, in the fifth-century-BC Athenian agora, the riotous eighteenth-century hustings of William Hogarth's *An Election* or the nineteenth-century debates between Abraham Lincoln and Stephen Douglas, one may not get enlightened deliberation, but one does see what the candidate is like.

The academic commentary on televised debates, from 1960 to the present, is often tinged with disappointment. The debate is neither a formal argumentative encounter between two speakers focused on a topic, nor the kind of relaxed conversation from which we can judge the characters and personalities of the candidates; questions are carefully selected to cover a range of disconnected topics, answers are brief and formulaic, and there is little chance for following up or rebuttal. Even brilliant speakers – and few candidates for president of the United States fall into that category – would find such a rigid format more of an obstacle course than an opportunity for display of their humanity.

Most of the academic writing on debates deals with one of three issues: who won, what works for candidates, and what would better inform the voters (for

121

references, see Benoit 2004; Louden 2006). The question of 'who won' – hotly debated from the moment the broadcast ends – proves remarkably hard to answer, because reports of responses are unreliable, and the final decision on voting involves many factors besides performance at debates (Lang and Lang 1978; Lanoue 1992; Friedenberg 1994; Munro *et al.* 2002; Seiter and Weger 2005). Even the effects of the Kennedy–Nixon Debates in 1960, the classic case of a broadcast debate, remain uncertain on closer scrutiny (Druckman 2003). The wider question of what kind of rhetorical performance is effective in winning votes also proves difficult to answer (Jackson-Beeck and Meadow 1979; Benoit and Wells 1996; Hart and Jarvis 1997). Is it more effective to talk about policies or personalities, to attack or to defend? Candidates who would seem to be excellent debaters (such as Al Gore) may come across as wooden and pompous, while candidates who may seem inept (such as George Bush) come across as firm and accessible. Detailed analysis of what was actually said may tell us little about outcomes if voters are responding to a general impression of 'accessibility', 'presidentialness' or composure under stress. A third line of research deals with the ways debates do or do not inform the voters (Jamieson and Birdsell 1988; Benoit 2000; Jamieson and Adasiewicz 2000). But often the voter is assumed to be an isolated individual seeking information for a rational choice between two candidates, eager for clarification through argument, as in the nineteenth-century debates (but perhaps without such a long attention span). But voters may be looking for impressions rather than information, and they form these impressions through a complex mediated encounter.

Instead of answering the questions of who won, what works, and what would be better, I focus on the interactions between the candidates, the questioners (in this case, members of the audience) and the moderator. I consider one broadcast election debate from 2004, drawing on discourse studies of debates (Clayman 1995; Beck 1996; Galasiński 1998; Bilmes 1999; Blum-Kulka and Liebes 2000; Bilmes 2001). The approach I take is broadly that of conversation analysis, the study of how participants in interaction organize their talk moment to moment and turn to turn (Hutchby and Wooffitt 1998; Silverman 1998; ten Have 1999).

Steps in analysis

1. How do questioners begin and end their questions? What *presuppositions* are involved? How does this framing of their turns display their role as questioners and maintain *face*?
2. How do candidates *address* the questioner and maintain face?
3. How do candidates display that they are addressing the topic and answering the question?
4. How do the candidates refer to each other and to themselves?
5. How do the candidates quote others?

6. How do candidates acknowledge and deal with the time restrictions of the debate format?
7. Where and how do candidates shift *register*?

These features, diverse as they are, all play some part in defining how the candidates present themselves, their relation to each other, and their awareness of the conventions of the genre, what Jack Bilmes calls 'interpersonal rhetoric' (Bilmes 1999) and Christina Beck calls 'social face' (Beck 1996). This self-presentation is not just a distraction from the serious political issues at hand, the who won, what works, and what's better: studies of responses to the debates suggest that the public watches for what they can learn about the candidates' personalities and their responses to pressure as well as for their views on the issues (Watts 2002).

Text and contexts

Like other contributions to this volume, I will draw on a heuristic framework that asks the textual analyst to consider: (1) the immediate co-text of any feature analyzed, (2) relations of this text to other texts, (3) the 'context of situation', the conventions of this genre and (4) broader socio-political and historical contexts (summarized from Chapter 1 in this volume, and Wodak and Meyer 2001:67).

First, the text I will consider is the video of the 8 October 2004 US presidential campaign debate, between the incumbent Republican George W. Bush and the Democratic challenger Senator John Kerry.[2] Transcription conventions are given in Table 6.1.[3] I chose this from the twenty-four US debates, and dozens in other countries, because of its somewhat unusual form. It is what is called a 'town hall format', recalling the days of face-to-face local democracy, because instead of a panel of journalists, members of the public (chosen as voters not strongly committed to one candidate or the other) ask the questions. The debate came one month before polling day, at a moment when the election was considered to be too close to call, and both campaigns were looking for a clear 'win' that would give their candidate momentum.

Table 6.1 Transcription convention for the 8 October 2004 US presidential campaign debate

Symbol	Function
.	pause
[ ]	uncertain transcription
/	overlapping with the following or previous turn
(( ))	transcriber's comments on gestures and camera

A transcript is available at the website of the Commission on Presidential Debates,[4] and the video is available from C-SPAN.[5] The transcript is sometimes inaccurate, and it lacks details on pauses, stresses, miss-starts, repetitions and overlaps. It was retranscribed to include these features, which are relevant to a discourse analysis approach.

One level of analysis of this text might involve using corpus tools to find keywords of each candidate: how Bush uses 'middle class' or 'liberal', and how Kerry uses 'plan' or 'tax cut'. In fact the blogger Cameron Marlow produced a keyword list for the first debate within days,[6] though he uses an algorithm ranking noun phrases by length and frequency, instead of comparing the frequencies of terms to those in a reference corpus, as would be done by for instance Wordsmith software (see Chapter 2 by Mautner in this volume). In a more interpretive analysis, one could code key arguments, kinds of appeals, such as attacking or defending (Benoit and Wells 1996; Benoit 2004), use of metaphors, or nonverbal features. One could also do more complex quantitative analyzes, for instance the approach of Roderick Hart and his colleagues (Hart and Jarvis 1997), in which they automatically score a text using a dictionary that categorizes various kinds of lexical items as showing certainty, optimism, activity, realism or community.

But there is in principle a problem with coding interactional data (and not just the more reductive automatic coding) in what Jack Bilmes (1999) calls 'categorize and count' methods. In many cases, the categories applied by analysts are just those that the participants – debaters, moderator, studio audience, home audience – are applying moment to moment. The form of an utterance in the transcript does not tell us what counts as a question, or whether it is an aggressive or soft question, or whether the response corresponds to the question, answers the question or evades it, and whether it is an accusation or a defence, agreement or disagreement. Instead, participants signal that they are taking the previous response as evasive. One can code utterances or words according to a schema, and can have multiple coders and achieve high interrater reliability, but one is still studying the perceptions of coders, in retrospect. An alternative would be to look at how participants do what they do, moment to moment, as I discuss under 'context of situation'.

Second, the text I am studying is linked to other texts (see *intertextuality*). I have suggested that debates, though watched by a mass audience, are only a small part of the campaign. The keywords one might find in the debate for each candidate take part of their meaning from echoes and inversions of earlier uses, by the candidates and others, in catchphrases, slogans and quotations through the campaign (for example, 'weapons of mass destruction', 'Patriot Act', 'No Child Left Behind'). And the debate broadcast itself is recontextualized in later texts, in quotations in the headlines the next day, commentaries over coming days, and summaries. In later comments and analyzes, all that remains of the 90-minute debate is some sound bites and one-sentence judgments (Glenn Reynolds's summary of bloggers' comments can be found on Instapundit).[7] Part of the analysis is showing what in the performance makes such sound bites, and not other parts, available for re-use (Clayman 1995).

Third, this chapter focuses on the context of situation, the conventions and constraints governing the encounter. As I have suggested, the context in the case of the presidential debates is complex. To begin with, the debates are not exactly debates. Soon after the Kennedy–Nixon debates in 1960, Auer (1962) called them 'The Counterfeit Debates', arguing that a *debate* should have five components: 'A debate is (1) a confrontation (2) in equal and adequate time (3) of matched contestants (4) on a stated proposition (5) to gain an audience decision.' The standard US presidential debate has no direct interaction between candidates, the time is severely limited, the topics shift after every few minutes, and the important 'audience decision' is the vote that follows weeks later. The only criteria met by these debates are that the candidates are evenly matched and have equal time. Some scholars prefer to call the debates 'joint press conferences' (Jamieson and Birdsell 1988).

Each debate is conducted under ground rules agreed by the two campaign organizations and the Committee for Presidential Debates (CPD) and written down in a Memorandum of Understanding (MoU). In 2004, the Memorandum of Understanding (Commission on Presidential Debates 2004) ran to thirty-two typed pages and specified, among other things, the topics of debates, the selection and form of questions, the role of the moderator, the exact time allowed for response (two minutes), the counter-response of the other candidate (one and a half minutes), and an extension (thirty seconds each). It also specified the design of the podiums and the chairs. It specifically did not allow the candidates to move outside their assigned space, bring notes into the hall, use visual aids, refer to people in the hall or ask their rival questions, other than rhetorical questions. It did allow them to take notes during the debate on a piece of paper with a writing implement of their choice. The sanction for violation of any of these rules was a heavy one: the moderator could pronounce, on live television (and in words also specified by the agreement) that the behaviour 'violates the rules agreed to by that candidate'. The camera was also strictly controlled; the MoU did not allow cutaways to the other candidate listening, reaction shots of the audience, or shots of the candidates' families (though as we will see, these restrictions were not always followed).

It may seem odd to turn to conversation analysis (Hutchby and Wooffitt 1998; Silverman 1998; ten Have 1999) when the debates are admittedly too constrained to count (by some definitions) as conversation. But there has been a useful line of research applying the insights of situated sequential analysis of everyday talk to the more rigid formats of institutional talk (Drew and Heritage 1992; Boden 1994), and more specifically broadcast talk (Scannell 1991; Hutchby 2006; Tolson 2006) and broadcast debates (Hutchby 1996; Thornborrow 2000; Ilie 2001; Clayman and Heritage 2002; Thornborrow 2002), and especially the excellent analyzes by Bilmes and Beck on US election debates (Beck 1996; Bilmes 1999; Bilmes 2001). Like any orators, the candidates use rhetorical appeals based on common topoi, use stylistic devices such as repetition and variation and metaphors, present themselves as good people and appeal to the emotions and interests of their audience. But they also use what Bilmes calls an 'interactional rhetoric' in which they are judged by their display of appropriate attitudes towards and moment-to-moment responses to the other participants, the moderator, questioners and opponent.

Fourth, features of the context of situation do not make sense without some account of the broader socio-political and historical context. The great significance accorded to the events leads us to a longer tradition of historical set-piece political debates, and the details of the MoU lead us to wider issues of the role of money and media in campaigns, the role of campaigns in the larger political system, and the model of the citizen as an informed consumer of political information. Televised debates are not an inevitable part of a presidential campaign (Jamieson and Birdsell 1988; Kraus 2000). They began in 1960 with the famous Nixon–Kennedy debates, which were made possible only by a suspension of broadcasting regulations that would have required the participation of all candidates, not just those of the major parties. Those debates had the candidates standing at podiums, responding to questions from journalists, a format that has been followed, with variations I will discuss, in all succeeding debates. There were no debates in the elections of 1964, 1968 or 1972, but they were started again in 1976 (Ford vs. Carter) and have continued in each election since. In some ways this persistence is surprising: there is usually a good reason for one side or the other not to participate, for instance an incumbent may not want to meet the challenger as an equal, or a candidate with more money may not want to give his or her opponent free air time. Only the danger of seeming to flee the debate ensures that the candidates do participate. From 1976 to 1984, the League of Women Voters sponsored the debates; they withdrew in 1988, citing undue pressure form the two campaigns in determining the format, and since then the debates have been sponsored by the Commission on Presidential Debates (CPD), with participation of the two political parties and support from corporate sponsors (this complex story gets an even-handed treatment in Kraus 2000).

The League of Women Voters was right; as we have seen, the two campaigns used the MoU to try to control the debate down to the smallest details. Morello traces how some of these constraints in the 2004 MoU resulted from incidents in earlier debates, unpredictable events the campaigns would now try to control (Morello 2005). For instance, when citizens were allowed to ask questions in the 1992 debates, they could also ask follow-ups that would be more likely to challenge the candidates; these were not allowed in 2004, and in fact the questioners had their microphones switched off as soon as the question was asked. Morello also tells about an incident in the 2000 debate in which Gore crossed over to Bush; in the 2004 MoU, the candidates were each assigned to a space, and the spaces could not overlap. We can see in these details the ways the two campaigns tried to anticipate all possible ways one candidate might gain an advantage over the other, or slip up and damage the message carefully produced over years of press conferences, public relations and advertising (Blum-Kulka and Liebes 2000).

Applying the framework to interaction in debates

The categories that follow draw on conversation analytic work on broadcast interviews. Debates are not interviews, but they have conventions that are in some ways similar: one set of people (journalists or chosen members of the public) has the role of asking questions, another set (the candidates) tries to show that they are answering the questions. In addition, as we have seen, the debates have strict time constraints, and the moderator and candidates sometimes acknowledge these limits, and refer to the complex format of the debate. As part of their engagement with this format, the candidates shift between different registers, signalling oratorical and conversational tones of voice. The framework I am following suggests we add another category of interaction, because the participants do not just interact with the other people who are in the room; they bring in other people by quoting them.

Asking the question

In most presidential debates, questions are asked by a moderator or by a panel of journalists. There have been many calls for the public to be allowed to ask questions, with the assumption that those questions might be less aggressive, less predictable and less a matter of professional display than those of the journalists (Jackson-Beeck and Meadow 1979; Carlin *et al.* 2001). But as I have noted, these members of the public were highly constrained: they were chosen to be uncommitted, their questions were submitted in writing and chosen and ordered by the moderator, and they were not allowed to follow up. Morello (2005) has commented on the form of the questions in this particular debate, arguing that the prevalence of future-oriented questions to Kerry, and past-oriented questions to Bush, gave Kerry an advantage. Instead of considering the form, I would like to consider the ways members of the public present what they are doing in their turn.

Questioners, nervous as they may be, are careful to present their entitlement to ask a question. In none of the eighteen questions does anyone offer a statement presenting themselves as entitled to speak because they have a distinctive experience or point of view (for instance as a veteran or an unemployed person). In that they are different from the public in vox pops, where the interviewee typically tries to show that they have good reason to speak of their opinions, experiences or feelings (Myers 2004). Questioners show they are aware that they have been chosen to ask a question, and a question is what they will produce. When there *is* a statement, it is always presented as the essential preface to a question:

EXAMPLE 6.1

Gibson: President Bush the next question is for you and it comes from Rob Fowler who I believe is over in this area
Fowler: President Bush . forty-five days after . (coughs) excuse me forty-five days after nine-eleven Congress passed the Patriot Act . which takes away checks on law enforcement and weakens American citizens' rights and freedoms especially Fourth Amendment rights . with expansions to the Patriot Act and Patriot Act Two . my questions to you is . why are my rights being watered down . and my citizens' around me . and what are the specific ju- . justifications for these [reforms]
Bush: [yeah] . I appreciate that erm . I really don't think your rights are being watered down (22:10)

The 'my question to you is' presents the arguable statement 'takes away checks on law enforcement' as part of the question. Even where the effect of the act is not a question, but a directive, the utterance is in interrogative form:

EXAMPLE 6.2

Gibson: Senator Kerry the next question will be for you and it comes from James . Varner who I believe is in this section Mr Varner . you need a microphone
Varner: thank you . erm . Senator Kerry . would you be willing to look directly into the camera . and using simple and unequivocal language . give the American people your solemn pledge not to sign any legislation . that will increase the tax burden on families earning less then two hundred thousand dollars a year . during your first term (21:54)

Varner's term is literally asking about Kerry's willingness to make such a pledge, not asking for information. Kerry responds by performing the act.

As the previous example shows, questioners sometimes pose potential threats to the candidate's *face*. One way they do this is by presenting themselves as speaking for others.

EXAMPLE 6.3

Gibson: the first question . is for Senator Kerry . and it will come for Che- . from Cheryl Otis who is right behind me
Otis: Senator Kerry . after talking with several co-workers and family and friends I asked the ones who said they were not voting for you why . they said that you were too wishy-washy . er . do you have a reply for them
Kerry: yes I certainly do (LAUGHTER) (laughs)(21:04)

Only two of the turns from members of the public are not formally questions, both to Bush. One of these turns follows a confused moment in which first Gibson and then Bush looked the wrong way for the questioner

---

EXAMPLE 6.4

Gibson: and the final question of the evening will be addressed to President Bush . and it will come from Linda Grabel . Linda Grabel's over here
Bush: put a head fake on us
Gibson: I do- (LAUGHTER) I got faked out myself
Bush: hi Linda
Grabel: President Bush . during the last four years you have made thousand of decisions . that have affected millions of lives . please give three instances . in which you came to realize you had made a wrong decision . and what you did to cre- to correct it . thank you
Bush: I er I have made a lot of decisions .(22:28)

Bush does not challenge the *presupposition* that he has made wrong decisions. Directives, questions with arguable presuppositions, and questions with elaborate prefaces might be seen as aggressive if posed in this way by journalists (Clayman and Heritage 2002). But the chosen members of the public present them as the right sort of turn for that slot, and as we will see, the candidates take them that way.

Addressing the questioner

The candidates are careful to address their remarks the questioner, in the first instance, and then to the studio audience. This is different from an interview, where the addressee is nominally the interviewer but actually the broadcast audience, or the broadcast speech where the candidate speaks directly to camera, addressing 'my fellow Americans'. In terms of Goffman's *participant roles* (Goffman 1981), Kerry signals the questioner as 'ratified participant', and by implication makes the moderator a bystander and the broadcast audience eavesdroppers, by beginning nearly every response with the questioner's first name, which he must have carefully written down:

EXAMPLE 6.5

Kerry: Anthony I would <u>not</u> (21:13)

Bush acknowledges the questioner in most cases by beginning, and even ending, his turn with a thank you:

EXAMPLE 6.6

Bush: right . thank you for that . er we have a deficit (21:48)

Though the address is always directed to the questioner at first, the candidates then turn to address the other people in the hall ('ladies and gentlemen'), and the moderator, Charles Gibson (Blum-Kulka and Liebes 2000). Here Kerry is completing the response quoted above, where he was asked to 'look into the camera' and make a pledge on taxes. In that specific case, the ability to speak to the whole nation, and in recorded form, rather than just to those in the room, is a way of putting the promise on the record. At the end of his description of his plans, he says:

EXAMPLE 6.7

Kerry: and looking around here at this group here . I suspect . there are only three people here who are going to be affected . the president . me . and Charlie I'm sorry . you too ((cut to a shot of Gibson, who is laughing))(21:55)

So Kerry has moved from addressing the questioner to addressing the camera, and then the studio audience, and finally, jokingly, the moderator. In all their forms of address, the candidates are anxious to show that they are capable of talking one-to-one to ordinary folk, and that they are treating these folk with proper respect.

Addressing the topic

Just as the candidates try to present themselves as answering the questioner, they try to show they are answering the question, not evading it or its potentially critical implications. There is a tension here, as in any political interview, between getting out the answers the candidate and his team have already prepared, and being seen to respond properly to the question. Kerry often says explicitly that he is answering, typically before or after he talks about something apparently unrelated:

EXAMPLE 6.8

Kerry: Robin I'm going to answer your question I'm also going to . talk . respond to what you asked Cheryl ((points to Cheryl)) at the same time (21:10)

After a digression, both candidates often return to a key word of the question; Kerry frequently signals this shift from introduction to question at hand with the discourse marker 'now':

EXAMPLE 6.9

KERRY: . . . that's the way we leave it . now with respect to the deficit (21:50)

He does the same when shifting from the current question to an earlier question

---

EXAMPLE 6.10

KERRY: . . . now to go back to your question Nikki (21:33)

As we have seen, many of the questions contain damaging presuppositions, but the candidates never challenge these presuppositions, as they might do in more adversarial encounters:

EXAMPLE 6.11

Farley: Mr President . since we continue to police the world how do you intend to maintain . our military presence without reinstituting a draft
Bush: yeah that's a great question thanks . er I hear there's rumors on the er . internets . that we're gonna have a . draft we're not going to have a draft ((gesture with flat hand)). period (21:28)

Instead of refuting the presupposition 'we continue to police the world', Bush calls this rather hostile challenge 'a great question'. Later in his turn he comes back to it, but by then 'your question' has been reformulated.

EXAMPLE 6.12

BUSH: . . . so to answer your question is . we're withdrawing . not from the world we're withdrawing manpower . . .((cut to shot of Kerry))

Of course marking the response as a relevant answer does not necessarily keep it from coming across as irrelevant or evasive to the audience in the hall or to viewers, but it does show respect for the question as well as for the questioner.

Only once does a candidate explicitly opt out of a question.

EXAMPLE 6.13

Michaelson: Mr President . if there were a vacancy in the Supreme Court . and you had the opportunity to fill that position today . who would you choose and why

Bush: (laughs) I'm not tellin' . (LAUGHTER) I really don't have a . haven't picked anybody yet . er . plus I want them all votin' for me . (LAUGHTER) (22:18)

Bush is joking (a shift of *register* indicated by his more relaxed pronunciation), but he makes the same assertion often made by members of the government, that the responsibilities of office forbid a full response. He goes on to rephrase the question in answerable form:

EXAMPLE 6.14

Bush: . . . er let me give you a couple of examples I guess of . the kind of person I wouldn't pick . . .

Though he is not answering the question as asked, he presents it is a way that makes such evasion potentially allowable, and reminds the audience that he is not just a debater here, he is The President.

Kerry twice responds to questions by referring to what he assumes are the moral values underlying the question, as a preface to disagreeing with what he takes to be the views of the questioner:

EXAMPLE 6.15

Gibson: Senator Kerry the next question is for you and it comes from Elizabeth Long
Long: Senator Kerry . thousands of people have already been cured . or treated by the
use of adult stem cells . or umbilical cord stem cells . however <u>no</u> one has been
cured . by using embryonic stem cells . wouldn't it be wise to use stem cells .
obtained with<u>out</u> . the destruction . of an embryo
Kerry: you know Elizabeth I really . respect . your . er . the feeling that's in your question I understand it . you know I I know the morality that's prompting that question . and I res<u>pect</u> it enormously (22:13)

The question is literally about a technical decision on which sorts of stem cells
should be used in treatment. But Kerry responds first to 'the feeling that's in
your question'. Even the opening hesitation (with a long pause after 'your')
suggests his respect, his reluctance to perform a dispreferred turn (see *preference structure*). He has to show he can deal properly with such deep differences in belief, for viewers who disagree with him, but also for viewers who
agree with him but want to see that he can maintain the questioner's social
face in the interaction.

Referring to the other candidate and to oneself

In earlier debates, candidates sometimes used their references and address to
the other candidate as part of their rhetoric, as when Senator Gore in 1992
referred to Vice President Quayle as 'Dan'. In 2004, the MoU specified that
candidates would say how they should be addressed. The moderator, of
course, sticks scrupulously to their choices. Only twice does a candidate
address the other candidate, rather than the questioner or the moderator, both
times Kerry to Bush:

EXAMPLE 6.16

Kerry: actually Mr President ((turns to Bush)) in nineteen ninety-seven we <u>fixed</u>
Medicare and I was one of the people in<u>vol</u>ved in it we not only fixed Medicare and
took it <u>way</u> out into the future . we did something that <u>you</u> don't know how to do
. we balanced the budget . . . (21:42)

This kind of direct address is just what the MoU tries to avoid, though it does
not in fact forbid it. But if there is little direct address, there is still room for
variation in forms of reference. Kerry nearly always refers, as agreed, to 'the
President'. Bush even refers this way to himself (six times):

EXAMPLE 6.17

BUSH: . . . of course I listen to our generals that's what a president does a president sets the strategy . and relies upon good military people to execute that strategy . . . (21:23)

Kerry also refers to 'a president' (four times), but always to set up an ideal that Bush does not meet.

EXAMPLE 6.18

KERRY: . . . I'm going to be a president who believes in science . . .(22:02)

Bush nearly always refers to Kerry as 'my opponent', rather than as 'Senator Kerry', so much so that Kerry makes an issue of it:

EXAMPLE 6.19

Kerry: well again er er i- i- the president just said categorically . my opponent's against this my opponent's against that . you know it's just not that simple . no I'm not . I'm against the partial-birth abortion . but . (22:27)

By making an issue of this form of reference, Kerry is offering a view of Bush as aggressive and querulous. In his own hesitant opening, he presents himself as thoughtful and conciliatory, someone who can appreciate the complexity of moral issues.

Quoting others

Intertextuality (see also Chapter 1 by Wodak) can be a way of bringing other voices into the room; the candidates regularly quote other people, especially those whose views might be distinct from their own.

EXAMPLE 6.20

KERRY: . . . Senator Richard Lugar the Republican chairman of the Foreign Relations Committee . said that the handling of the . reconstruction aid in Iraq by this admin- istration . has been incompetent . those are the Republican chairman's words (21:13)

Or they quote people with some unquestionable experience and authority on an issue, as when Kerry, continuing the response to the question on stem cell research quoted above, quotes the actor Michael Fox about his experience of Parkinson's Disease:

EXAMPLE 6.21

Kerry: . . . but like Nancy Reagan . and so many other people you know I was at a . at a forum with Michael J Fox the other day in New Hampshire . who's suffering from Parkinson's and . and he wants us to do <u>stem</u> cell . embry<u>on</u>ic stem cell . and this fellow stood up . and he was quivering his whole body was . was was . shaking from . the nerve disease the muscular disease that he had . and and he said to me and to the whole hall . he said you know . don't . don't take away my <u>hope</u> . because my <u>hope</u> is what keeps me going (22:13)

Kerry dramatizes the scene and style of delivery (without doing an impression that would be in bad taste) to enlist this voice to support his position as a moral position. Bush does a similar sort of dramatization using reported speech:

EXAMPLE 6.22

Kerry: . . . he <u>didn't</u> he broke his word
Gibson: /[Mr President]
Bush: /[I remember] sitting in the White House . looking at those generals . saying do you have what you need . in this war . do you have what it <u>takes</u> . I remember going down to the <u>base</u>ment of the White House the day we committed our troops . as last resort . looking at Tommy Franks and the generals on the ground . asking them do we have the right plan . with the right troop level . and they looked me in the eye and said yes sir Mr President . of course I listen to our generals that's what a president does (22:23)

Unusually, Bush overlaps the moderator instead of waiting for his turn, a form that is typical in responses to serious accusations (Kerry had said 'he broke his word'). Like Kerry in his use of Michael Fox, he sets the scene for the reported speech. And he ends to making explicit what is implicit in his remembering these apparently exact words and the exact circumstances in which they were said – that he listens to the generals.

The candidates also quote each other, out of context of course, ironically.

EXAMPLE 6.23

Bush: he complains about the fact our troops don't have adequate equipment . yet
he voted against the eighty-seven billion dollar supplemental I sent to the
Congress and then issued . one of the most amazing quotes in political history . I
actually did vote for the eighty-seven billion dollars . befo- before I voted against
it . . . (21:31)

This is the second time in the debate that Bush has used this quotation of
Kerry; this time he signals more strongly the intended effect by saying it is 'one
of the most amazing quotes in political history'. It is used to support the Bush
campaign's main charge, at this point, that Kerry changes his mind ('flip
flops'). Kerry also quotes Bush against himself:

EXAMPLE 6.24

Kerry: thank you Charlie . erm . a few years ago when he came to office the president
said . these were his words . what we need . are some good conservative judges on
the courts . . . (22:21)

Saying 'these were his words' signals that there is something problematic in the
words – the way they conflict with what Bush has just said, that there was 'no
litmus test' for appointment of judges. Of course the opponent can try to correct the impression given by ironic quotation, as Kerry tries to do in his next
turn after Bush's quotation on the vote. But with no chance to interrupt, he
has to come back while responding to another point, too late, when denials
may sound digressive, querulous and ineffective.

References to time

As we have seen, the time allotted to each answer is strictly controlled. And
the candidates do generally stick to the time – rather better than academics do.
They have a system of green, yellow and red lights on the cameras, so the moderator does not usually need to signal time is up. There is only one point in the
transcript when the moderator does cut a candidate off, and we see that it is
presented as a *Face* Threatening Act, because Gibson apologizes, even as he
overlaps Kerry's closing:

EXAMPLE 6.25

Kerry: . . . I voted for the balanced budget in ninety-three and ninety-seven . we did it
. we did it . /[and I was there]
Gibson: /[thirty seconds] . I'm sorry thirty seconds Mr President
Bush: yeah I mean he- he's got a record he's been there for twenty years (21:59)

Just before this there is a moment Bush thinks his time is up when it is not:

EXAMPLE 6.26

Bush: . . . and I suspect given his record he's going to raise taxes . is my time up yet
Gibson: no you can keep /[going]
Bush: /[keep] going . good(LAUGHTER)
Gibson: you're on /[a roll]
Bush: /[he] looked at me like my clock was up . I er . I think that er the way to grow
this economy is to keep taxes low (LAUGHTER) (21:59)

Bush asks, Gibson answers and goes on to encourage Bush to continue, Bush
overlaps with repetition to check, Gibson overlaps with further encourage-
ment, and Bush provides an account for all this before continuing with his
turn. This complex checking back and forth that suggests the extreme delica-
cy with which both candidates and moderator treat the time limits:

There are other moments when there is confusion about whether there will
be an extension, or about where the questioner is, and there is even an
exchange of gestures at the end, each candidate conceding to the other, when
the moderator suggests that it was agreed that Kerry would be first to conclude (one of the issues specified in the MoU). For our purposes, what is
important is the care the candidates and moderator show in observing the
exact specifications of the format. There is little of the overlapping typically
found in interviews (Clayman and Heritage 2002) or found in earlier town-
hall-style debates where direct interaction between candidates was allowed
(Beck 1996; Bilmes 1999, 2001), and what overlaps do occur are with the
moderator, not the members of the public asking questions. Apparently it is
more important to display the proper demeanour of respect and self-control
than to show the enthusiasm and sincerity that transgresses the conventions.

Oratory and conversation

Commentators on the debates often complain that the candidates have prepared answers. One indication of this preparation is when they use oratorical

devices such as contrasts and three-part lists (Atkinson 1984). Both candidates make frequent use of contrastive structures:

EXAMPLE 6.27

KERRY: ... these are the differences now the president has presided over th- an economy where we've lost one point six . million jobs . the first president in seventy-two years to lose jobs . I have a plan to put people back to work that's not wishy-washy ... (21:04)

Both candidates use three-part structures:

EXAMPLE 6.28

Gibson: [well I want to get] into the issue of /[the back-door draft]
Bush: /[you tell Tony Blair] we're going alone (LAUGHTER) (2.0) tell Tony Blair we're going alone . tell Silvio Berlusconi we're going alone . tell Aleksander Kwasniewski of Poland we're going alone ... (21:32)

This is a particularly emphatic turn, overlapping the moderator when Gibson has clearly signalled his intention of asking a follow-up question. Again Bush is presenting himself as reacting quickly and directly to an implied accusation. The oratorical drive to three-part lists is so strong that at one point, when Kerry gets stuck, he continues to fish around for an item to complete his list before settling for 'anything':

EXAMPLE 6.29

Kerry: ... and I believe if we have the option which scientists tell us we do . of curing Parkinson's . curing diabetes . curing . er . a a a . a you know . some kind of a of of a . er s- p- you know . paraplegic or quadriplegic or . er . er you know a spinal cord injury anything . that's the nature of the human spirit I think it is respecting life . to reach for that cure ... (22:13)

Of course neither Kerry nor Bush gets the applause that intended to follow such devices in, say, a conference speech; the audience is not allowed to respond, and that may be part of the reason such devices may seem overblown in this context.

As if to balance the oratorical register, candidates also use devices that mark a shift to a register appropriate to more informal interaction. There are colloquial expressions:

EXAMPLE 6.30

Kerry: . . . and it's the president's fiscal policies . that have driven up the biggest deficits in American history he's added more debt to the debt of the United States in four years . than . all the way from George Washington to Ronald Reagan put together . go figure (21:43)

'Go figure' here is typical of the use of colloquialisms; it comes after a very complex and rather academic assertion about budget figures, as if such high-flown talk had to be undercut. Bush tends to more casual speech when he is put on the spot, which is why one may need to transcribe the talk fairly carefully; we have already seen 'we're gonna have a . draft' and 'I'm not tellin''. This is not the way Bush always talks; it is a way of signalling informal tone in a particular utterance.

Both candidates also use (rather laboured) jokes; I have quoted Kerry's (rather unwise) comment that he, Bush and Gibson were the only ones in the room who would have to pay more in his tax plan. I will give just one more example, from Bush. Despite the rules about the cameras not showing reaction shots, Bush's face had been seen in the first debate (in this second debate, the non-speaking candidate is seen an average of once every turn). Bush was criticized in the press for 'scowling'. At one point in the second debate, Bush begins:

EXAMPLE 6.31

Bush: that answer almost made me want to scowl (LAUGHTER) (4.0) he keeps talkin' about let the inspectors do their job . . . (22:27)

Joking shows one is relaxed under stress, and it softens the aggression directed at the other candidate. The shifts of register, along with the constant address to the audience that I discussed earlier, are attempts to produce the sense of casual interaction. The candidates and their advisers realize that the oratorical style of party conference speeches backfires in a debate, and particularly in a debate with a town hall format that sets of expectations of informal interaction. Successful modern politicians, real (Franklin Roosevelt, Ronald Reagan, Tony Blair) and fictional (James Stewart in *Mr Smith Goes to Washington*, Martin Sheen in *The West Wing*) master the use of informal markers in formal settings.

Debates and other genres

As I noted in the introduction, analysts of debates are nearly always disappointed. One reason may be that they judge the debates against various ideal genres, the big speech, the honest chat and reasoned deliberation. But debates aren't a setting for extended development of complex arguments, or for revelation of the candidate's true self. It is probably best to see them in relation to a range of other broadcast genres all of which raise the sorts of issues I have discussed – questions and answers, topic, quoting, timing and tone. We might think of these genres as a continuum from speeches (for instance at party conventions) which are more oratorical, to genres such as interviews involving questions from the public, which are supposed to be more conversational. Of course it is not that simple, because conversational features enter even the most formal genres, and implicit rules govern even informal genres.

In the past, politicians had to master one main genre, the speech. Now successful politicians have to perform until close media scrutiny in a range of genres (Table 6.2; see also Meyrowitz 1985). And the conventions of these genres shift constantly, for instance as the rules of the debates are tightened up, while the conventions of interviewing are loosened.

One use of the study of questions and answers in these genres is to make suggestions for the formats of future debates and the preparation of future candidates (Jackson-Beeck and Meadow 1979; Carlin *et al.* 2001; Morello 2005). But all commentators who are not themselves running campaigns would like to see less controlled, less predictable discussions, and believe such discussions would better serve the voters by providing a wider range of information about the candidates and their policies. Seen from this point of view, broadcast political debates, in any format, are an ongoing struggle between broadcasters and the public on one hand and politicians and their advisers on the other, on who speaks when for how long about what, and with what comeback.

A more useful critical approach might be to make viewers more aware of the ways their evaluations of the candidates' personalities depend on the 'interactional rhetoric' of the encounters. The viewer's impression that a candidate is affable, unpretentious, stiff, aggressive or presidential is produced in specific moves the candidates make in interactions with the audience, the moderator, and each other (even where they aren't supposed to be interacting with each other at all). Voters are notoriously skeptical about what candidates say. They would be wise to be a bit more skeptical about how they say it, and about their own abilities to interpret the manner of the candidates as mediated by television. Viewers may need to question the belief, reinforced by chat shows, reality TV and glimpses of the backstage of politics and sports, that they can have access to what candidates are really like.

Table 6.2 Genres of campaign talk

	Questioner	Address to audience	Audience participation	Constraint of topic	Constraint of time	Rhetorical vs. Conversational tone
Party political advertisement (e.g. US TV spots)	None	Implicit	Not	None	Yes	Rhetorical/conversational
Broadcast of a speech (e.g. conference speech)	None	Yes	Yes	None	Not explicitly stated	Rhetorical
Broadcast debate (e.g. Bush–Kerry)	Moderator or chosen audience members	Yes (to moderator and audience)	No	Topics specified, but shifting	Explicitly stated	Rhetorical/conversational
Parliamentary debate (e.g. UK PM's Questions)	Member of the parliament as specified	Yes (formally, to the speaker)	Yes	Explicit specification of topics	Governed by parliamentary rules	Rhetorical
News interview (e.g. BBC Newsnight)	Journalist	No (talk for overhearing audience)	No	Implicitly need to display relevance	Implicit – signalled by the interviewer	Conversational
Broadcast with questions from the public (e.g. BBC Question Time)	Representative members of the public	Yes	Yes (in some formats)	Implicitly need to display relevance	Implicit	Conversational

Notes

1. This chapter was prompted by discussions in October 2004 at the Lancaster University 'Language–Ideology–Power' Research Group. My thanks to Johnny Unger.
2. Special thanks to Claire Roberts of Lancaster University, who prepared a detailed transcript of the whole debate, making this study possible. I added further details to the parts I have quoted of her transcription
3. Since transcripts have different lines and pagination, I give references with an approximate figure for when they occurred in the debate, Eastern Standard Time (the debate began at 9 pm).
4. See http://www.debates.org/pages/trans2004c.html
5. See internet archive: http://www.archive.org/details.php?identifier=presidential_debate_10_8_04&from=mainPicks
6. See http://overstated.net/2004/10/01/presidential-debate-analysis
7. See http://www.instapundit.com/archives/018329.php

Key readings

Clayman, S.E. and Heritage, J. *The News Interview: Journalists and Public Figures on the Air* (Cambridge: Cambridge University Press, 2002).
Coleman, S. *Televised Election Debates: International Perspectives* (New York: St. Martin's Press, 2000).
Hutchby, I. *Media Talk: Conversation Analysis and the Study of Broadcasting* (Maidenhead: Open University Press, 2006).
Jamieson, K.H. and Birdsell, D.S. *Presidential Debates: The Challenge of Creating an Informed Electorate* (New York: Oxford University Press, 1988).
Tolson, A. *Broadcast Talk: Spoken Discourse on TV and Radio* (Edinburgh University Press, 2006).

References

Atkinson, J.M. *Our Masters' Voices: The Language and Body Language of Politics* (London: Methuen, 1984).
Auer, J. 'The Counterfeit Debates', in S. Kraus (ed.) *The Great Debates: Background, Perspective, Effects* (Bloomington: Indiana University Press, 1962), pp. 142–9.
Beck, C.S. ' "I've Got Some Points I'd like to Make Here" ': The Achievement of Social Face through Turn Management in the 1992 Vice Presidential Debate', *Political Communication* 13 (1996), 165–80.
Benoit, W.L. 'Let's Put "Debate" into Presidential Debates', *Rostrum* 74 (2000), 21–24.
Benoit, W.L. *Political Campaigns: The Messages and Their Analysis* (from http://presidentialcampaign2004.coas.missouri.edu/, retrieved 6 December, 2006) (2004).
Benoit, W.L. and Wells, W.T. *Candidates in Conflict: Persuasive Attack and Defense in the 1992 Presidential Debates* (Tuscaloosa: University of Alabama Press, 1996).

Bilmes, J. 'Questions, Answers, and the Organization of Talk in the 1992 Vice Presidential Debate: Fundamental Considerations', *Research on Language and Social Interaction* 32 (1999), 213–42.

Bilmes, J. 'Tactics and Styles in the 1992 Vice Presidential Debate: Question Placement', *Research on Language and Social Interaction* 34 (2001), 151–81.

Blum-Kulka, S. and Liebes, T. 'Peres vs. Netanyahu: Television Wins the Debate, Israel 1996', in S. Coleman (ed.) *Televised Election Debates: International Perspectives* (London: Macmillan, 2000), pp. 66–91.

Boden, D. *The Business of Talk* (Cambridge: Polity, 1994).

Carlin, D.B., Morris, E. and Smith, S. 'The Influence of Format and Questions on Candidates' Strategic Argument Choices in the 2000 Presidential Debates', *American Behavioral Scientist* 44 (2001), 2196–218.

Clayman, S.E. 'Defining Moments, Presidential Debates, and the Dynamics of Quotability', *Journal of Communication* 45 (1995), 118–57.

Clayman, S.E. and Heritage, J. *The News Interview: Journalists and Public Figures on the Air* (Cambridge: Cambridge University Press, 2002).

Coleman, S. *Televised Election Debates: International Perspectives* (New York: St. Martin's Press, 2000).

Commission on Presidential Debates. *Memorandum of Understanding* (from http://opendebates.org/news/documents.html) (2004).

Drew, P. and Heritage, J. (eds) *Talk at Work: Studies in Interactional Sociolinguistics* (Cambridge: Cambridge University Press, 1992).

Druckman, J.N. 'The Power of Television Images: The First Kennedy–Nixon Debate Revisited', *Journal of Politics* 65 (2003), 559–71.

Friedenberg, R. V. (ed.) *Rhetorical Studies of National Political Debates 1960–1992* (Westport, CT: Praeger, 1994).

Galasiński, D. 'Strategies of Talking to Each Other: Rule Breaking in Polish Presidential Debates', *Journal of Language and Social Psychology* 17 (1998), 165–82.

Goffman, E. *Forms of Talk* (Oxford: Blackwell, 1981).

Hart, R.P. and Jarvis S.E., 'Political Debate: Forms, Styles, and Media', *American Behavioral Scientist* 40 (1997), 1095–122.

Hutchby, I. *Confrontation Talk : Arguments, Asymmetries, and Power on Talk Radio* (Mahwah, NJ: Erlbaum, 1996).

Hutchby, I. *Media Talk: Conversation Analysis and the Study of Broadcasting* (Maidenhead: Open University Press, 2006).

Hutchby, I. and Wooffitt, R. *Conversation Analysis: Principles, Practices and Applications* (Malden, MA: Polity 1998).

Ilie, C. 'Semi-Institutional Discourse: The Case of Talk Shows', *Journal of Pragmatics* 33 (2001), 209–54.

Jackson-Beeck, M. and Meadow, R.G. 'The Triple Agenda of Presidential Debates', *Public Opinion Quarterly* 43 (1979), 173–80.

Jamieson, K.H. and Adasiewicz, C. 'What Can Voters Learn from Election Debates?', in S. Coleman (ed.) *Televised Election Debates: International Perspectives* (London: Macmillan, 2000), pp. 25–42.

Jamieson, K.H. and Birdsell, D.S. *Presidential Debates: The Challenge of Creating an Informed Electorate* (New York: Oxford University Press, 1988).

Kraus, S. *Televised Presidential Debates and Public Policy* (Mahwah, NJ: Erlbaum, 2000).

Lang, G.E. and Lang, K. 'Immediate and Delayed Responses to a Carter–Ford Debate: Assessing Public Opinion', *Public Opinion Quarterly* 42 (1978), 322–41.

Lanoue, D.J. 'One that Made a Difference: Cognitive Consistency, Political Knowledge, and the 1980 Presidential Debate', *Public Opinion Quarterly* 56 (1992), 168–84.

Louden, A. *Political Debates: Selected Bibliography* (from http://www.wfu.edu/~louden/Political%20Communication/Bibs/DEBATES.html, retrieved 6 December 2006) (2006).

Meyrowitz, J. *No Sense of Place: The Impact of Electronic Media on Social Behavior* (New York: Oxford University Press, 1985).

Morello, J.T. 'Questioning the Questions: An Examination of the "Unpredictable" 2004 Bush–Kerry Town Hall Debate', *Argumentation and Advocacy* 41 (2005), 211–24.

Munro, G.D. *et al.* 'Biased Assimilation of Sociopolitical Arguments: Evaluating the 1996 U.S. Presidential Debate', *Basic and Applied Social Psychology* 24 (2002), 15–26.

Myers, G. *Matters of Opinion: Talking about Public Issues* (Cambridge: Cambridge University Press, 2004).

Scannell, P. *Broadcast Talk* (London: Sage, 1991).

Schrott, P.R. 'Electoral Consequences of "Winning" Televised Campaign Debates', *Public Opinion Quarterly* 54 (1990), 567–85.

Seiter, J.S. and Weger, H., Jr 'Audience Perceptions of Candidates' Appropriateness as a Function of Nonverbal Behaviors Displayed during Televised Political Debates', *Journal of Social Psychology* 145 (2005), 225–35.

Silverman, D. *Harvey Sacks: Social Science and Conversation Analysis* (Cambridge: Polity, 1998).

ten Have, P. *Doing Conversation Analysis: A Practical Guide* (London: Sage, 1999).

Thornborrow, J. 'The Construction of Conflicting Accounts in Public Participation TV', *Language in Society* 29 (2000), 357–77.

Thornborrow, J. *Power Talk: Language and Interaction in Institutional Discourse* (Harlow: Longman, 2002).

Tolson, A. *Broadcast Talk: Spoken Discourse on TV and Radio* (Edinburgh: Edinburgh University Press, 2006).

Watts, M. 'Watching Debates: A Focus Group Analysis of Voters', *Campaign & Elections* 23 (2002), 27–32, 44.

Wodak, R. and Meyer, M. (eds) *Methods of Critical Discourse Analysis* (London: Sage, 2001).

Analyzing Research Interviews

Jackie Abell and Greg Myers

Introduction

Much of the research in the social sciences starts with questions and answers, whether in survey research, semi-structured interviews, interviews repeated over time in panel studies, focus groups, casual conversations as part of ethnographies or recordings made for oral history. Even relatively small research projects produce dozens of hours of recording and millions of words of transcripts. The usual approach to these data is to reduce what the participants said to some sort of content categories. This process may involve summarizing themes common to many of the transcripts, and perhaps quoting a few passages from the transcripts to illustrate or support the researchers' assertions. In quantitative research, the analyst may develop a system of codes to ensure that all sections of the transcripts are treated in the same ways by all researchers (Bauer 2000). In reports of such studies, the reader may hardly be aware of what the interviews were like, moment to moment.

An alternative way of approaching research interviews is to see them as a form of interaction that can be analyzed in the same ways one might analyze talk between a doctor and a patient, or an interviewer and interviewee on the news, or for that matter an ordinary conversation at a bus stop or coffee machine. The participants, both interviewer and interviewee, are taking their turns at appropriate times, relating one turn to the last and the next, strategically presenting themselves to the other, and making assumptions about what sort of event this is.

EXAMPLE 7.1

From: Edley (2001:199)

1. Nigel: Give me an imaginary picture of a feminist.
2. Adrian: I seem to think of a feminist person as like ugly women (.) with like shaved hair (.) stuff like that you know (.) who can't get a chap and so they think 'I'll become a feminist'

---

3. Nigel: Right
4. Adrian: Lesbians (.) that sort of thing (.) I don't know.

Drawing on Example 7.1, this could be summarized in some coding system as 'physical appearance' or 'feminist = ugly' or in other ways. But that would be to ignore what Nigel and Adrian are doing in their talk. In what circumstances can one give another person a directive such as in turn 1? What is the effect of Adrian's hedging such an opinion at the beginning of turn 2 ('I seem to think')? What is the effect of 'you know' – does the interviewer know? What is the function of the narrative and reported thought, 'I'll become a feminist'. What is the effect of Nigel saying 'Right' in turn 3, just there, and how does Adrian respond to that in turn 4? What is 'that sort of thing'? And why does Adrian end 'I don't know' – or rather, why does Nigel treat this as marking an ending? Edley quotes the whole exchange, not just Adrian's turn 2, so he allows us to see it as an interaction between two young males who are strangers to each other and who have constrained roles in this interaction.

There is, of course, a place for content coding, if one wants to know the range of different views expressed in a set of interviews, or how widely one view is expressed, or how the holding of a view correlates with other factors, such as age, gender or experience (Bauer 2000). But all such coding assumes that for each question the meaning stays the same in each interview because the context of utterance stays the same, and assumes that one knows, reading the transcript, what this context was. If one goes back and looks not only at what was said, but at how it was said, one will be able to consider much less of the data, but will be able to give a more detailed analysis, situated in the particulars of each interview.

In this chapter we review some of the disciplinary approaches applying this kind of detailed discourse analysis to interviews, and relate some of this work to the levels of analysis applied in other chapters in this book: each unit can be related to the rest of that text, to other texts, to the immediate situation in which it was produced, and to the wider historical and socio-political context of this situation.

Approaches to discourse analysis in different disciplines

In the methodological literature of the social sciences there are many insightful comments on the wording of interview questions and responses.[1] Most of these comments are aimed at improving reliability by ensuring uniformity, and enhancing validity of traditional instruments by removing a potential source of distortion. They treat interviews as something different from conversation, simpler and more controllable, with the emphasis on the interviewee's side of the interaction. As Thompson puts it in a handbook of oral history methods: '[An] interview is *not* a dialogue, or a conversation. The whole point is to get the informant to speak. Your role is above all to listen . . . The time for conversation is later on, when the recorder is switched off'. (Thompson 2000:238)[2]

It is only in the last twenty years that the complexities of the interaction have been seen as an opportunity for researchers, rather than as a problem that hinders the efficient extraction from subjects of attitudes or information. There are several different strands to this approach, and it has raised different issues in different disciplines, such as science studies, social psychology, linguistics, women's studies and oral history. We can think of these disciplines as raising issues about the collaborative ordering of social interaction, the construction of versions of reality, the methodology of social research and the ethical and epistemological issues underpinning a project.

Approaches from *conversation analysis* (CA) (see Hutchby and Wooffitt 1998; Silverman 1998; ten Have 1999; Peräkylä 2004) run through many of these studies of interviews. CA looks in detail at the sequence of talk in interaction to see ways participants organize mundane conversation, how they indicate who should speak when, and how one turn at talk relates to what comes before and after it. The CA approach does not define questions in terms of their grammatical structure (such as subject–verb inversion, or other), but looks at the ways they are treated by the participants, as the first part of a two-part sequence, an *adjacency pair*. Some kinds of turns are regularly followed by another kind of turn, such as an answer. Of course a question may not be followed by an answer, or by the kind of answer the questioner expected (see *preference structure*) – and the participants typically acknowledge that something unexpected is going on, for instance by starting a turn with a delay or 'well . . .' or using hedging, caution or an explanation. Researchers have also applied CA to doctor–patient interaction, broadcast political interviews, classroom talk, courtroom cross-examination, and other forms of institutional interaction (see Boden and Zimmerman 1991; Drew and Heritage 1992; McHoul and Rapley 2001), In institutional contexts such as these, there are constraints on participants' roles (usually one asks questions and the other doesn't), on the sequence of turns and on the ways participants interpret turns (in terms of the implicit or explicit purpose of the interaction).

For CA, research interviews are not a simpler and more controllable form of conversation, but a complex hybrid of conventions from everyday talk and from this specific genre (Suchman and Jordan 1990; Houtkoop-Steenstra 2000). For instance, in everyday talk, a question may be followed by an answer which may be followed by some sort of evaluation or comment from the questioner. These third turns are often missing in interviews, where the interviewer may go on right after the answer to ask another question (Antaki and Rapley 1996). In Example 7.1, Nigel's 'Right' does not necessarily mean he agrees with Adrian's view; it signals that he is not going to take a turn here, so Adrian can continue talking. Adrian pauses twice in his response. Nigel has said nothing after 'Lesbians', so Adrian then reformulates this as the more general 'that sort of thing'. In the continued absence of any audible response from Nigel, Adrian offers a downgraded 'I don't know', a typical way of closing a turn and finally giving up the floor. The particular views expressed are embedded in a complex interaction, as Nigel prompts candidate answers from Adrian, who, in producing them, monitors how they are received by Nigel. As such, both interviewer and interviewee work to make the interview happen as an event.

One of the influential early applications of CA to social science research interviews was in the sociology of scientific knowledge. Gilbert and Mulkay (1984) did interviews with scientists involved in an important discovery, and found different accounts of what they and other scientists had done in these events and why. They could have tried to choose between these accounts, and assemble a definitive explanation of what had happened. Instead, they analyzed the ways scientists used these accounts in the interview, for instance in the course of explaining why two scientists could disagree. Gilbert and Mulkay identified two *interpretative repertoires*: empiricist (explaining behaviour in terms of the facts of nature) and contingent (explaining behaviour in terms of social and institutional factors). An interviewee might explain the view of another scientist using the contingent repertoire by referring to their training, their need to get research grants, or their desire for publicity. However, he or she could explain his or her own view using an empiricist repertoire, as following from the structure of the molecule and the progress of a research programme. These repertoires do not necessarily correlate with two kinds of scientists or two views of the discovery; an interviewee may use both. An analyst identifies repertoires not by grammatical structures or content words but by their place in the interaction and the function they perform. In this case the repertoires are a response to the interviewer's challenge, in implying that science could produce contradictory results.

Social psychology has a long tradition of study of the sorts of actions one might expect from interviewees in research interviews: giving accounts, making attributions, recalling memories, constructing categories and stereotypes, and expressing and defending attitudes. Most of these studies are experimental and quantitative, but over the last twenty years some social psychologists have reinterpreted these concepts in terms of the ways they are used in interaction and persuasion (see: Billig 1987; Potter and Wetherell 1987; Antaki 1994; Edwards 1997; Antaki and Widdicombe 1998). For instance, Wetherell and Potter (1992) studied interviews with people in New Zealand about the boycott of a visit of a rugby team from South Africa, which was at the time of the study still under apartheid. They found a range of interpretative repertoires, and devices for expressing what might seem to be racist views while presenting oneself as not a racist. This line of research leads away from trying to find a single underlying attitude, deciding who is really racist and who is not, and towards understanding the functions of racist or non-racist statements in discourse, for the individual speaker and a wider ideological moral code. Recent work has considered shifting presentations of identities by people talking in a group, and interactions between these groups and an interviewer who may be seen as an outsider bringing their own expectations and predictable views (Abell, Locke *et al.* 2006). Nigel Edley, in the study from which we quoted in Example 7.1, takes a similar approach, identifying two repertoires used by his interviewees, one that explains feminism in terms of women's desire for equality, and one that explains it in terms of women's failed heterosexuality. Both repertoires are used as these young men position themselves in relation to each other and to this interviewer.

The discourse analysis of research interviews in linguistics came first, not through CA but through a concern with the collection of valid survey data. Labov and other sociolinguists (1972) had shown that the distribution of some variables depended on the context, so that for instance a New Yorker might pronounce the /r/ after a vowel while reading a word list, but not pronounce it in casual conversation when they weren't monitoring what they were saying. Sociolinguists looked for ways of eliciting more or less natural speech, for instance by prompting subjects to tell narratives. But Wolfson (1976) and others raised the issue of just what sort of speech event a sociolinguistic interview is; for instance, she noted that the openings of narratives prompted in interviews are different from those in conversation. Schiffrin and others re-analyzed interviews that had originally been conducted to elicit evidence for studies of sociolinguistic variation, finding this time around that they had complex discourse structures as the interviewees related to the mostly but not entirely silent interviewer. Schiffrin noted for instance the way having an argument can serve as a kind of sociability (Schiffrin 1984), or the circumstances in which one person can speak for another (Schiffrin 1993). The emphasis in interactional sociolinguistics has moved from trying to find some 'natural' form of talk to analyzing the different constraints of various speech events.

Much of the current toolkit of analysts of research interviews comes from these lines of work in CA, the sociology of scientific knowledge, social psychology and linguistic discourse analysis. Other lines of research methodology, in anthropology, women's studies and oral history, focus on ethical issues. Briggs's classic *Learning How to Ask* (1986) traces his gradual acquisition of the cultural competence needed even to begin asking about the Native American culture he was studying. As the title suggests, the entitlement to ask questions, which he as an academic researcher had taken for granted, needed to be earned over the course of years of learning and engagement. Anthropologists typically have a much longer engagement with the people they study than do social scientists, who tend to do one-off research interviews, and they often write up their interactions in a form that highlights the different cultural perspectives and the asymmetries of power and knowledge (another example is Basso 1996). Feminist and cultural studies researchers, though their methods and aims may differ from those of the anthropologists, also highlight the power relations implicit in a researcher eliciting and using the talk of others, and in juxtaposing academic frameworks of knowledge with popular or vernacular knowledge (for a review see Kitzinger 2004). These concerns do sometimes, but not always, carry over into the analysis.

Oral historians are a special case in their taking up of discourse-analytic approaches to their data, because of their focus on the authenticity of neglected voices. In earlier work, the aim was to produce the effect of a monologue, in which the interviewee could be heard to speak from the past to the present. Thus interviewers were trained to intervene as little as possible, and to keep such interventions inaudible, and transcripts did not usually include backchannel utterances. More recently, researchers have seen the interaction as contributing to the interviewee's self-presentation, not interrupting it; analyzes take up issues of narrative, and treat the interviewees as artfully crafting an identity in a specific context, often for an interviewee who is younger, who comes from elsewhere, or who has different experiences.

The different disciplines that have contributed to the discourse analysis of research interviews look at various features in the data, as we will see in the next section. They have different emphases: conversation analysis is part of a radical shift in what social sciences study, social studies of science are concerned with the production of knowledge, discursive psychology critiques the concepts developed in social psychology, and taken up in other academic areas, sociolinguists raise issues of naturalism and methodology, anthropologists and feminists raise issues of power and difference, and oral historians use voices to challenge a documentary version of history seen from above. But they share an implicit or explicit critique of social science methods that abstract away from the contexts of interaction and cover up the processes by which academic claims are developed.

Contexts for discourse analysis of research interviews

The different disciplines reviewed so far have identified various features for discourse analysts to study in research interviews: turn-taking, preference structure, categorization, topoi or commonplaces, repertoires, accounts, narratives. There are already good methodological guides for most of these approaches; instead of going into detail about any one of them, we could give an overview of the kinds of context they address. Following some of the other chapters in this collection (see Chapter 1 by Wodak), we will organize our discussion on the following levels:

1. the immediate, language or text internal co-text;
2. the intertextual and interdiscursive relationship between utterances, texts, genres and discourses;
3. the extralinguistic social/sociological variables and institutional frames of a specific 'context of situation' . . .;
4. the broader socio-political and historical contexts (Wodak 2001:67).

In terms of research interviews, study of the *co-text* involves relating each utterance to what comes before and after it, and to the other utterances in the interview transcript. *Intertextual and interdiscursive relationships* include links between the talk in an interview and other talk, as in the use of keywords or topoi. The *context of situation* concerns the frame participants have for this kind of interaction, such as their expectations of the role of the interviewer or facilitator. The study of *socio-political and historical contexts* raises the question of how this kind of interview is possible (or impossible) and what sorts of knowledge and power relations it presupposes. We will consider each of those levels of context while drawing on Example 7.2.

EXAMPLE 7.2

Hermes, in *Reading Women's Magazines* (1995), is one of the few researchers in any discipline to give large parts of an interview transcript in an appendix, showing how she excerpted comments that she could use in her argument and allowing us to see what we are calling here the co-text. Here is an excerpt in which she has put in bold the parts she coded as dealing with her topic, women's magazines. Mary has been talking about reading a book first loaned to her and then given to her by her neighbour, about women growing older. She has been laughing about this choice of reading matter, which implicitly involves admitting that she is concerned with her age. Here Joke, the interviewer, comes in:

Joke: [I laugh.] Yeah, so can I ask you how old you are?
Mary: Me? I will be sixty-three in October.
Joke: So you're a Scorpio
Mary: That's it, yet! Yes it is, yes. When you pinch, when you pinch, they say, they bite! [She laughs.]
Joke: I know, my father is a Scorpio.
Mary: Is he?
Joke: Yes.
Mary: We're all good teachers, Scorpios! [She laughs.]
Joke: Do you read things like that, you know, the stars and . . .
Mary: Oh yes, **I always read my stars, I do.** I've been to twenty fortune-tellers, you know, I've been with people and that, and they'd say to me, 'Well you know,-we'll pay for it, pay for you, if you come with us', sort of thing. Some of them are six pounds a day! I said I would not waste money on that you know. **But, eh, anyway, I like the stars. I like to read the gardening in the . . . I do like the gardening. I don't do any knitting, but I crochet.**
Joke: Oh, right, that's a kind of embroidery, or . . .?
Mary: I do, I used to do embroidery, crocheting is different. Crocheting . . . you do it with a crochet pin.
Joke: And is it . . . you make a sort of lace?
Mary: That's it! Like old lace, look . . . this . . . here. That's crocheting, it is, yes. I make, eh . . . you make cushion covers and blankets and things like that, you know. **And if there are any crocheting patterns in, I like to have a look at those, sort of thing.**
Joke: You take them out? Do you have the patterns out of the magazine?
Mary: **Sometimes, it depends on what I want, you know, things. Some things are beyond me, you know. [She laughs].** (Hermes 1995:170, bold in original)

Co-text

The first step in most analyzes of interviews it to extract bits out of their immediate co-text, so the first step in a discourse analysis is to put them back, looking at what comes just before and after the quoted bits in the transcript. One
simple approach to co-text is the concordance, checking what sorts of words
typically go with a selected term (McEnery and Wilson 2001). Here for
instance starting with 'I always read my stars', we might look at what collocates with *read* throughout the interview. In the quoted passage, there is 'I
don't read serials', 'I read books', 'I'd read little bits', 'I read my stars', 'to read
the gardening', 'reading the letters'. There are also other verbs used for con-
suming magazines: 'they get used', 'she has *Women's Realm*', 'have a look at
those'. It is hard to tell how this exercise would turn out, from the bit of transcript here, but it might be that *read* is invested mainly with positive associations, and that it implies serious attention, while other verbs may signal for
other, more casual uses of the magazines.

While co-text refers to the immediate textual collocations of an expression,
it may also cover the CA approach that looks at the preceding and following
turns. For instance, in this passage we can see the way the construction of
topic is done collaboratively. Let's start with the coded passage, 'I always read
my stars, I do'. This is prompted by Joke's question, 'things like that, you
know, the stars and . . .', referring back to their previous talk about her being
a Scorpio: 'things like that, you know, the stars and' is presented as a category that Mary will recognize, which she does. Mary elaborates with another
example of 'things like that', going to fortune-tellers. This is relevant to Joke's
question, and the previous talk about Scorpios, even though it does not seem
to be directly related to the overall topic of the interview: how she reads magazines. Mary then changes the topic herself, back to the magazines, marking
clearly that she is closing one topic and opening another that is relevant: 'But,
eh, anyway, I like the stars. I like to read the gardening.' The 'anyway' suggests
a return to a previous topic. 'I don't do any knitting, but I crochet' completes
a list of three – stars, gardening, crochet – that fits together as a series of possible columns she could read. Joke's response is an 'oh' indicating that this is
something new to her (Heritage 1984), a 'right' indicating her receipt of this
information, and a tentative offer of a possible category, 'a kind of embroidery' (Hester and Eglin 1997). This leads them into talk about crochet, but
Mary leads it back to talk about magazines. For all the wandering of the
unstructured interview, as in a casual conversation, both participants are careful to indicate that they are on topic, and to show they share the same set of
categories.

Analysis of the co-text goes beyond the immediately adjacent turns. An
analyst might for instance pick up the reference at the end 'some things are
beyond me' (here, because of her eyesight) and connect them to many references through the quoted transcript to her age and the ages of others. One
might pick up the reference to money ('six pounds a day!') and link it to other

references in the same interview about saving money (not surprising for a woman on a small fixed income). But one need not just look for consistency across an interview. Hermes refers in her methodological note to the danger of reducing her interviewees to 'positions' (Hermes 1995:184). That is why she instead categorizes her findings in terms or interpretive repertoires, such as the 'repertoire of practical knowledge,' and 'the repertoire of emotional learning and connected knowing'. The quoted passage might seem to be a clear example of 'practical knowledge'. But Hermes uses it, instead, to show an underlying tension (Hermes 1995:48), that Mary is interested in such columns in magazines even though she can no longer see well enough to enjoy crocheting. Or one might find a tension between talking about horoscopes and 'things like that' as a sceptic who would never pay a fortune-teller, and as an eager participant in chat about Scorpios. An approach through repertoires acknowledges this tendency to tensions (Potter and Wetherell 1987; Wetherell and Potter 1992) and contradictions (Billig 1987; Billig, Condor *et al.* 1988) in people's talk, as they orient to the ever-changing local context of the interaction.

Intertextual links

The analysis of the co-text focuses on the transcript itself. But participants can bring other voices into the interaction, in quotations, commonplaces and other forms of *intertextuality*. Mary refers to a saying about Scorpios: 'When you pinch, they say, when you pinch, they bite!' This evokes a whole discourse in which people just know, from shared experience, what Scorpios (or people born under other star signs) are like. And she uses direct reporting of speech to re-enact her situation when people invite her to come to a fortune-teller. The report is presented not as their actual words but as an example of what people would generally say ('sort of thing'). But she also presents it with discourse markers that make it sound like speech ('well you know'). Reported speech allows participants to set up opposing positions, dramatize situations, try out hypotheticals and present evidence to support their views.[3]

Intertextuality need not involve direct quotation of another person; interviewees often invoke generally used arguments or *topoi* (Myers and Macnaghten 1998; Reisigl and Wodak 2001; Myers 2007). If we look back to Example 7.1, we see that Adrian is invoking a compressed form of argument that goes something like this:

- All relations between men and women are fundamentally sexual.
- All (normal) women want male approval.
- Feminists do not want male approval.
- Feminists must not be normal women.
- Feminists must not be capable of sexual relations with men (because they are undesirable or they do not themselves desire men).

But Adrian does not have to explain this step by step; he assumes it is a form of argument available to his interviewer, that just needs a phrase like 'shaved hair' to invoke the whole set of shared attitudes. Commonplaces may be notable by the absence of fully formed statements of shared knowledge in the text; participants may feel they need only give a hint for the others to fill in the gaps. Commonplaces, like reported speech, are used at specific points in talk for specific functions – for instance responding to a challenge or closing off an interactionally problematic topic.

Context of situation

The term 'context of situation' refers to all the conditions immediately surrounding an act of speech (Goodwin and Duranti, 1992:14–15, trace how this term is taken from Malinowski via Halliday). In the case of an interview, these include the place and time of the interview, the references to texts, objects and activities in the surroundings, the face relations between the interviewer and the interviewee, their understandings of the purpose of the interview, and the sort of speech event they think they are engaged in. All these issues are of course part of the planning of the interview, but they are also part of the analysis.

So, Hermes for instance accounts in detail for her interview methods: the way she contacted interviewees, the interview schedule, the sequence of questions. The genre here is obviously an interview, in that Joke is asking Mary a series of questions, and Mary does not usually ask any back (though as we will see there is an exception to this rule). We can also see how she leads discussion back to specific kinds of information, such as the question at the end of the quoted passage about taking pages out of the magazine. Mary also seems to grant an overall purpose to the interaction, as when she interrupts her comments about fortune-telling to return to magazines. They follow the conventions of a genre in which each participant is assigned a role.

But it is also clear even from this bit of transcript that these interviews are not impersonal encounters with someone with a clipboard collecting information: they are informal talks over a cup of tea, and the participants carefully maintain – and enjoy – the experience of chatting. We see that in the way Joke volunteers the comment about her father's astrological sign. Joke can guess at what crocheting is, and Mary can pick up an example that is to hand to show what it is. There are four episodes of transcribed laughter: Joke at the beginning laughing at Mary's comment about telling friends facts from the book about older women, Mary twice laughing about her astrological sign, and at the end Mary laughing after admitting that she can no longer do some of these crochet patterns. Mary goes on to say how her worsening vision is keeping her from crocheting as she used to do, and after this passage shared laughter plays a role in a move out of troubles talk (Jefferson 1984). Laughter is used as part of the interaction, not just as a response to it (Glenn 2003).

The clearest indication of the flexibility of their roles is the way, in an earlier part of the transcript, Mary asks Joke about *her* reading. This reversal of roles happens now and then in research interviews. I can recall a focus group of mothers breaking off their talk about children to ask the moderator if *he* had any children (no, but he had a dog). That kind of reciprocity is just what is missing, not only in research interviews, but in most institutional encounters. But the gap between interviewer and interviewee can be an opportunity. Joke can draw on the resource of being different – Dutch rather than British, a generation or two younger than Mary, an academic with her own interests – and Mary responds to this difference, for instance by explaining what crochet is. Similarly, focus group interviewers may present themselves as strangers so that participants explain local issues (demonstrations, a power plant, ethnic divisions, unemployment) on the record; they talk about what would in other situations be too obvious to need to be said. The oral historian Roy Hay found his ignorance proved to be useful in interviewing Clydeside shipbuilders:

> On many occasions older workers have greeted my naïve questions with amused tolerance and told me 'Naw, naw laddie it wasn't like that at all', followed by a graphic description of the real situation. (*Source:* Thompson 2000:223)

The situation of sociability, though it works well for Hermes, is not the only possible kind of situation for interviews, nor is it necessarily always the most productive. Attempts to create a sense of solidarity with interviewees may backfire (Abell, Locke *et al.* 2006).

For instance, one commonly observed feature in studies of racist discourse is that interviewees try to present themselves as non-racist (Wetherell and Potter 1992). But such findings assume a certain kind of interaction in which interviewees are careful about the image they present to outsiders. The assumed identity of the interviewer (as liberal, older, associated with the university) may prompt displays of attitudes that are anything but subtle. In Example 7.3 the apparently innocuous question about political arrangements sets a group of young women off on a kind of game of increasingly extreme expressions of dislike of various national groups.

EXAMPLE 7.3

1   Susan: So wh- what do do you think about Scotland having their own
2   parliament?
3   Chloe: What?
4   Susan: You know, eh Scottish people, they've recently got got their own
5   parliament uh and Wales have got an Assembly

6   Gem: I hate the Welsh
7   ((laughter))
8   Katie: Yeah. Sheep-shaggers.
9   ((laughter))

(Condor 2006).

They continue with a series of increasingly virulent denigrations of the French, Chinese and Pakistanis, all with a chorus of laughter. Condor asks about the kind of exchange here, and the interviewer's role as audience to it. A research interview, like any other social encounter, is open to the participants constantly shifting redefinitions of what is going on here.

Another example of the issues of 'context of situation' is provided by an interview conducted for the classic oral history *The Edwardians* (Thompson 1975). We have used the project's transcripts,[4] but have listened to the sound file (also available online), have added in square brackets the responses of the interviewer, and have added in parentheses the parts of the transcript not included in the sound file. The excerpt comes at the end of a long standardized interview (see Example 7.4).

EXAMPLE 7.4

Interviewer: Do you think your parents had any disputes over religion or differences of opinion?

Interviewee: Never. No. I never heard them have any disputes at all. One thing as a boy I didn't like and it sticks in my mind today. I came to the conclusion that church-goers were something like the railway carriages were at one time – 1st, 2nd and 3rd class. [yes] You see, my Mother was a person of the lower class – was a poor woman – [yes] and she and her friends were all poor but they were great church-goers, regular church-goers, kindly gentle people. [yes] (But they had to sit in the middle of the church or rather at the back. I say 'middle' because there wasn't so many going at that time.) They had to sit in the back pews [yes] in the middle of the church were the local shopkeepers and people who were considered to be a little bit superior to the others – better educated, perhaps. [yes] And right at the top of the church, behind where the choir used to sit were the local farmers, the local bigwigs, you see. [yes] Posh [yes] people. [yes] [yes] And when people left the church, although as I said, he was a nice old kindly vicar, he didn't seem to have any time for the lower classes. [no] Mother and her friends would pass out of the church door – the vicar would stand near the church door – and he would just nod and smile, perhaps not that, even. But when the higher class people came out he would shake hands and beam [yes] to everyone of them as if they was somebody far superior to my Mother and her friends, [yes] the poor, the very poor.

(Interviewer: Very unchristian.

Interviewee: Yes.) And I didn't like that. I thought my Mother was worth a handshake as well as the rich.

While we don't know much about this particular interview, one of the 500 done for this project, some aspects of the context of situation are apparent from the transcript and the sound file. There is a domestic setting (on the sound file one hears, under it all, an old clock ticking). The interviewer asks a standard interview question about a sensitive personal issue (disagreements between parents over religion or other opinions) and the interviewee responds instead with a comment on social class, which he presents as relevant to this question ('one thing as a boy I didn't like and it sticks in my mind today'). The interviewer punctuates the following narrative with (untranscribed) minimal responses, and only when the story is complete gives an evaluation ('very unchristian'), just where a narrative typically has such a slot. This excerpt comes at the end of the interview, where, after answering so many questions about daily life, the interviewee asserts his own opinion: he is not just a source of facts; he has his own interpretations of the time.

Sociopolitical and historical contexts

Condor's example reminds us that the origins, the framing and perhaps the effects of a research interview go well beyond the immediate context of situation. On the most basic level, interviewers and interviewees bring to the interview assumptions about the attitudes and identity of the other, and about the purpose of the interview. These assumptions may not be correct, but they shape everything else. To take the most obvious example, a young interviewee may monitor their expressions on out-groups in deference to an interviewer from the university – or may exaggerate these expressions in playful taunting of the interviewer's sensibilities, as in Example 7.3. Briggs (1986) notes that the researcher trying to enter such close-knit communities has to have cultural capital that is not provided just by institutional connections. The way the interview goes is not *determined* by class or gender or ethnic or generational identities, but these identities may emerge as relevant as the talk develops.

The whole genre of the research interview is contingent on a socio-political and historical context in which institutions ask individuals for their opinions, these opinions are aggregated for purposes the interviewees may never know about, and there is a promise that there will be no consequences for the interviewee (Myers 2004, 2005). Interviewees may be aware of this kind of speech event from broadcast interviews, market research focus groups, government consultation exercises, or political polls; usually they do not ask much about what all this is for. It is only when the interviewer enters a community that feels threatened, stigmatized, marginalized, powerless or misrepresented that the tacit assumptions underpinning the exercise may come to the surface: Why me? Who are you? Who will read this? What will happen? Hermes (1998:, see Example 7.2) found her informal style hard to reproduce when she approached women in the Surinam and Antilles communities in Amsterdam, because they had good reason to be wary of outsiders asking questions. The interviewer may suddenly become aware of the resemblance of what he or she is doing to other sorts of work, the queries of social service or law enforcement officers, the support offered by counsellors or therapists, the attempts of parties and campaigns to enrol support. Often it is only in the interviews that don't work for the interviewer that these possible alternative views of the situation become apparent. Researchers like Agar, Basso, Hermes and Condor have used such awkward moments to interrogate the uses of their own research.

Issues in analysis and explanation

The approaches to research interviews we have outlined have different aims, but they all share an interest in the interview as one kind of interaction, in which both or all participants construct the event moment to moment, and there are complex shifts in the roles and relations of interviewer and interviewee(s). They share a belief that detailed analyzes of the interaction can improve the researcher's understanding of (1) what the questions and answers mean for the participants, not just for the researchers, (2) how the expressions used link to other talk and other discourses and (3) how the participants are constructing this particular event and their roles in it. The analysis also leads them out to a wider set of issues: (4) how such an interview becomes possible, how it is used in academic knowledge and how that knowledge is used in social change.

- Researchers across a range of disciplines would, we think, agree about the importance of linking analysis at all four levels. But they disagree about the nature and directions of these links.
- Does one start with the co-text – whether concordances, sequences or narratives – and generate the relevant identities and categories from them, or does one start from what one knows about the encounter and the sociopolitical context, and use that to guide interpretation of the text?
- Are the intertextual links, such as reported speech and topic, reflections of underlying ideologies, or are they creative and even playful individual uses of language?
- Granted that the conventions of everyday conversation be applied to interviews, does this strange and constrained genre of the interview tell us anything about how people talk in everyday conversation?
- As we have seen, these interviews clearly have links to wider socio-political issues – gender equality, ethnic conflict, consumer culture, class divisions. But what is the nature of those links. Are the interviews evidence for social change, or responses to it, or attempts to shape it?

The most basic issues raised by many of these researchers are who and what these interviews are for. Attention to research interviews as interaction opens up many of the traditional ethical and political issues around research on language: how the experience is seen by participants, how their words are transformed in academic genres, how academic texts construct knowledge and how that knowledge does or does not have an effect back in the participants' world. Of course the same ethical and political issues apply to any social science research, but they arise with particular clarity in interview research, where the whole academic project can be traced back to a situated encounter, face-to-face contact, and their words.

Notes

1. See, for example, Lazersfeld (1944); Payne (1951); Merton, Fiske, *et al.* (1956); Sudman and Bradburn (1982); Becker (1998).
2. Italics in original.
3. See also Holt (1996); Buttny (1997); Buttny (1998); Myers (1999); Matoesian (2000).
4. The transcripts are available online at http://www.qualidata.ac.uk/edwardians/original/introduction.asp

Key readings

Briggs, C.L. *Learning How to Ask* (Cambridge University Press, 1986).
Houtkoop-Steenstra, H. *Interaction and the Standardized Survey Interview: The Living Questionnaire* (Cambridge: Cambridge University Press, 2000).
Hutchby, I. and Wooffitt, R. *Conversation Analysis: Principles, Practices and Applications* (Malden, MA: Polity, 1998).
Wetherell, M. and Potter, J. *Mapping the Language of Racism: Discourse and the Legitimation of Exploitation* (London: Harvester Wheatsheaf, 1992).

References

Abell, J. *et al.* 'Trying Similarity, Doing Difference: The Role of Interviewer Self-Disclosure in Interview Talk with Young People', *Qualitative Research* 6 (2006), 221–44.
Antaki, C. *Explaining and Arguing : The Social Organization of Accounts* (London: Sage, 1994).
Antaki, C. and Rapley, M. '"Quality of life" talk: The Liberal Paradox of Psychological Testing', *Discourse & Society* 7(3) (1996), 293–316.
Antaki, C. and Widdicombe, S. *Identities in Talk* (London: Sage, 1998).
Basso, K.H. 'Wisdom Sits in Places: Notes on a Western Apache Landscape', in S. Feld and K.H. Basso (eds) *Senses of Place* (Santa Fe, NM: School of American Research Press, 1996), pp. 53–90.
Bauer, M.W. 'Classical Content Analysis: A Review', in M.W. Bauer and G. Gaskell (eds) *Qualitative Researching with Text, Image, and Sound* (London: Sage, 2000), 131–51.
Becker, H.S. *Tricks of the Trade: How to Think About Your Research While You're Doing It* (Chicago, IL: University of Chicago Press, 1998).

Billig, M. *Arguing and Thinking: A Rhetorical Approach to Social Psychology* (Cambridge: Cambridge University Press, 1987).

Billig, M. *et al.* (eds) *Ideological Dilemmas: A Social Psychology of Everyday Thinking* (London: Sage, 1988).

Boden, D. and Zimmerman, D. (eds) *Talk and Social Structure: Studies in Ethnomethodology and Conversation Analysis* (Cambridge: Polity, 1991).

Briggs, C.L. *Learning How to Ask* (Cambridge University Press, 1986).

Buttny, R. 'Reported Speech in Talking Race on Campus', *Human Communication Research* 23(4) (1997), 477–506.

Buttny, R. 'Putting Prior Talk into Context: Reported Speech and the Reporting Context', *Research on Language and Social Interaction* 31(1) (1998), 45–58.

Condor, S. 'Public Prejudice as Collaborative Accomplishment: Towards a Dialogic Social Psychology of Racism', *Journal of Community and Applied Social Psychology* 16(1) (2006), 1–18.

Drew, P. and Heritage, J. (eds) *Talk at Work: Studies in Interactional Sociolinguistics* (Cambridge: Cambridge University Press, 1992).

Edley, N. 'Analysing Masculinity: Interpretative Repertoires, Ideological Dilemmas, and Subject Positions', in M. Wetherell, S. Taylor and S. Yates (eds) *Discourse as Data* (London: Sage, 2001), pp. 189–228.

Edwards, D. *Discourse and Cognition* (London: Sage, 1997).

Gilbert, G.N. and Mulkay, M. *Opening Pandora's Box: A Sociological Analysis of Scientists' Discourse* (Cambridge: Cambridge University Press, 1984).

Glenn, P. *Laughter in Interaction* (Cambridge: Cambridge University Press, 2003).

Goodwin, C. and Duranti, A. 'Rethinking Context: An Introduction', in C. Goodwin and A. Duranti (eds) *Rethinking Context: Language as an Interactive Phenomenon* (Cambridge: Cambridge University Press, 1992), pp. 1–42.

Heritage, J. 'A Change of State Token and Aspects of Its Sequential Placement', in J.M. Atkinson and J. Heritage (eds) *Structures of Social Action: Studies in Conversation Analysis* (Cambridge: Cambridge University Press, 1984), pp. 299–345.

Hermes, J. *Reading Women's Magazines* (Cambridge: Polity, 1995).

Hermes, J. 'Gender and Media Studies. No Woman, No Cry', in J. Corner, P. Schlesinger and R. Silverstone (eds) *International Media Research: A Critical Survey* (London: Routledge, 1998), pp. 65–95.

Hester, S. and Eglin, P. (eds) *Culture in Action: Studies in Membership Categorization Analysis* (Washington, DC: University Press of America, 1997).

Holt, E. 'Reporting on Talk: The Use of Direct Reported Speech in Conversation', *Research on Language and Social Interaction* 29(3) (1996), 219–45.

Houtkoop-Steenstra, H. *Interaction and the Standardized Survey Interview: The Living Questionnaire* (Cambridge: Cambridge University Press, 2000).

Hutchby, I. and Wooffitt, R. *Conversation Analysis: Principles, Practices and Applications* (Malden, MA: Polity, 1998).

Jefferson, G. 'On the Organization of Laughter in Talk about Troubles', in J.M. Atkinson and J. Heritage (eds) *Structures of Social Action: Studies in Conversation Analysis* (Cambridge: Cambridge University Press, 1984), pp. 346–69.

Kitzinger, C. 'Feminist Approaches', in C. Seale, G. Gobo, J.F. Gubrium and D. Silverman (eds) *Qualitative Research Practice* (London: Sage, 2004), pp. 125–40.

Labov, W. *Sociolinguistic Patterns* (Philadelphia: University of Pennsylvania Press, 1972).

Lazersfeld, P. 'The Controversy over Detailed Interviews: An Offer for Negotiation', *Public Opinion Quarterly* 8 (1944), 38–60.

Matoesian, G.M. 'Intertextual Authority in Reported Speech', *Journal of Pragmatics* 32 (2000), 879–914.

McEnery, T. and Wilson, A. *Corpus Linguistics: An Introduction* (Edinburgh: Edinburgh University Press, 2001).

McHoul, A. and Rapley, M. (eds) *How to Analyse Talk in Institutional Settings* (London: Continuum, 2001).

Merton, R.K., Fiske, M. and Kendall, P.L. *The Focused Interview: A Manual of Problems and Procedures* (New York: Free Press, 1956).

Myers, G. 'Functions of Reported Speech in Group Discussions', *Applied Linguistics* 20(3) (1999), 376–401.

Myers, G. *Matters of Opinion: Talking about Public Issues* (Cambridge: Cambridge University Press, 2004).

Myers, G. 'Applied Linguistics and Institutions of opinion', *Applied Linguistics* 26(4) (2005), 527–44.

Myers, G. 'Commonplaces in Risk Talk: Face Threats and Forms of Interaction', *Journal of Risk Research* 10(3) (2007) , 285–305.

Myers, G. and P. Macnaghten. 'Rhetorics of Environmental Sustainability: Commonplaces and Places', *Environment and Planning* 30(2) (1998), 333–53.

Payne, S.L. *The Art of Asking Questions* (Princeton, NJ: Princeton University Press, 1951).

Peräkylä, A. 'Conversation Analysis', in C. Seale, G. Gobo, J.F. Gubrium and D. Silverman (eds) *Qualitative Research Practice* (London: Sage, 2004), pp. 165–79.

Potter, J. and Wetherell, M. *Discourse and Social Psychology: Beyond Attitudes and Behaviour* (London: Sage, 1987).

Reisigl, M. and Wodak, R. *Discourse and Discrimination: Rhetorics of Racism and Anti-Semitism* (London: Routledge, 2001).

Schiffrin, D. 'Jewish Argument as Sociability', *Language in Society* 13(3) (1984), 311–35.

Schiffrin, D. 'Speaking for Another' in Sociolinguistic Interviews: Alignments, Identities, and Frames', in D. Tannen (ed.) *Framing in Discourse* (Oxford University Press, 1993), pp. 231–63.

Silverman, D. *Harvey Sacks: Social Science and Conversation Analysis* (Cambridge: Polity, 1998).

Suchman, L. and Jordan, B. 'Interactional Troubles in Face-to-Face Survey Interviews', *Journal of the American Statistical Association* 85(409) (1990), 232–41.

Sudman, S. and Bradburn, N. *Asking Questions* (San Francisco, CA: Jossey-Bass, 1982).

ten Have, P. *Doing Conversation Analysis: A Practical Guide* (London: Sage, 1999).

Thompson, P. *The Edwardians: The Remaking of British Society* (London: Weidenfeld & Nicolson, 1975).

Thompson, P. *The Voice of the Past: Oral History*, 3rd edn (Oxford University Press, 2000).

Wetherell, M. and Potter, J. *Mapping the Language of Racism: Discourse and the Legitimation of Exploitation* (London: Harvester Wheatsheaf, 1992).

Wodak, R. 'The Discourse-Historical Approach', in R. Wodak and M. Meyer (eds) *Methods of Critical Discourse Analysis* (London: Sage, 2001), pp. 63–94.

Wolfson, N. 'Speech Events and Natural Speech: Some Implications for Sociolinguistic Methodology', *Language in Society* 5(2) (1976), 189–209.

Analyzing Focus Group Discussions

Michał Krzyżanowski

Focus groups and their foci

As many recent publications suggest (see Barbour and Kitzinger 1999; Bloor *et al.* 2001; Fern 2001; Macnaghten and Myers 2004; Myers 2004), *focus groups* have recently become one of the key methods of qualitative exploration in the social sciences. They have been used for different purposes in a variety of (disciplinary and interdisciplinary) research settings, and depending on those purposes, focus groups may be defined in a variety of ways. Nonetheless, there are several core definitions of focus groups which, pointing to their main advantages and virtues, describe the actual 'what' of the focus group research. And so, while Myers defines a focus group as 'a discussion held for research purposes' (2004:23), Morgan and Spanish claim that focus groups 'bring to gather several participants to discuss a topic of mutual interest to themselves and to the researcher' (1984:253). Other key theoreticians and practitioners of focus groups similarly define them as 'group discussions exploring a specific sort of issues' (Kitzinger and Barbour 1999:4).

Yet it seems that what uniquely and specifically constitutes focus group research is their actual 'nature'. In fact, unlike other methods of (collective) interviewing (see Chapter 7 by Abell and Myers), focus groups are characterized by the 'explicit use of group interaction to generate data' (Kitzinger and Barbour 1999:4); that is, within focus groups participants are expected to interact with one another (and not only with the person moderating a group) and thus to discuss the issues or topics that arise or are presented by the moderator. This in turn explains the designation of the focus groups as such; that is a 'group is "focused" in the sense that it involves some kind of collective activity' (Kitzinger 1994:103). This activity might pertain to either discussing different issues right away or performing simple group-tasks which are to facilitate a group debate on a particular topic – for example 'viewing a film, examining a single health education message' (ibid.). In so doing, focus groups are set 'to explore a specific set of issues such as people's views and experiences' (ibid.), while their other unique aspect lies in the fact that within them not only differing assessments of different (public and private) issues are discussed, but also 'meanings that lie behind those group assessments' (Bloor *et al.* 2001:4) are revealed in an informal way. In other words, *focus groups are used (1) whenever one is exploring shared (collective) or individual opinions and (2) whenever one is willing to empirically test whether those beliefs and opinions are well grounded and stable, or whether they are prone to change in the situation of interaction with others, who are possibly seen as equals (hence excluding the principle of power) and are able to challenge and modify a participant's views.*

While in different strands of the social sciences there is frequent debate on how to treat and analyze the empirical material yielded in the course of focus groups in order to effectively reveal the said *meanings* that lie behind social perceptions of different issues (see below), it must be stressed that those issues themselves have also evolved. Previously, many social science researchers have used focus groups to reveal opinions on strictly individual experiences such as those of, for example, health problems (Morgan and Spanish 1984) or marriage issues (Suter 2000), and in turn have used the focus group-based interactions to assess the commonality of individual experiences.

More recently, however, focus groups have been applied to discuss issues of an ever wider (collective) social and public interest and were treated as means of investigating the growing number of different social contexts (see Hollander 2004). Kitzinger (1994:103) refers to examples of other studies on foci such as contraception, drunk driving, nutrition and mental illness, as issues recently studied through focus groups. Just like Bruck and Stocker (1996), Kitzinger specializes in her research on the focus group-based analysis of media audiences by highlighting 'controversial' topics like the role of the media in shaping and changing social understanding of HIV and AIDS (see Kitzinger 1994).[1] The trend developed even further in the most recent studies, where one can see a much clearer departure from private to public areas of social life: for example, the interest in 'public foci' continued with the recent, seminal works by Myers (2004) and Macnaghten and Myers (2004) who, in their focus groups, examined public opinions on different environmental problems. By the same token, the interests of other studies reach even further towards the social and political 'macro' (as well as to the even more abstract issues) by trying to investigate issues like national identity and its crisis in the late-modern era (see Wodak *et al.* 1999; Benke 2003; Kovács and Wodak 2003).

EXAMPLE 8.1   **'Voices of migrants' as a research focus explored through focus groups**

Below, we analyze a set of focus groups which were organized in the course of a cross-national research project investigating institutional patterns and politics of racial discrimination.[2] We focus explicitly on just a strand of the research within that project, specifically five focus groups with migrants organized in Austria in 2003. The focus groups were organized in order to examine the so-called 'voices of migrants' which was understood as a set of discourse-based experiences of migrants collected on their contacts with Austrian institutions and members of Austrian society throughout a certain duration of time (see Example 8.1). The analysis of those individual as well as, in our case, also collectivized experiences, helps deconstruct various discursive phenomena which shape and reconstruct racial and discriminatory practices prevalent in Austrian society. However, unlike what would usually be the case with discourse-based research on migration, discrimination and so on (see Reisigl and Wodak 2001) those practices are not investigated directly from the point of view of their elements and constituents. Rather, they are approached from the paradigm of the opinions expressed within the said focus groups, and of those who experience those practices (in this case, migrants living in Austria).

Exploring key features of focus groups

Some key features or components of focus groups, which will now be discussed in detail, are elements that are both the primary interest of a respective study, and function in a mutually interdependent manner. These include: (1) *the role of the moderator*, (2) *the role of the participants (and their selection)*, (3) *the role of the discussed topics* and (4) *the role of the communicative dynamics taking place during the course of a focus group discussion*. The mutual interplays between those elements as described below are also presented in Figure 8.1.

First, unlike in other methods where the person leading the process of interviewing is defined as the interviewer (thus the one asking questions), those individuals leading focus groups are usually defined as either *moderator(s)* or *facilitator(s)* (see Kitzinger 1994; Bloor *et al.* 2001). These names are very symptomatic for the role of the moderator/facilitator: s/he is supposed to steer and facilitate the process of the discussion rather than actually 'ask the participants questions'. Thus, the role of the moderator is only to present key *topics* be discussed within a focus group; one may say that the moderator is metaphorically hidden behind the topics which are supposed to frame the debate and which shall, above all, be debated by the participants. Differently put, the moderator is first and foremost responsible for overseeing the general development of the *communicative dynamics* taking place in the course of a focus group (see below), while s/he must not take the leading position in the discussion. On the contrary, s/he should primarily listen to participants and, plainly speaking, keep the discussions focused on the subject of investigation.

While the general aim of the focus group sessions is that they be 'conducted in a relaxed fashion with minimal intervention from the facilitator' (Kitzinger 1994:106), it is frequently the case that the moderator must, ideally in a subtle manner, intervene in the discussion. Such interventions must take place when the moderator required to urge 'the debate to continue beyond the stage it might otherwise have ended, challenging people's taken for granted reality and encouraging them to discuss the inconsistencies both between the

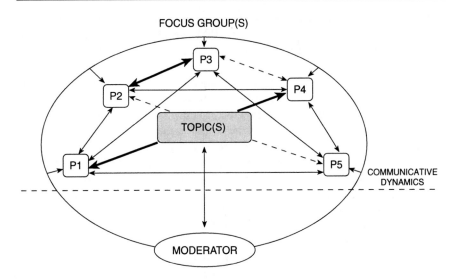

Figure 8.1 Interplays between key elements of focus groups (P = participant; arrows indicate possibility of a diverse intensity of interpersonal exchanges between participants)

participants and their own thinking' (ibid.). On the other hand, apart from these interventions into the contents of the discussions, the moderator is also frequently forced to intervene in order to maintain a balance within the communicative dynamics. Hence, the moderator must also 'seek to avoid the over-determination of the group by particular individual members' (Bloor *et al.* 2001:49). In other words, s/he must not only assure that the most outspoken participants do not dominate the discussion, 'but also seek to encourage contributions from the more timorous' (ibid.).

It appears that the core element of the focus groups is the *communicative dynamics* . These dynamics are crucial to the overall development of the discussion and it is within these dynamics that interactions between the participants can yield a possibly far-reaching diversification of views and opinions. The communicative dynamics are to be created and sustained (see below) in the course of the discussion by the *participants*; they remain key actors in the focus group process while the moderator, as much possible, should remain outside the dynamics (see Figure 8.1). Second, the participants also contribute to the communicative dynamics either by stating their own opinions on the previously introduced topics or by challenging the opinions expressed by others.

The (process of) framing focus groups

For reasons of space, this chapter cannot discuss in further detail all of the technicalities of organizing and conducting the focus groups (for closer and elaborate description of those see for example Krueger 1994; Kitzinger and Barbour 1999; Macnaghten and Myers 2004), yet the (dicourse) analytic focus of the present study requires us to discuss, at least briefly, the process of framing the focus groups.

The latter, which (in a very plain language) boils down to the act of 'asking the right questions', must always be informed by the overall theoretical and practical design of the research, in which focus groups are selected as (one of the) tools of investigation. Each of the overall aims and theoretical underpinnings of one's project, as well as its expected or hypothesized outcomes, would direct the researchers and organizers of focus groups as to how the latter should be framed and why. Thus, while no actual 'general prescription' may be provided with regard to the framing of focus groups, and only some general steps in such framing may be defined as largely universal, one may turn to the example of the previously described focus groups on 'voices of migrants' to show the process of their framing.

First, the process of framing begins with the *overall theoretical background* and the *research design (research questions)* of a project. In the case of the aforementioned research in Austria, the overall aim was to investigate:

1. what are the qualitative aspects of migrants' experiences in the country to which they migrated (Austria), especially considering the harsh anti-immigration policies introduced in the country at the end of the 1990s and the widely known anti-foreigner moods prevalent among the country's 'native' society, as well as
2. how those experiences can be informative as to which forms of inclusion/exclusion are taking place in relation to migrants, based on their contacts with Austrian state institutions and in their everyday contacts with 'ordinary' members of Austrian society.

Those (overall) research questions were obviously fuelled by the theoretical background of this project. The former constituted a combination of several theoretical accounts which, inter alia, pertained to the following issues: the discursive construction of racism and discrimination (see for example Reisigl and Wodak 2001), theoretical accounts on the constructions of 'everyday' and 'institutional' racism (see Carmichael and Hamilton 1967; Essed 1991; Wieviorka 1995), theories on the genesis of racism or discrimination (Joppke and Lukes 1999), as well as many other broader and more complex theories on modern democracy and state formation in the European context and and the role of immigrant groups within this context. Of further relevance were theories on intergroup contacts and community-building (see Delanty 2003), as well as those pertaining to right-wing politics and their impact on the changing social views on immigration (see for example Rydgren 2005).

Following the project's key research questions and its theoretical background (both of which clearly predisposed using focus groups as the key research methods), the *set of specific areas of inquiry* was devised during the second step of framing focus groups. Those areas pertained to different layers of social reality which were defined as particular contexts or loci in which migrants interact with the 'host' society and state system. There were five key identified areas of inquiry, which included: (1) perceptions of the host country, (2) the labour market and the workplace, (3) education, (4) the extreme right and (5) coping with racism. Those areas pertained not only to certain physical or institutionalized spaces (as is the case with areas 2 and 3), but also to the specific sets of situations or to the actual perceptions of migrants, all of which were defined as pivotal for the formation of migrants' experiences in Austria.

Finally, having designated the key areas of inquiry of the described focus groups, a third step in the framing took place. Within the latter, diverse *area-specific questions* were formed and those, in turn, were eventually asked to the focus group participants by way of different general and particular questions (see Example 8.3 below). By introducing the questions to the focus groups participants, all of the areas of inquiry were hence elaborated upon by the speakers, while their discursively constructed perceptions of the areas helped the researchers test in which of the areas (and why/how) positive and negative migrant experiences were formed.

Approaching and analyzing focus groups

Prior to proceeding to an exemplary analysis of the textual material obtained from the previously discussed migrant focus groups, one must emphasize that there are several ways of approaching focus groups in different disciplines (which, in turn, defines the types and categories of analysis eventually applied).

Within the social sciences, as well as in other disciplines recently interested in focus groups (including health research and marketing research), the analysis of the focus group material is frequently limited to its very general information level and used to support other types of analyzes. One may therefore claim that the material is not in fact analyzed, and remains only an auxiliary source of information obtained otherwise through questionnaires, individual interviews and the like (see Krueger 1994; Bloor *et. al* 2001; Fern 2001). The majority of such studies, which treat focus groups in this 'general' way, frequently refrain from actually describing their methodology or categories of analysis and refer only to their generally interpretative questions (sometimes described as 'guiding questions', such as, 'who had voice to speak and who not' or 'what was promoted and what was underplayed' – Smit and Cilliers 2006:308, quoting Cheek 2000) as those guiding their analysis. Some of these studies also claim that the type of analysis they perform may be defined as *content analysis*, though it must be noticed that the understanding of the latter is far from the similarly named text-analytic method which does posses several strictly defined analytical categories such as subject/theme, direction, norms, values, and means (for further details see Holsti 1969; Titscher *et al.* 2000).

A radically different situation occurs in linguistically based analyzes of the focus group material, where, unlike in other approaches, one can speak of a clear recognition of focus groups as a specific *genre*. For example, in the tradition of the sociolinguistic narrative analysis (see Smith 2006), focus groups tend be treated as *(group and individual) narratives*.[3] Within individual narratives, the recent emphasis has mainly been on analyzing how, within the process of focus groups, different identities are formed in the course of the obtained narratives. For example, by applying such categories as 'affective community space and time' (Kaneva 2006:2) it has been traced how the narratives displayed via focus groups are informative for the 'intersection of memory and identity' (ibid.:2) and for the differentiated construction of spatial and temporal realities of the speakers[4] displayed in different linguistic constructions of temporality and (dis)placement (as well as in other narrative-analytic categories originally proposed by Labov and Waletzky 1967).

On the other hand, within the ethnomethodologically based tradition of conversation analysis (CA) which has been applied very widely in the analyzes of focus groups (see Macnaghten and Myers 2004; Myers 1998, 1999, 2004), focus groups have been approached as *a form of (localized) verbal interactions* which, accordingly, have not been examined from the point of view of 'what was said' (Macnaghten and Myers 2004:74) but much rather from the point of view of 'how it was said' (ibid.). Therefore, the interest of the CA has been devoted only partially to the actual contents of the textual material obtained via focus groups, while the main focus was directed towards the local 'sequential organisation of focus-group interaction' (Myers 1998:86). Therefore, the CA-based analysis aims at 'patterns that can indicate what the participants think they are doing here, the relation of the moderator to the participants, and of the participants to each other, to the topic and to the conventions of the group' (ibid.). In other conversational-analytic approaches to focus groups as a type of verbal interaction, the analyzes have also focused on some more concrete linguistic categories. For example Myers (1999) shows how the usage of different forms of reported speech by the focus group participants can be indicative of shifts in 'setting (shifting to a different time and place), factuality (evidence that something was indeed said), positioning (whether the speaker or group identifies with what is said or not), wording (stepping back to look how it was said)' (ibid.:381). Other CA-based studies (see for example Myers 1999) also show how topics are indeed shaped, introduced, acknowledged, closed and interpreted in the course of the focus group-based interaction, or, how different verbal/linguistic elements, defined as 'markers' (ibid.; see also Schiffrin 1988), can signalize agreement/disagreement between the speakers or between the speakers and the moderator.

Thematic structures in focus group discourse: example of analysis

This chapter offers a way of analyzing the textual material from focus groups which, to a certain extent, builds on the linguistic explorations proposed thus far (see above). This approach has recently been developed within the discourse-historical tradition of critical discourse analysis (see Wodak 2001; Reisigl and Wodak 2001; also Chapter 1 by Wodak in this volume). Within the latter, an application of the in-depth content-analytical approach has been presented by way of examining two different levels of textual representation: (1) the general level of the key topics of discourse stratifying its contents and (2) the in-depth level, which focuses on discourse elements such as rhetoric, different argumentation patterns and other means of linguistic realization supporting the key arguments.

In a broader sense, the critical-analytic, two-level examination of focus group material concentrates on how focus groups may help reveal the discursive character and embedding (that is, discursive construction or construction in/through discourse) of such issues as for example national and other identities (see Wodak *et al.* 1999; Kovács and Wodak 2003). In those studies, focus groups have been applied in order to depict constructions of different forms of social, political and other identities within the so-called 'semi-private' sphere of the society, that is the sphere which is at the borderline between public/collective views and the views of selected small-scale groups or individuals. Those focus group-based examinations of the 'semi-private' have usually been supplemented by other investigations of, for example, the analyzes of constructions of different views and opinions in the public sphere analyzed through various instances of political language (political speeches, interviews with politicians and so on), as well as by analyzing the language/discourse of the media. However, the parts of the critical-analytic research devoted to focus groups remained central in several studies, since, through the focus groups, one could map out the ways in which the public sphere influences (and changes) individuals' views on politics and society and how, conversely, the ideas crucial to the 'social' (individual) level penetrate, as much as possible, into politics, into the media and into other constituents of the public sphere.

As both levels of the critical-analytic examination of the focus group material (the thematic and the in-depth analysis; see above) cannot be presented here in detail owing to limitations of space, the main interest of the present examination is in its 'first level', that is the analysis which pertains to identifying key themes of the analyzed instances of discourse, as well as to mapping links between those themes. However, while the second in-depth level of the analysis is omitted here, it is crucial to refer to other studies in which such in-depth examination of the same empirical material has been undertaken (see Krzyżanowski and Wodak 2007).[5]

Returning to our analysis of the first level of the textual representation of the material generated through focus groups, one must first define the basic analytic category that is central here, in this case *'discourse topics'* (for different conceptions see van Dijk 1982; Brown and Yule 1983). The discourse topics are perceived here from the point of view of text semantics as 'expressed by several sentences of discourse . . . by larger segments of the discourse or by the discourse as a whole' (van Dijk 1984:56). In this vein, discourse topics are seen as 'the most "important" or "summarizing" idea that underlies the meanings of a sequence of sentences . . . a "gist" or an "upshot" of such an episode . . . it is what such passage is *about*' (ibid.; original emphasis). In the analysis presented below, a distinction is introduced between two main types of these basic analytical categories. The first group, that is the *primary topics*, are the ones which, in the process of thematically semi-structuring (or framing) discussions and interviews, were put ('given') under discussion by the moderators through the use of general topics that framed the discussions. The other group of *secondary topics* includes the topics which were developed by the participants through their utterances during discussions, and were brought into discourse in a manner which transcended the primary, structuring topics. The aforementioned group dynamics frequently played a pivotal role in the discursive development of the secondary topics.

EXAMPLE 8.2   Selecting an appropriate transcription convention

As the analysis of the focus groups studying the 'voices of migrants' was focused predominantly on eliciting textual material presenting different views and opinions of various topics related to migration, discrimination and so on, it did not need to focus on the actual structure of interaction taking place in a focus group and other elements which would otherwise need to be included in the transcript. Therefore, a simplified transcription convention was applied (see Table 8.1.) which was largely based on the so-called 'half interpretative working transcription system' or 'HIAT' (see Ehlich and Rehbein 1976; Ehlich and Redder 1994). The applied transcription convention, while not excluding crucial non- or para-verbal elements of interaction, was focused primarily on (a) textual material as such and (b) additional elements of speech and behaviour which significantly influenced the textual level (for example emphases, rising and falling intonation, overlapping speech as an example of reaction to statements by other participants and so on).

Table 8.1   Transcription convention in focus groups on 'voices of migrants'

Symbol	Function
M1, M2 (or other)	Speakers
(.)	Short pause
(6.0), (8,0), (9,0) . . .	Longer pause
	(six seconds, eight seconds, nine seconds, . . .)
(incomp. 6.0)	Incomprehensible elements of speech
[	Overlapping speech
Mhm. Eeeeeh	Para-verbal elements
((leans back)),((laughs))	Non-verbal behaviour
[Heimat]	Elements of original language (difficult to translate)
I would not say so	Normal speech
THIS	Accentuated/stressed element of speech
(↑)	Rising intonation (if significant)
(↓)	Falling intonation (if significant)

Note: See also Example 8.2.

Primary discourse topics (Step One)

The primary discourse topics (see Table 8.2.) were selected as the general frames of the presented focus group discussions. Those topics were devised in the process of designing the research in the aforementioned project as a set of (six) basic areas in which migrants are in contact with various levels and arenas of the Austrian social state and political system and were therefore treated as pivotal for migrant experiences within them.

During the focus group discussions, those topics were introduced by means of different general and particular questions posed to the participants who were further responsible for discussing those topics with other partakers in their focus groups. Depending on the progress of discussions, not all general questions were posed, while, whenever necessary, additional prompts (particularly in the form of descriptions of various frequent 'real-life situations' and in the form of presenting different 'artefacts') were given to the participants.

Table 8.2   Primary discourse topics in the focus groups on 'voices of migrants'

Topic I	T-I	Perceptions of the Host Country
Topic II	T-II	Labour Market / Workplace
Topic III	T-III	Education
Topic IV	T-IV	Extreme Right
Topic V	T-V	Coping with Racism
Topic VI	T-VI	Improving Tolerance and Anti-Racism

Example 8.3 presents an extract from the focus groups guidelines and lists the questions and prompts which, whenever necessary, were applied when discussing the first of the aforementioned primary topics. Importantly, one of the general questions posed within the first primary topic includes examples of two (on the one hand 'negative' and on the other hand 'positive') prompts which were used to facilitate the discussion on the so-called 'negative' and 'positive practices' towards migrants which they might encounter in Austria. The introduction of such different types of prompts was applied additionally to assess whether 'positive' or 'negative' examples would cause the most heated reactions and accounts of experiences among the focus group participants.

EXAMPLE 8.3   Questions and prompts in a primary discourse topic

Primary topic I

Perceptions of the host country

General question I/I
How much and where exactly do you have contact with members of Austrian society?

General question I/2
Do you feel welcome in Austrian society?

Prompts to general question I/2

(a) 'Negative prompt'
Passport and customs controls which take place on the night trains passing through the Austrian–German border. Those controls, which are within the Schengen zone and should not in principle take place at all, are performed only at the ethnic selection basis, that is only those passengers who, by their appearance, look 'non-Austrian' or 'non-European' are controlled. The controls usually end up with very overt, radical, discriminatory actions performed by the officials against ethnically non-white passengers.

(b) 'Positive prompt'
Presenting participants the information package file which was sent out to all newly (officially) settled foreigners by the city of Vienna. The package, with a set of welcoming notes and numerous instances of helpful and practical pieces information, is fairly handy to many foreigners who are still not well acquainted with everyday activities at the Viennese institutions of, for example, education, labour market and so on

General question I/3
Do you think the fact that whether you are welcome/unwelcome in Austria depends on your particular location – living in the city of Vienna/Innsbruck? (Would the situation be different if you lived elsewhere in Austria?)

General question I/4
How about your relatives (for example children) or friends living in Austria?

General question I/5
How does it correspond with your previous experiences (if there are any) gained in living abroad?

Example 8.4 presents how, after a general introduction to the discussion and introducing the first primary frame by the moderator (MK), the primary topics were further developed by different participants (M1, M2 and M3). As one can see, responding to the general question listed above (see Example 8.3), the participants clearly pointed to different areas in which they interact with Austrians (among the listed milieus are: work, casual contacts, education and so on) and thus they developed the said primary topic by introducing another theme (the latter is further defined as a secondary topic – see below) which clearly pertains to the issue of 'social contact'. That topic emphasizes that migrants living in Austria gather the majority of their experiences through interpersonal contacts with the 'ordinary members' of the Austrian society. Crucially, while developing the topic of social contact, the participants emphasize that their interactions with 'Austrians' are limited to milieus in which the interaction must take place (work, education and so on), thus also showing that any other forms of contacts (for example, private contacts and the like) are not prevalent between the migrants and the 'natives'.

EXAMPLE 8.4   Development of a topic (extract from transcript)

MK: No no (.) no no just just wha what's what's the f-the most frequent occasion for your contact with Austrians
[
M2: Work
[
MK: Work (1.5) aha (0.5) for all of you (1.0)
M3: No (.) for me I I (.) I do not have many contacts with with with Austrians in work (.) my only contacts are just casual contacts with ahm people who might quite new within jobs or in (.) ah who come to do some work or (unread.0.5) all but ah I has I has scarcely any contact with Austrians (1.0)
MK: So those are just everyday-everyday situations (1.0)
M3: Yah yah (1.0)
MK: Casual contacts (0.5) ahm okay (1.0)
M1: Yeah my (0.5) ah myself I have a (0.5) a great (0.5) ah contact with the normal Austrian people because since a these ah (2.5) exactly (unread.1.0) twenty years now in Austria (1.0) and at the beginning at (1.0) I studied at university of Vienna (1.0) and then after when I got national citizenship (0.5) five years ago then I went to the military and then (.) this I my (.) contact to Austrian (0.5) ah students (.) people at the workplace sometime because during the (2.0) summer I used to work at the (1.0) some factories and some (0.5) institutions an then (1.0) yeah

---

Obviously, this last example constitutes only a strand of the entire response of the participants to the 'given' primary topic on 'perceptions of the host country' (in this case, the listed response constitutes only about 5 per cent of the entire transcript), while it also crucially represents one of the first issues discussed and therefore still takes place under the involvement of the moderator. However, the extract provided emphasizes how the topics themselves are developed within the focus groups and how the issues placed under discussion by the moderators are further developed by the participants themselves.

Secondary discourse topics (Step Two)

In the following step of the thematic analysis of contents, the main aim is to devise the list of the 'secondary topics' – topics which, in discussing the matters framed by the 'primary topics' (see above), were put forth by the participants themselves. Discussing the lists of topics must be performed in a gradual manner. This discussion occurs first with regard to each of the focus groups in question, and second with regard to all of the focus groups organized in the course of the research, where, desirably, the similar guidelines, frames and general questions (together with respective prompts) were used. In any case, devising the list of secondary topics, which can cross-section the primary ones in the individual groups as well as in the entire set of groups organized in the course of one's research, helps in assessing which issues are in fact crucial for migrants in their functioning in the 'host societies' (in our case Austria). Therefore, the lists of the secondary topics may sometimes differ significantly from those of the primary ones. Yet if this is the case then the secondary topics will prove that the preconceptions about migrants and their reality – reflected in the lists of the primary topics and treated by the researchers as touching upon the key areas which, from their perspective, might be important – may sometimes be misleading. Thus the discourse-based designation of the secondary topics will prove what types of experiences migrants possess in both negative and positive terms, the former referring to discrimination and exclusion, the latter to openness and tolerance. Additionally, this will demonstrate in which areas of their social functioning (institutions or everyday contacts) those experiences would frequently be acquired.

Table 8.3 Secondary discourse topics in the focus groups on 'voices of migrants'

Topic 1	T-1	Social Contact
Topic 2	T-2	Perception of Migrants
Topic 3	T-3	Citizenship and Collective Identification
Topic 4	T-4	Ethnicity and Religion
Topic 5	T-5	Language
Topic 6	T-6	Prejudices
Topic 7	T-7	Austrian Radical-Right Politics
Topic 8	T-8	Media and the Public Sphere
Topic 9	T-9	Integration

Table 8.3 presents a list of secondary topics that were developed in the course of any of the focus group discussions with migrants in Austria. As the list suggests, the secondary topics differed from the original lists of the primary topics (see above), thus proving that the 'issues' identified as crucial by migrants were different from those which were privatized by the researchers.

Connections between primary and secondary discourse topics (Step Three)

It is crucial, however, for the thematic analysis presented not to stop at the level of devising different lists of, respectively, primary and secondary discourse topics. On the contrary, the analysis must proceed further in order to 'map' thematic links that existed between primary and secondary topics (at the linguistic level), and thus to help the researchers locate varying contexts and areas in which different issues become prominent and different experiences are gathered (at the 'real-life' level).

Let us first explore how different primary topics (marked with Roman numbers in Table 8.2 and in Figure 8.2.) triggered the development of different secondary topics (marked with Arabic numbers in Table 8.3 and in Figure 8.2.). For example, within the primary topic T-I described above, the strongest thematic interconnection (established through the statistical frequency of

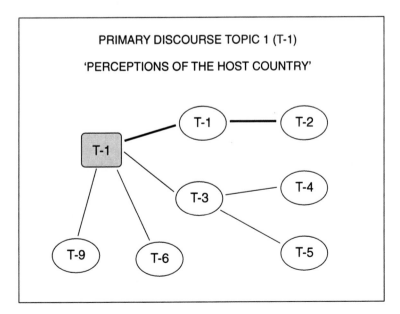

Figure 8.2   Thematic interconnections of the primary discourse topic I (T-I)

referring to the topic in all focus groups – marked with bold lines in Figure 8.2) appeared with regard to the secondary topic T-1 (social contact), which was also further frequently connected with T-2 (Austrian perception of immigrants). Also, T-I often triggered discussion on the issues of citizenship and collective identification (T-3), which brought about further discussions on the problems of ethnicity and religion (T-4), as well as on language (T-5). T-I was also intermittently connected directly with issues such as prejudices (T-6) and integration (T-9).

As one can see, the map of development of the primary topic (T-I) into different secondary topics (T-1, T-2, T-3 and so on) clearly points to the core issues which were pointed out with regard to the overall frame emphasized by the primary topic ('perception of the host country') and how different issues identified through secondary topics were further connected between one another. Based on the example of the strongest primary–secondary connection mapped out above, one can infer that in general the perceptions of the host country in the Austrian case depend on everyday social contacts between migrants and the natives (T-1), while the latter are (further) particularly crucial for the overall perceptions of migrants by the Austrians (T-2). In a similar way, one can map an interconnection (though, of a lesser salience) between the problems of collective identification of migrants and the issue of citizenship (T-3) and how those issues are, in turn, further fuelled by two crucial aspects of migrants' ethnicity and religion (T-4) as well as by language (T-5). These connections between identification and citizenship on the one hand, and ethnicity/religion and language on the other, were crucial for migrants. They claimed that being both identified as a foreigner or native and being granted citizenship (which would emphasize one's membership in the broadly defined Austrian community) was very much dependent on their ethnicity, religion and native language. This, in turn, emphasized that migrants were aware of the widely known discriminatory ideologies prevalent in Austria (as a homogeneous 'white' country characterized by Christianity and by the severe repercussions of the use of German language in a variety of settings).

Alternatively, one might also look at the interconnections between primary and secondary topics in a way different from the method used above. Thus, by looking at whether (how and when) secondary topics were called upon in realizations of different primary ones, one is able to see whether particular issues identified by migrants within secondary topics were of importance in the analyzed focus group material in different areas predefined by the primary discourse topics.

Table 8.4 outlines the links between secondary and primary topics and points to the differentiated use of the former in the realization of the latter. As one can see, some of the secondary topics (such as for example 'T-2: perception of migrants' or 'T-7: Austrian radical-right politics') were used only in the realizations of selected primary topics (the analyzed 'T-I: perceptions of the host country' and 'T-V: coping with racism'). On the other hand, several

Table 8.4   Links between secondary and primary discourse topics in the focus groups on 'voices of migrants'

Secondary topics	Primary topics						
T-1	T-I	T-II		T-IV			
T-2	T-I						
T-3	T-I	T-II			T-V		
T-4	T-I	T-II			T-V		
T-5	T-I	T-II	T-III	T-IV	T-V	T-VI	
T-6	T-I	T-II	T-III		T-V		T-VI
T-7					T-V		
T-8				T-IV	T-V	T-VI	
T-9	T-I		T-III	T-IV			T-VI

secondary topics (such as 'T-5: language' or 'T-6: prejudices') were used extensively in different forms while responding to the primary frames. The latter clearly points to the importance of different issues in different contexts and allows drawing different types of conclusions. For example, the significant omnipresence of the issue of language (T-5, identified in the realizations of all primary discourse topics) points to the fact that the latter, 'the native-like knowledge of the German language', must be seen as a key that allows migrants a full entry into various domains of social reality, in both its everyday and institutional meaning. This, in turn, allows one to conclude that the explicit recent migrant-related policies of the Austrian state system, based particularly on the issue of language as a quasi-marker of belonging and non-belonging, are finding their ways into a variety of social and institutional milieus where 'the language' is being perceived as pivotal both by 'ordinary' members of society and by the Austrian institutions regulating education and the labour market, as well as by the Austrian media and politics.

Conclusions

We have examined above the key elements of focus groups as well as of selecting ways for their eventual analysis. In particular, the example presented, of analyzing key discourse topics of the material generated through a set of focus group discussions, shows that the latter are an effective tool for investigating different issues, including those targeted in the presented material as 'voices of migrants'. As shown in the presented case, focus groups can effectively be used when investigating the discourse-based, semi-private experiences of migrants on such issues as discrimination and exclusion in different levels of social organization. These include everyday interactions with other 'ordinary' members of society, as well as institutions (particularly those pertaining to the labour market and to education) and different constituents of the public sphere, including politics and the media.

We have seen that focus groups are an effective tool in investigating the relation between discourse and society, in particular of discourse's role in producing, sustaining and reproducing an ideologically based social status quo. Thus, we may say that focus groups are effective when analyzing those discursive practices which help produce and reproduce unequal power relations between (for instance) 'social classes, men and women, and ethnic/cultural majorities and minorities through the ways in which they represent things, as well as position people' (Fairclough and Wodak 1997:258).

Accordingly, the analysis of experiences or 'voices' of migrants allows one to discover, uncover and deconstruct the forms of such (discursively shaped) inequalities taking place at an institutional level of the (Austrian) state system. Such a focus group-based analysis, it is argued, may supplement 'primary' analyzes of institutionalized, discriminatory practices rooted in the legal and organizational frames of the labour and education system (in Austrian case, see Wodak *et al.* 2003).

Additionally, by looking past the focus groups, into the experiences of those who, on a daily basis, have to cope with various forms of inequality and exclusionary institutions, one is able to draw a clear map of those practices (as identified in, for example, different discourse topics), which affect the migrants' living and working conditions as well as, in a broader perspective, the ongoing (discourse-based) construction of their 'non-belonging' as part of an 'outgroup' (Reisigl and Wodak 2001) in a European society.

Notes

1. The studies on media audiences were among the first research foci explored in the social sciences through focus groups by the group around Robert K. Merton and Paul Lazarsfeld who defined them as 'focused interviews' (Merton *et al.* 1956). The approach of examining media audiences through focus groups was also followed later on in a majority of settings, as was the case with for example the research in Austria conducted by Bruck and Stocker (1996) which inspired the later critical-analytic studies which applied focus groups to the exploration of Austrian national identity (see Wodak *et al.* 1999).

2. The data used in this chapter come from an EU Fifth Framework Research Project 'The European Dilemma: Institutional Patterns and Politics of Racial Discrimination', coordinated by Masoud Kamali (Uppsala University, Sweden; see www.multietn.uu.se) in 2002–5. The project investigated socio-political developments and attitudes towards migration as well as mechanisms of social exclusion of migrants in eight European countries (Austria, Cyprus, France, Germany, Italy, Poland, Sweden and UK). The author participated in the project within the 'Austrian partner institution' located at the Research Centre 'Discourse, Politics, Identity' and Department of Linguistics, University of Vienna. For results, see Krzyżanowski and Wodak (2008).

3. See also Squire (2005) for the description of growing social-scientific interest in narratives.
4. Kaneva (2006) adopts those analytical categories from Halbwachs (1980).
5. Different linguistic categories which can be used for such in-depth (strictly linguistic) analyzes can also be found in other parts of this volume (for example, see Chapter 2 by Mautner).

Key readings

Barbour, R.S. and J. Kitzinger (eds) *Developing Focus Group Research: Politics, Theory and Practice* (London: Sage, 1999).
Bloor, M., Frankland, J., Thomas, M. and Robson, K. *Focus Groups in Social Research* (London: Sage, 2001).
Macnaghten, P. and Myers, G. 'Focus Groups', in C. Seale, G. Gobo, J.F. Gubrium and D. Silverman (eds) *Qualitative Research Practice* (London: Sage, 2004), pp. 65–79.
Myers, G, 'Displaying Opinions: Topics and Disagreement in Focus Groups', *Language in Society* 27 (1998), 85–111.
Wodak, R., de Cillia, R., Reisigl, M. and Liebhart, K. *The Discursive Construction of National Identity* (Edinburgh: Edinburgh University Press, 1999).

References

Barbour, R.S. and Kitzinger, J. (eds) *Developing Focus Group Research: Politics, Theory and Practice* (London: Sage, 1999).
Benke, G. 'Somehow EmotionallyIf We Lose Neutrality That Makes Me Afraid', in A. Kovács and R. Wodak (eds) *NATO, Neutrality and National Identity* (Vienna: Böhlau, 2003), pp. 347–407.
Bloor, M, Frankland, J., Thomas, M. and Robson, K. *Focus Groups in Social Research* (London: Sage, 2001).
Brown, G. and Yule, G. – *Discourse Analysis* (Cambridge University Press, 1973)
Bruck, P.A. and Stocker, G. *Die ganz normale Vielfältigkeit des Lesens. Zur Rezeption von Boulevardzeitungen* (Münster: Lit Verlag, 1996).
Carmichael, S. and Hamilton, C. *Black Power: The Politics of Liberation in America* (New York: Vintage, 1967).
Cheek, J. *Post-Modern and Post-Structural Approaches to Nursing Research* (Thousand Oaks, CA: Sage, 2000).
Delanty, G. *Community* (London: Routledge, 2003)
Ehlich, K. and Redder, A. 'Einleitung', in A. Redder and K. Ehlich (eds) *Gesprochene Sprache – Transkripte und Tondokumente* (Tübingen: Niemeyer, 1994), pp. 1–17.
Ehlich, K. and Rehbein, J. 'Halbinterpretative Arbeitstranskriptionen (HIAT)', *Linguistische Berichte* 45 (1976), 21–41.
Essed, P. *Understanding Everyday Racism* (London: Sage, 1991)
Fairclough, N. and Wodak, R. 'Critical Discourse Analysis', in T.A. van Dijk (ed.) *Discourse as Social Interaction* (London: Sage, 1997), pp. 258–84.
Fern, E. *Advanced Focus Group Research* (Thousand Oaks, CA: Sage, 2001).
Halbwachs, M. *The Collective Memory* (New York: Harper & Row, 1980).

Hollander, J.A. 'The Social Contexts of Focus Groups', *Journal of Contemporary Ethnography* 33(5) (2004), 602–37.

Holsti, O.R. *Content Analysis for the Social Sciences and Humanities* (Reading, MA: Addison-Wesley, 1969).

Joppke, C. and Lukes, S. *Multicultural Questions* (Oxford: Oxford University Press, 1999).

Kaneva, N. 'Memories of Everyday Life in Communist Bulgaria: Negotiating Identity in Immigrant Narratives', *Colorado Research in Linguistics* 19 (2006), 1–15.

Kitzinger, J. 'The Methodology of Focus Groups: The Importance of Interaction between Research Participants', *Sociology of Health and Illness* 16(1) (1994) 103–21.

Kitzinger, J. and Barbour, R.S. 'Introduction: The Challenge and Promise of Focus Groups', in R.S. Barbour and J. Kitzinger (eds) *Developing Focus Group Research: Politics, Theory and Practice* (London: Sage, 1999), pp. 1–20

Kovács, A. and Wodak, R. (eds) *NATO, Neutrality and National Identity* (Vienna: Böhlau, 2003).

Krueger, A. *Focus Groups: A Practical Guide for Applied Research* (Thousand Oaks, CA: Sage, 1994).

Krzyżanowski, M. and Wodak, R. 'Multiple/Collective Identities, Migration and Belonging', in C-R. Caldas-Coulthard and R. Iedema (eds) *Identity Trouble: Critical Discourse and Contested Identities* (Basingstoke: Palgrave Macmillan, 2007), pp. 95–119.

Krzyżanowski, M. and Wodak, R. *The Politics of Exclusion. Debating Migration in Austria* (New Brunswick, NJ: Transaction Publishers, 2008).

Labov, W. and Waletzky, J. 'Narrative Analysis: Oral Versions of Personal Experience', in J. Helm (ed.) *Essays on the Verbal and Visual Arts* (Seattle: University of Washington Press, 1967), pp. 12–44.

Macnaghten, P. and Myers. G. 'Focus Groups', in C. Seale, G. Gobo, J.F. Gubrium and D. Silverman (eds) *Qualitative Research Practice* (London: Sage, 2004), pp. 65–79.

Merton, R.K., Fiske, M. and Kendall. P., *The Focused Interview: A Manual of Problems and Procedures* (Glencoe, IL: Free Press, 1956).

Morgan D.L. and Spanish, M.T. 'Focus Groups: A New Tool for Qualitative Research', *Qualitative Sociology* 7(3) (1984), 253–70.

Myers, G, 'Displaying Opinions: Topics and Disagreement in Focus Groups', *Language in Society* 27 (1) (1998), 85–111.

Myers, G. 'Functions of Reported Speech in Group Discussions', in *Applied Linguistics* 20(3), (1999), pp. 376–401.

Myers, G. *Matters of Opinion: Talking about Public Issues* (Cambridge: Cambridge University Press, 2004).

Reisigl, M. and Wodak, R. *Discourse and Discrimination* (London: Routledge, 2001).

Rydgren, J. (ed.) *Movements of Exclusion: Radical Right-Wing Populism in the Western World* (New York: Nova Science, 2005).

Schiffrin, D. *Discourse Markers* (Cambridge: Cambridge University Press, 1988).

Smit, B. and Cilliers, F. 'Understanding Implicit Texts in Focus Groups form a Systems Psychodynamic Perspective' *The Qualitative Report* 11 (2) (2006), 302–16.

Smith, J. 'Narrative: Sociolinguistic Research', in K. Brown (ed) *Encyclopedia of Language and Linguistics*, vol. 8 (Amsterdam: Elsevier, 2006), pp. 473–76.

Squire, C. 'Reading Narratives', *Group Analysis* 38 (1) (2005), 91–107.

Suter, E.A. 'Focus Groups in Ethnography of Communication: Expanding Topics of Inquiry beyond Participant Observation', *The Qualitative Report* 5 (1 and 2) (2000), http://www.nova.edu/ssss/QR/QR5-1/suter.html

Titscher, S., Meyer, M., Wodak, R. and Vetter, E. *Methods of Text and Discourse Analysis* (London: Sage, 2000).

van Dijk, T.A. *Text and Context: Explorations in the Semantics and Pragmatics of Discourse* (London: Longman, 1982).

van Dijk, T.A. *Prejudice in Discourse* (Amsterdam: John Benjamins, 1984).

Wieviorka, M. *The Arena of Racism* (London: Sage, 1995).

Wodak, R. 'The Discourse-Historical Approach', in R. Wodak and M. Meyer (eds) *Methods of Critical Discourse Analysis* (London: Sage, 2001), pp. 63–94.

Wodak, R., de Cillia, R., Reisigl, M. and Liebhart, K. *The Discursive Construction of National Identity* (Edinburgh: Edinburgh University Press, 1999).

Wodak, R., Ulsamer, F. and Krzyżanowski, M. *Report on 'Discriminatory Landscapes' in Institutional Areas of Education and Labour Market in Austria.* Prepared for the European Commission (DG Research) within the EU-FP5 Research Project 'The European Dilemma: Institutional Patterns and Politics of Racial Discrimination' (Vienna: University of Vienna, 2003).

Discourse Analysis and Ethnography

Florian Oberhuber and
Michał Krzyżanowski

9

What is ethnography?

The study of ethnography has changed significantly in recent years. Once associated with studies of distant, non-European cultures, ethnography has now firmly established its place 'at home' (Burgess 1984). In other words, it has become a way of critically investigating 'our own' so-called modern or Western societies. Hence, ethnography has ceased to be associated with its objects of study (that is, with 'who' or 'what' is studied) and has become a designate of a certain research perspective (thus, related to a certain 'how') which implies 'taking a distance' to whatever field (familiar or exotic) one wants to study (Abélès 1991:343).

Second, ethnography has crossed disciplinary boundaries. 'Going in the field' is no longer the exclusive prerogative of professional anthropologists. Other disciplines increasingly accommodated and adapted ethnographic methods for their own purposes; sociology, sociolinguistics, discourse studies, education, administrative studies, nursing, cultural studies, social psychology and other disciplines now routinely integrate elements of the ethnographic toolbox into their own approaches and research designs.

As this chapter discusses uses of fieldwork strategies in discourse-oriented research, our perspective on ethnography is characterized by a specific focus. First, we do not necessarily presuppose the traditional anthropological field experience of one or more years of intensive participant observation, but also reflect on more limited encounters with the field of study (see below). Second, we are examining research which often does not share the epistemological and theoretical commitments of anthropology, but places ethnography to work in the context of other analytical and interpretative strategies.[1] Third, the focus of this chapter is limited to research on (political, corporate, media, administrative and so on) organizations. We believe that this object-field lends itself particularly well to demonstrating how the study of discourse can be enhanced by an ethnographic analysis of particular socio-cultural locales.

In what follows, we look first at some of the major topics and concepts in studies on organizational discourse.[2] Then, crucial issues in fieldwork research are discussed from a practical point of view, followed by a discussion of the problem of how to interpret and integrate ethnographic data in discourse-oriented research. The final section gives an overview of quality criteria for ethnographic research to reflect upon the ways the ethnographic endeavour implies a particular commitment to reflexivity in social-scientific research.

Analyzing organizational discourse

It is now widely accepted within discourse studies that an analysis of linguistic elements of discourse presupposes a proper appraisal of their context of production and reception (see van Dijk 1985; Drew and Heritage 1992; Panagl and Wodak 2004; Blommaert 2005). This seems to be especially evident for the field of organizations. The latter have been defined for instance as 'material practices of text and talk set in currents of political economy and socio-history' (Boje *et al.* 2004:571). In such organizational settings, linguistic exchange is oriented towards predefined goals and there exist several 'external constraints' on contributions: that is, one cannot say and do anything everywhere, and different subcontexts (for example, informal vs. plenary meetings in organizations) require and allow for different kinds of talk and behaviour limited by different types of official and latent rules (see Drew and Heritage 1992). Furthermore, discourse in organizations is articulated by a number of routines and practices that contribute to the ongoing reproduction of the organization; such practices are 'distributed across a variety of "places" . . . and representation systems' (Streeck 1996:366), that is they are embedded within a multitude of spatial, material and technological conditions.

The study of organizational practices has been one of the major issues in discourse-oriented social research on organizations (see Linde 2001:519–21), which very frequently integrated both anthropological and sociological (as well as other social-scientific) perspectives. The pioneering study by Boden (1994) for instance drew on conversation analysis and ethnomethodology to analyze business meetings, in an attempt to demonstrate how talk is employed to perform various actions, such as to 'review, reassess, reason, instruct, revise, argue, debate, contest, and actually *constitute* the moments, myths and, through time, the very *structuring* of the organisation' (ibid.:8). Wodak (1996), in her study of clinical discourse, drew on observations of entire mornings, as well as interviews with patients, doctors and administrators. Other fields of enquiry have included decision-making processes, negotiations, talk in professional settings or in school and workplace settings (for an overview see Drew and Sorjonen 1997; Muntigl 2000).

Another key focus of organizational research has been the representative function of talk, that is the constitutive role of meaning 'in the reproduction and maintenance of institutions, as well as contestation and changes in the institutions' self-representation' (Linde 2001:520). Again, such research interests correspond to an ethnographic perspective, since it does not focus so much on the formal organization of interaction, communication and hierarchy, but rather targets the organization's human and cultural dimensions (Bellier 2002:207).[3]

Czarniawska (1997) for instance studied the role of stories/narratives for managing social change in organizations on the basis of discourse materials about Swedish public organizations, ranging from reports or budgets to autobiographies and informal conversations. Based on a three-year field study including extensive observations of meetings, training programmes or the work of sales agents, Linde (1993) and colleagues looked at narratives in an American insurance company. Furthermore, interest on representations also focused on the concept of identity, which is crucial in both anthropology and discourse analysis (see Answorth and Hardy 2004). Wodak (2003, 2004) for instance drew on data from semi-structured interviews to study the competing national and institutional identities that politicians and officials orient themselves towards in the organizational context of the European Union.

Finally, research on key concepts in discourse analysis, such as power and ideology, also demonstrates a need for an analysis to include a perspective on the ways texts are disseminated by, and implemented in, the actual work of organizations (see Oberhuber, 2008). As Muntigl (2000:2) argued with respect to research on policy-making in the European Union, 'it is not sufficient merely to examine policy as an outcome'; rather, the researcher needs to study the whole process from agenda-setting to policy formulation, decision and implementation. Thus Wodak (2000, 2000a) for instance studied the transformation and recontextualization of different elements of discourse in various stages of the work of an EU committee on employment policy (see Example 9.1). Fairclough (2005) recently looked at neo-liberal discourse in bureaucratic settings and on governance as complex network relationships between genres.

EXAMPLE 9.1   Ethnography and the transformation/recontextualization of discourse

Wodak (2000:73–115) presents how, at different stages of the ethnographically studied committee meetings of the European Union's Competitiveness Advisory Group (CAG, consisting of EU-officials, trade-union and employers' representatives), various elements of discourse (coming from different sources and members of the committee) are used in the co-construction of an EU-policy paper on unemployment. In the process, different forms of text-transformation (such as 'new sequence, addition, deletion and substitution', ibid.) undergo different changes which are proposed and (re)drafted by different officials involved in the committee. Below, we present two versions of one paragraph of the policy paper on unemployment studied by Wodak. The paragraph discusses the issue of 'globalization' and its impact on changing economic and social cohesion, resulting in growing unemployment. Below, Text 1 presents one of the first drafts of the paragraph, whereas Text 2 presents its final version. In the texts, one can observe different processes of transformation: some elements are deleted, while others are merged with one another, added or substituted (for the exact description of those processes and for other versions of the drafts of the document, see Wodak 2000).

Text 1: Original draft of the paragraph on 'Globalization' of the EU-CAG Paper on Unemployment (from Wodak 2000:100):

1. But it [globalisation] is also a demanding one, and often a painful one.
2. Economic progress has always been accompanied with destruction of obsolete activities and crea-tion of new ones.
3. The pace has become swifter and the game has taken on planetary dimensions.
4. It imposes on all countries – including European countries, where industrial civilization was born – deep and rapid adjustments.
5. The breadth and urgency of the needed adaptations are indistinctively perceived by public opinion, which explains a widespread sense of unease
6. The duty which falls on governments, trade unions and employers is to work together
   – to describe the stakes and refute a number of mistaken ideas;
   – to stress that our countries have the means to sustain high ambitions; and
   – to implement, without delay and with consistency, the necessary reforms.

Text 2: Final version of the paragraph on 'Globalization' of the EU-CAG Paper on Unemployment (from: Wodak 2000:101)

1. But (globalisation) is also a demanding process, and often a painful one.
2. Economic progress has always been accompanied by destruction of obsolete activities and creation of new ones.
3. The pace has become swifter and the game has taken on planetary dimensions.
4. It imposes deep and rapid adjustments on all countries – including European countries, where in-dustrial civilization was born.
5. Social cohesion is threatened by a widespread sense of unease, inequality and polarization.
6. There is a risk of a disjunct between the hopes and aspirations of people and the demands of a global economy.
7. And yet social cohesion is not only a worthwhile social and political goal; it is also a source of ef-ficiency and adaptability in a knowledge-based economy that increasingly depends on human quality and the ability to work as a team.
8. It is more than ever the duty of governments, trade unions and employers to work together
   – to describe the stakes and refute a number of mistakes;
   – to stress that our countries should have high ambitions and they can be realized; and
   – to implement the necessary reforms consistently and without delay.
9. Failure to move quickly and decisively will result in loss of resources, both human and capital, which will leave for more promising parts of the world if Europe provides less attractive opportunities.

From a research-design perspective, the ways ethnography is applied in discourse research depend on the issues approached and the questions asked. On the one end of an ideal continuum, ethnography might be employed as an element of the process of gathering discourse material, that is the researcher contacts and interviews people in the field with the aim of collecting documents he or she would not have access to otherwise (Weimer and Vining 2004:296–310). On the other end of the scale, there is the traditional in-depth ethnographic experience which consists of participation in the field over an extended period of time, and which involves an open process of data collection and theory-building.

In both cases, a principal issue for ethnographic research is the conceptualization of the field one engages with 'It is no longer a question of studying a local community or 'a people': rather, the anthropologist is seeking a method for analyzing connections between levels and forms of social process and action, and exploring how those processes work in different sites – local, national and global' (Shore and Wright 1997:14).

Interactions have to be grasped at different levels and sites, and the articulation of local cultural worlds with macrolevel structures, dynamics and discourses has to be scrutinized. As Agar argues (1996:13), such a concept of fieldwork involves 'a variety of "found" data from several different social locations, all of which have become "local" with reference to the ethnographer'. These sets of data could include for instance population or economic statistics, mass media debates, legal and administrative regulations, as well as microlevel instances of discursive action in various locales and situations.

In the field: gathering and analyzing ethnographic data

From a research-practical perspective, *ethnography can be defined as the engagement of a researcher with his or her subject at the local level. Such an endeavour implies a commitment to actually 'being there in the field', that is being with the people one wants to study, to interact with them and participate in the routines of their everyday life.* In other words, 'the conditions of fieldwork . . . require the researchers to engage in face-to-face contact with subjects rather than assume an impersonal detached approach' (de Laine 2000: 1).

At the beginning of each ethnographic experience, researchers need to plan and negotiate their *access* to the field. This often poses significant practical problems, especially with the study of formal organizations, as the access to the latter is usually formally controlled and can be denied for various (often unspecified) reasons. Therefore it is often necessary to establish contacts to an upper-rank official prior to entering the field. Such a person, besides granting access, can also introduce the researcher to those in the field and solicit cooperation on behalf of 'the natives'. One's own (academic) institutional affiliation can be important for persuading officials to grant access. In this respect, establishing contacts to academic colleagues who have already done work in the respective organization is often very helpful.

Comment: Access to the field

One of the benefits of a good entrée in the field is a chance to gain access to important resources available at the field site itself. In our own research at the European Union's Convention on the Future of Europe (2002–03), being able to use internal telephone lines when arranging interviews with persons working for EU institutions turned out to be crucial, since they would immediately see on their displays or fax machines whether someone was calling 'from the inside' or 'from the outside'. Also, access to offices and facilities such as copying machines or computers can be very helpful for recording observations on site or just for retreating for a while to rest or work on fieldnotes.

On the other hand, ethnographers have often pointed to the problematic side of gaining access through superior officials. For instance in corporations such a position can create resistance on the side of employees. Superiors might want to use ethnography as a means of gaining information about the team they manage, while employees might want to use the researcher to strengthen their position with the superior. Establishing relations of trust ('rapport') is crucial in this respect, as is time in the field as well as close relations with individuals from all aspects of the life of the organization (see Bellier 2002:213–21; for a critical view on objectivist stances to observations see Angrosino and Mays de Pérez 2000).

Finally, gaining access to and negotiating the researcher's role in the field is not only a preliminary condition for actual research, but is already part of it since 'it is in these encounters that the most dramatic differences between the ethnographer's culture and the informant's culture will be apparent. The surprises, differences, misunderstandings and such that occur in these encounters may foreshadow major research concerns and issues; however, in the beginning, researchers may not know how to interpret what these differences reveal about themselves and their informants. This is why it is extremely important to take detailed field notes in the beginning of one's fieldwork' (Schwartzmann 1993:48).

Many ethnographers recount a large degree of confusion in the initial stages of the research with regard to what to observe and what questions to ask. Therefore, difficulties in orienting oneself in the field can be considered an integral element of the fieldwork experience itself. *As a researcher you are a stranger in the group you want to study. Just as you observe others and try to figure out what they are up to, you are likewise being studied and interpreted* (see also Agar 1996). Listening and observing are the main occupations in these early days, in order to keep the research process as open as possible. This constitutes a key difference between ethnographic and other forms of social research. As Spradley (1980:32) put it, in ethnography, 'both questions and answers must be discovered in the social situation being studied'. In a similar vein, the ethnographer's task is usually conceptualized in terms not of translating and interpreting the field according to the researcher's categories but rather of understanding the knowledge and practices that participants share and use to interpret their experiences.

Turning to the techniques of data-gathering, such a stance implies that in fieldwork everything encountered has to be treated as potentially meaningful (see Shore 2000:7–8; Krzyżanowski and Oberhuber 2007). Research practice does not in principle differ in this respect from everyday 'methods' we use to make sense of and orient ourselves in an alien environment, that is we look around, try to 'read' what occurs to us, and ask questions. Accordingly, we formulate hypotheses which help us to create new situations and questions. From an interpretative perspective, fieldwork can thus be understood as a process in which the researcher learns to interpret and follow the rules that govern the practices of the field and to understand (and make explicit) its structures of meaning.

In discourse-oriented research, (formal) interviews and (informal) conversations will most likely be the primary data used. Again, the open format of such interviews is crucial (especially in the early stages of a project), as they allow informants to discuss matters and concepts important to them, rather than to the researcher. Whyte (1984:102) suggests encouraging informants to comment on their feelings and experiences using examples: 'When the informant expresses an attitude apparently unconnected with any event already described, I say something like this: 'That's interesting. Have you had some experience that has led you to feel this way'? Almost invariably the informant will respond with an account of one or more relevant experiences'.

Stories have been described by ethnographers as important elements of organizational reality used by people to make sense of their world and that can contribute to 'shape and reshape the way the individuals experience their organization' (Schwartzmann 1993:44). *Events and routines* are another type of activity that has been fruitfully studied. As Giddens argued (1984:36), all 'social systems, no matter how grand or far-flung, both express and are expressed in the routines of daily social life'. In organizations, such routines are the key means of ordering and framing people's interactions with each other. Moreover, following Latour and Woolgar

(1986), social action in organizations can be seen not only as interactions between individuals, but also as embedded within a multitude of ecological (spatial, material, semiotic) conditions which, in turn, determine how the individuals (inter)act.

The *observation of behaviour* (and of the settings in which it takes place) will often be an important part of the study of practices in organizations – alongside and complementing interviewing. Standardized observational schemes can be used in such contexts; however, in discourse-oriented research observations will more likely play a supplementary role. First, they are an important way of contextualizing interview and textual material. Second, what people know about their practices, and, furthermore, what they can or want to tell about them, need not coincide with what they are actually doing. Hence, even when talk is treated 'as the primary area for systematization' observations can be used both as a contextualization and as an 'input into talk and as test of the result of talk' (Agar 1996:157).

Given the complexity of organizations as a field of study, strategies for narrowing down the data and increasing focus will certainly become an issue in the course of the research process. From a systematic point of view, selection strategies can be geared towards locations, time, events or people. From a practical perspective, though, more important than systematic sampling is an awareness of choices to be made in the research process, and a commitment to transparency and reflexivity with respect to those choices.

The concept of *theoretical sampling* caters to this need of openness and flexibility within the research process on the one hand and avoidance of opportunistic sampling on the other. The key idea of theoretical sampling is to look for representativeness not in terms of a population but rather in terms of concepts, that is, the researcher does not count individual occurrences but he or she looks for incidents and events that will 'maximise opportunities to discover variations among concepts' (Strauss and Corbin 1998:201). Clearly, this kind of sampling cannot be designed from scratch but evolves with the research process in which relevant concepts are gradually discovered. This implies that analysis should be performed immediately after data collection in order to guide further sampling choices. While the sampling strategy is open in the beginning, in order to generate as many categories as possible, over time it becomes more focused, aiming at 'developing, densifying, and saturating those categories' (ibid.:203).

Finally, a crucial issue throughout the research process is the *recording, management and interpretation of data*. Taking fieldnotes is part and parcel of the daily routine of fieldwork as a craft. Bernard (2002) recommends systematically setting aside two or three hours a day for working on notes: 'The faster you write up your observations, the more detail you can get down. More is better. Much more is much better' (ibid.:373). Indeed, taking fieldnotes makes the difference between everyday observation and a controlled method.

Comment: Functions and types of fieldnotes

The two main *functions of fieldnotes* are: (a) to allow for a systematic reflection on your experiences in the field and to plan the further steps of your research and (b) to assure a scrupulous documentation of the unfolding of the research process for later analysis (that is to be able to reconstruct different elements of the research process 'later on', thus within your eventual analysis). Therefore notes are crucial to help develop the research while it is still 'in the making' as well as reflect upon it (for example write a paper, thesis and so on) when the research activities in the field are terminated.

There are different *types of fieldnotes* which help you fulfil the enumerated functions in a variety of ways. Bernard (2000) distinguishes four different kinds of notes: (a) *jots* used to note down observations while still in the field, (b) a *diary* which is personal and deals with your own feelings and thoughts as the 'research-instrument', (c) a *log* used for planning activities for each day of your fieldwork, and (d) *fieldnotes proper*, that is descriptive notes, methodological reflections and analytical notes (the latter are often lengthy pieces of theoretically oriented reflections on certain key aspects of the field and they will most likely be part of the research papers you produce at the end of your work).

As one can see from the diverse types and functions of notes used during/for the ethnographic research in the field, the interpretative work is taking place from the very beginning of one's encounter with the field and it is strongly intertwined with all the stages of the process of data-gathering. Consequently, unlike many different approaches which undertake data interpretation only after research is completed, ethnography is not a linear research process that would either start with or lead to theories and hypotheses. On the contrary, ethnography must be seen as cyclical, where learning about the field, formulating hypotheses and confronting them with the data are activities performed throughout the entire ethnographic experience.[4] Or, differently put: in ethnography 'the research does not proceed in a straight line, but in a series of loops, because each step leads the researcher to reflect upon, and even revisit, earlier steps' (Delamont 2004:223).

Interpreting ethnographic data in discourse-oriented research

After weeks or months spent 'in the field', the researcher comes back to the office with packs of notebooks and documents, observations and interpretations typed in his or her computer, as well as other material, such as tape-recorded interviews or photographs and other artefacts collected in the field. This section discusses three strategies in which (such) ethnographic data is put to work in the context of discourse-oriented research. First, ethnography can be employed to establish the context of the discourse one wants to study.

The second strategy consists of using the knowledge gained in fieldwork to show how more general discursive processes and structures play out in a specific locale. The third one, finally, puts ethnography to work for studying the ways in which language is articulated with and realized in the studied social practices.

For example, in their investigation of European Union discourses on un/employment, Muntigl *et al.* (2000) analyzed and compared decision-making processes in the European Parliament and in small networks/committees of the European Commission. Working from their linguistic perspective, they focused on such issues as argumentation patterns, the recontextualization of meaning in negotiation processes, or interdiscursive relations of discourses on un/employment and their ideological dilemmas. At the centre of their research were textual data, such as parliamentary debates and policy papers. On the other hand, these detailed discourse-analytical analyzes were informed by an ethnographic case-study which involved the observation of meetings and debates, interviews with EU officials, staff and politicians, the collection of documents and the 'shadowing' of one member of the European Parliament (MEP) during several of his working days (see also Wodak, forthcoming). Only through such a study of the European Union 'from the inside', the authors claim, was it possible to understand the discursive practices of policymaking in the respective field of employment, and thus to ask the right questions and to select the right documents to more closely analyze these at the textual level. Reflecting on the significance of the said fieldwork experience, Gilbert Weiss (2000:70) argues: 'To be sure, not all the data collected during our stays in Brussels entered into the present book . . . On the other hand, even those ethnographic experiences . . . which are not directly followed up here, are indirectly very relevant for the case study presented in this book because . . . they helped us to draw a closer and better understanding of a subject as complex as EU decision-making and organizational discourse. In this sense, we will most likely use for instance the interview data to complement textual and other data types as part of a case study rather than a primary focus.'

In line with an argument put forward by Michael Agar (1996:8), this contextual use of fieldwork can be labelled 'encyclopaedic' ethnography since it is about gathering as much background knowledge about a field as possible. In the case of formal organizations, this could be information on the organization's history, on its structures, practices and routines, on key groups and their conflicts, on core concepts used within the organization and their meanings, on latent rules and myths and so on. 'The ethnographic product is the knowledge that you, the outsider, have learned, knowledge that helps understand the world within which those "others" live' (ibid.)

Only through *detailed contextual knowledge* can the specific texts studied and questions asked be evaluated properly as to the role they play in an organization. A failure to achieve such a contextualization of discourse may on the other hand lead to the analysis yielding results which are artificial, since it does not incorporate the actual significance of discourse in the daily life of an organization. Codes of conduct in businesses for instance lend themselves perfectly to an analysis of discursive structures. On the other hand, only an ethnographic type of investigation can find out whether, and in what ways, such codes of conduct are actually used and referred to by various participants, that is it allows linking the study of (discursive) structures to individual agency and daily practices.[5]

A second strategy for integrating discursive and ethnographic approaches can be thought of in terms of 'bringing discourse in place'. In our own research on the European Convention (Krzyżanowski and Oberhuber 2007), we proposed to analyze EU institutional reform and constitutional debates by looking at the Convention on the Future of Europe as a specific locale and a key moment in this process. This entailed gathering information locally, at the site of the Convention, that is not only to study its official discourse and self-presentation (for example in the media), but also to conduct interviews with those involved and to make observations in various formal and informal settings. Through this approach, we aimed at complementing our understanding of the EU as a set of institutions and as a structure of governance (at the macrolevel) with an account of its actual practices and its culture for dealing with and transforming conflict and contingency at the microlevel.

Against the backdrop of such a detailed appraisal of the locale of the Convention, our analysis of Convention discourse looked at the multiplicity of ways of making meaning of Europe/the EU by various actors and texts. Thus, while previous research mainly focused on ideas and images of constitutional discourse at a general level (by analyzing textual data such as party programmes or official documents), our research project proposed a more agency-oriented and situated approach. To be sure, bringing discourse in place and focusing on concrete institutions, events and actors forecloses making general claims about the European Union as an object of study. On the other hand, it allows one to see how the individual agency of those involved in a particular 'nexus of practice' (Scollon and Scollon 2004) may influence the production of discourse within particular social and political conditions, and it furthermore allows one to see how the individual experience of social (or political) actors may influence the form of such a practice in general, and its constitutive discourses in particular (see Example 9.2).

EXAMPLE 9.2   Nexus of practice and the discourse-ethnographic study of the European Convention

In their recent proposal of an inherently ethnographic 'nexus-analysis', Scollon and Scollon (2004) focus on various micro- (social and political) loci where different discursive practices meet to create practice-bound networks (see also Scollon and

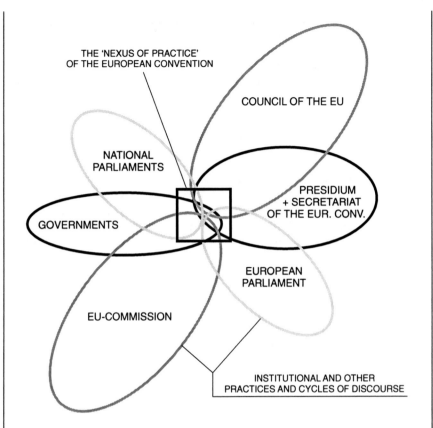

THE 'NEXUS OF PRACTICE'
OF THE EUROPEAN CONVENTION

COUNCIL OF THE EU

NATIONAL
PARLIAMENTS

PRESIDIUM
+ SECRETARIAT
OF THE EUR. CONV.

GOVERNMENTS

EUROPEAN
PARLIAMENT

EU-COMMISSION

INSTITUTIONAL AND OTHER
PRACTICES AND CYCLES OF DISCOURSE

Figure 9.1 Nexus of practice of the European Convention

Scollon 2003). Within their conception, Scollon and Scollon see 'nexus analysis as the mapping of semiotic cycles of people, discourses, places, and mediational means' involved in certain practices (2004:vii). Those performing 'nexus analysis', they argue, must see themselves 'as ethnographers' while their main interest should be located 'in social action' (ibid.).

In Figure 9.1, we present a graph (adopted from a general outline of 'nexus analysis' proposed by Scollon and Scollon 2004:28) which points to different institutional and other cycles of discourse which cross-sect within the nexus of the 2002–3 European Convention (for further details see Krzyżanowski and Oberhuber 2007). The graph implies that one must not only take into account the official discourses of the Convention (as well as the immediate institutional context of their production and reception). It is also necessary to examine and interpret different types of discourses produced within other institutional spaces (such as academic networks, the European Parliament and other bodies) and eventually represented in the Convention and recontextualized within its (discursive and other) practices.

At the level of data analysis, this approach was operationalized by linking the ethnographic dimension of our study of the European Convention (its organizational and communicative setup as well as the social practices of various actors and groups) with the analysis of discourse data. For example, in a set of interviews with Conventioners common positions were found which reflected a more abstract and deeply rooted conception of the nature of the European Union in terms of a certain vision of progress. Such vision was repeatedly used in Convention discourse to justify and legitimize claims about institutional reform. At the same time, it could be demonstrated how this set of linguistic practices would serve as a positive identity-marker setting an in-group apart from an out-group and hence, at the level of social practices, help build alliances in the very heterogeneous social context of the Convention and contributed to the overall process of consensus-building.

The said temporal notion of the European Union can be found in academic and political discourses from the very beginning of the integration project and has been analyzed by Petr Drulàk (2003) in terms of a sedimented metaphor of 'Europe as a flow'. Below, selected examples from various genres and discourses within the nexus of practice of the European Convention are provided (for details see Krzyżanowski and Oberhuber 2007:85–91):

1. Interview LUX-JS: one will not have a finality in Europe; it will always develop further.
2. Interview UK-AD: Mr Blair and friends have got to confront but if Britain is going to be a part of this thing or not but it it is also clear that it Britain should not block the process of integration of all the rest if they wish to continue (unread 2.0) which they do.
3. Interview IRL-JC: I would see EPP as a (.) party which should be to the forefront promoting greater community integration and therefore the community method.
4. Gisela Stuart (2003): From my experience at the Convention it is clear that the real reason for the Constitution – and its main impact – is the political deepening of the Union. This objective was brought home to me when I was told on numerous occasions: 'You and the British may not accept this yet, but you will in a few years' time.'
5. Joint parliamentarian declaration (2003)[6]: There must be no retreat from the Convention's already modest proposals for its extension of QMV [qualified majority voting] in the fields of tax, social security or criminal justice. The Passerelle provisions, triggered by a unanimous decision of the European Council, as well as in enhanced cooperation, must be maintained as a key element of the evolutive nature of the Constitution.

Finally, our third ideal-typical strategy of combining ethnographic and discourse-oriented research aims at conceptualizing the articulations and interrelations of discursive and social practices.[7] With respect to this objective, the writings of Michel Foucault were particularly influential. Foucault himself had set out with analyzes of the internal structures and formative principles of discourse, and only later turned to social practices and institutions. From the very beginning, however, he vigorously defended a view of discourse as not being representative, that is mirroring reality, but as productive, that is constituting reality and, above all, human subjects (see Foucault 1982). An important expansion of such a perspective was achieved when Foucault began excavating the practical dimension of the discursive processes of the production of subjects, namely power. With his perhaps most famous concept of power/knowledge, he coined an influential term for this new focus. Foucault (1977:27) writes: '[P]ower and knowledge directly imply one another ... there is no power relation without the correlative constitution of a field of knowledge, nor any knowledge that does not presuppose and constitute at the same time power relations.'

By emphasizing the dialectical relations between regimes of power on the one hand and orders of discourse on the other, Foucault pointed to the many pathways that language can take in influencing social reality. For Foucault, power, understood as the structuring of a possible field of action, can be literally everywhere. It circulates throughout the entire social field, even in its tiniest and apparently most trivial extremities. Thus, it is important to focus on the concrete, local techniques and micropractices of power. Furthermore, such local '*dispositives*' of power are always conceived as connected with a set of discursive practices.

A similar perspective was also developed in critical discourse analysis (CDA) with its notion of 'language as social practice' (Fairclough and Wodak 1997) contributing to the reproduction of society, and its emphasis on the context of language use as well as the problem of conceptualizing the 'mediation between the social and the linguistic' (Chouliaraki and Fairclough 1999; see also Wodak 2006). Within CDA in general (see Wodak 1996; also Chouliaraki 1995; Sarangi and Slembrouck 1996; Iedema 1997, 2003; Fairclough 2005) it has been argued that 'multiple genres and multiple public spaces are studied, and intertextual and interdiscursive relationships are investigated' (Wodak 2001:69). In particular within the CDA's discourse-historical approach (see for example Muntigl *et al.* 2000; Krzyżanowski 2005; Krzyżanowski and Oberhuber 2007) various, mainly institutional, milieus of language use have been studied to discover how different genres acquire different pragmatic roles and meanings in different contexts.[8]

Recent interest in 'social construction' within policy studies provides an example of the combination of discourse-oriented research and ethnographic perspectives in political science research. Scholars of European studies for instance attempted to open up the black box of institutions and negotiations and to focus on the microlevel dynamics of social interaction and their institutional environments (for a literature review see Jupille *et al.* 2003; Checkel 2004). Such efforts included the adoption of linguistic concepts such as 'speech community' or 'shared language' in order to explain how language permits the reduction of contingency, and thus successful cooperation in complex political organizations. Furthermore, the so-called cognitive metaphor theory first formulated by Lakoff and Johnson (1980) has been applied in political science research for looking at the ways in which language shapes the manners of thinking and acting of political elites and civil servants (see Schön 1979; Schäffner and Wende 1995; Drulák 2004; Lakoff 2004).

Maarten Hajer's book *The Politics of Environmental Discourse* (1995) set a milestone for the discursive turn in policy analysis. Focusing on the case of the regulation of the problem of acid rain in Great Britain and the Netherlands, Hajer highlighted the constitutive function of discourse in defining and framing public policy: 'ecological problems do not pose institutional problems by themselves, but only to the extent that they are constructed as such' (Hajer 1995:40). The ways the problem of acid rain is framed by certain actors always already implies certain policy-relevant recommendations. A focus on the critical limits of emissions that nature can endure, for instance, clearly favours an end-of-pipe-oriented regulatory regime. Thus Hajer (1995:30) conceives of discourse as an 'organizing principle for the innovation of institutional procedures', while he also suggests that 'We will speak of discourse institutionalization if a given discourse is translated into institutional arrangements, that is if the theoretical concepts of ecological modernization are translated into concrete policies ... and institutional arrangements' (ibid.:61).

At the methodological level, Hajer implemented this research programme by studying the construction of the acid rain problem both at the level of programmatic statements (such as memoranda) and at the level of concrete practices (such as regulatory regimes). The author analyzed a wide variety of genres, including conference proceedings, scientific reports, mass media coverage of crucial events, parliamentary debates and many others. Moreover, he paid attention to all kinds of practices involved in the construction of the acid rain problem. The restructuring of ministerial departments for instance is used as an indicator for changing conceptions of environmental regulation. The practices and main concepts organizing the negotiations between the government and representatives of industry are looked at (drawing on interviews with officials). The contribution of 'subpolitical' practices like tree health surveys, excursions and public awareness campaigns for the 'public construction of damage' are analyzed. Hajer even goes to great lengths to reconstruct the story lines informing the setup and model assumptions of the Dutch Priority Programme on Acidification, and he also dissects the practices of translating scientific knowledge into policy-relevant information.

Assessing the quality of research and the principle of reflexivity

Turning to the evaluation of ethnographic fieldwork within discourse research, positivist ideals such as objectivity, validity and reliability will often not be suitable criteria. Ethnography seeks to reconstruct and understand the specificity of the worlds it purports to study; it does not strive for general and replicable results. Furthermore, the researcher is inextricably part of the research process. Data-gathering in fieldwork is always selective, and it is subjective since it necessarily reflects the particular experience of each researcher in and with his (or her) field. Doing away with subjectivity, thus, seems to be a futile endeavour, and consequently the quality of research has been conceived of and evaluated along different lines (see Angrosino and Mays de Pérez 2000; Steinke 2000):[9]

- First, transparency is the primary condition of possibility for the evaluation of the quality of research. This entails the detailed documentation of the research process with respect to the researcher's theoretical presuppositions, his or her research objectives, the methods of data-gathering, recording and analysis, and the decisions taken in the research process, with respect to choosing research sites and sampling.
- Second, the methods and cases chosen should be adequate in relation to the object-field and the questions asked: the object defines the methods to be used, and not vice versa.
- Third, ethnographic interpretation and theory-building should be grounded in the data themselves, that is the perspectives and concepts employed in the field, and not be derived from predefined models.
- Fourth, data should be gathered which is suitable to actually challenge the previous knowledge (or prejudices) of the researcher, that is to avoid 'fitting the data to illustrate a theory'. Thus for instance sampling should include extreme or contrasting cases to test the distribution of patterns in the field (or falsify a hypothesis).
- Fifth, good ethnographic research depends upon systematic self-reflection of the researcher: this could include observing yourself (for instance by using a fieldwork diary), making personal conditions and interests explicit, and systematically reflecting on the development of the relations to the people you observe and work with.

With respect to the use of ethnography within discourse-oriented research, other more specific criteria can be added which concern the level of integration of the various discursive and non-discursive data in the analysis. As Agar (1996:37) has stated, one of the secrets to good qualitative research 'lies in its reliance on different sources, all of which support one's conclusions'. Choosing the right kind of data and coming up with ways to analyze them which will allow drawing connections is part of the singular and creative element of each research project.

The latter aspect once again points to *reflexivity*: clearly, the choice for an ethnographic encounter with one's object-field implies privileging a flexible and situated approach over the authority yielded by the application of a set of well-established and seemingly rigorous methods of 'scientific' data-gathering and analysis. Grant and Hardy argued (2004:9) that qualitative research strategies provide 'researchers with the opportunity to reflect on the ambiguous and constructed nature of the data with which they must work, while at the same time allowing them space for freer and bolder ways of interacting with the material'.

In other words, such research opens itself up to the language and self-interpretations of a field with a view to making the structures of the natives' world explicit. Consequently, the 'subjects' one works with, and their behaviour, are not reified by the scientific gaze, but they are confronted with the possibility for change. Thus, critical awareness of the ways in which research interacts with practice, or is geared towards it or integrated with it, constitutes another important element of researchers' reflexivity.

Notes

1. Traditionally, ethnography has been defined as the work of 'understanding another way of life from the native point of view' (Spradley 1980:3), that is bringing the others' 'ways of understanding into awareness, making them explicit and public, and building a credible argument that what one learned should be believed by others who were not present' (Agar 1996:1).
2. In recent years, discourse has become increasingly prominent in research on organizations. This is reflected for instance by the launch of a biennial conference series on organizational discourse in 1994, the establishment of the International Centre for Research in Organizational Discourse, Strategy and Change in 2001 (http://www.management.unimelb.edu.au/icrodsc), or the publication of a number of special issues of journals in the fields of organizations and discourse – for example see *International Journal of the Sociology of Language* 166; *Organizational Studies* 25(1); *Academy of Management Review* 29(4); *Human Relations* 53(9). For reviews of this quickly expanding literature see Wodak (1996); Drew and Heritage (1997); van Dijk (1997); Iedema and Wodak (1999); Linde (2001); Grant *et al.* (2004).
3. Such a focus was already implied in early human-relations research on industrial settings which developed notions such as formal and informal organization. The latter was understood as 'the actual personal interrelations existing among the members', as opposed to 'those patterns of interaction prescribed by the rules and regulations of the company', the 'policies which prescribe the relations that obtain ... within the human organization', and the technical dimension of organization (Roethlisberger and Dickson 1939:566).
4. Agar (1996:35–9) draws on the concept of abduction in order to demonstrate the specific research logic of ethnography: 'Abduction is about the imaginative construction of a *p* that implies an observed *q*.' In other words, abduction is about inventing concepts that will account for a set of data. Thus, abduction is a creative process. There always remains a gap between what one observed and how it is interpreted. To bridge that gap, one cannot draw on a strictly determined logical inference (such as induction or deduction) but one has to argue in terms of the added explanatory value of the interpretation.
5. A paradigmatic study of this kind is Orr's (1996) investigation of the unofficial ways in which service technicians fix particular problems – as opposed to what official documentation requires.

6. Joint Declaration addressed to the European Council by Parliamentary members of the European Convention, reunited in Brussels on Friday 5 December 2003, http://europa.eu.int/futurum/documents/other/oth051203_en.pdf
7. As Fairclough and Wodak (1997:258) put it: 'Describing discourse as social practice implies a dialectical relationship between a particular discursive event and the situation(s), institution(s) and social structure(s) which frame it: the discursive event is shaped by them, but it also shapes them. That is, discourse is socially constitutive as well as socially conditioned – it constitutes situations, objects of knowledge, and the social identities of and relationships between people and groups of people. It is constitutive both in the sense that it helps to sustain and reproduce the social status quo, and in the sense that it contributes to transforming it. Since discourse is so socially consequential, it gives rise to important issues of power.'
8. Elsewhere in CDA, it was argued that 'in analysing language-in-society, the focus should be on *what language use means to its users* . . . Consequently, we need to find out *how* language matters to people. The "insider's view" . . . is a crucial tool in understanding the dynamics of language in society and it is the cornerstone of ethnography)' (Blommaert 2005:14; original emphasis). In a similar vein, it has also been suggested that 'we have to be aware that *language operates differently in different environments*, and that, in order to understand how language works, we need to contextualise it properly, to establish the relations between language usage and the particular purposes for which and conditions under which it operates' (ibid.; original emphasis).
9. See also Wodak (2001) for a methodological programme of the discourse-historical approach.

Key readings

Agar, M.H. *The Professional Stranger: An Informal Introduction to Ethnography*, 2nd edn (San Diego, CA: Academic Press 1996).
Bellier, I. and Wilson, T.M. (eds) *An Anthropology of the European Union: Building, Imagining and Experiencing the New Europe* (Oxford: Berg, 2000).
Grant, D., Hardy, C., Oswick, C. and Putnam, L. (eds) *Handbook of Organizational Discourse* (London: Sage, 2004).
Krzyżanowski, M. and Oberhuber, F. *(Un)Doing Europe: Discourses and Practices of Negotiating the EU Constitution* (Brussels: PIE-Peter Lang, 2007).
Muntigl, P., Weiss, G. and Wodak, R. *European Union Discourses on Unemployment* (Amsterdam: Benjamins, 2000).

References

Abélès, M. *Quiet Days in Burgundy: A Study of Local Politics* (Cambridge: Cambridge University Press, 1991).
Agar, M.H. *The Professional Stranger: An Informal Introduction to Ethnography*, 2nd edn (San Diego, CA: Academic Press 1996).

Ainsworth, S. and Hardy, C. 'Discourse and Identities', in D. Grant, C. Hardy, C. Oswick and L. Putnam (eds) *Handbook of Organizational Discourse* (London: Sage, 2004), pp. 153–74.

Angrosino, M.V. and Mays de Pérez, K.A. 'Rethinking Observation: From Method to Context', in N.K. Denzin and Y.S. Lincoln (eds) *Handbook of Qualitative Research*, 2nd edn (Thousand Oaks, CA: Sage, 2000), pp. 673–702.

Bellier, I. 'In and Out, Fieldwork in a Political Space: The Case of the European Commission', *Österreichische Zeitschrfit für Politikwissenschaft* 31(2) (2002), 205–16.

Bernard H.R. *Handbook of Methods in Cultural Anthropology* (Oxford: AltaMira, 2000).

Bernard, H.R. *Research Methods in Anthropology: Qualitative and Quantitative Methods* (Walnut Creek, CA: Altamira, 2002).

Blommaert, J. *Discourse. A Critical Introduction* (Cambridge: Cambridge University Press, 2005)

Boden, D. *The Business of Talk: Organizations in Action* (Cambridge: Polity, 1994).

Boje, D., Oswick, C. and Ford, J.D. 'Language and Organization: The Doing of Organization', *Academy of Management Review* 29 (2004), 571–7.

Burgess, R.G. *In the Field: An Introduction to Field Research* (London: George Allen & Unwin, 1984).

Checkel, J. T. 'Social Constructivisms in Global and European Politics (A Review Essay)', *Review of International Studies* 30(2) (2004), 229–44.

Chouliaraki, L. and Fairclough, N. *Discourse in Late Modernity: Rethinking Critical Discourse Analysis.* (Edinburgh: Edinburgh University Press 1999)

Chouliaraki, L. 'Regulation in "Progressivist" Pedagogic Discourse: Individualized Teacher–Pupil Talk', *Discourse and Society* 9(1) (1995), 5–32.

Czarniawska, B. *Writing Management: Organization Theory as a Literary Genre* (Oxford: Oxford University Press, 1999).

de Laine, M. *Fieldwork, Participation and Practice: Ethics and Dilemmas in Qualitative Research* (London: Sage, 2000).

Delamont, S. 'Ethnography and Participant Observation,' in C. Seale, G. Gobo, J.F. Gubrium and D. Silverman (eds) *Qualitative Research Practice* (London: Sage, 2004), pp. 217–30.

Drew, P. and Heritage, J. *Talk at Work: Interaction in Institutional Settings* (Cambridge: Cambridge University Press, 1992).

Drew, P. and Sorjonen, M. 'Institutional Dialogue', in T.A. van Dijk (ed.) *Discourse as Social Interaction* (Newbury Park, CA: Sage, 1997), pp.92–118.

Drew. P. and Heritage, J. (eds) *Talk at Work: Interaction in Institutional Settings* (Cambridge: Cambridge University Press, 1997).

Drulák, P. *Metaphors Europe Lives By: Language and Institutional Change of the European Union.* Working Paper SPS no. 2004/15 (Florence: European University Institute, 2004).

Fairclough, N. and R. Wodak. 'Critical Discourse Analysis', in T.A. van Dijk (ed.) *Discourse as Social Interaction: Discourse Studies – A Multidisciplinary Introduction*, vol. 2 (London: Sage, 1997), pp. 258–83.

Fairclough, N. 'Critical Discourse Analysis in Transdisciplinary Research', in R. Wodak and P. Chilton (eds) *A New Agenda in (Critical) Discourse Analysis: Theory, Methodology and Interdisciplinarity* (Amsterdam: Benjamins, 2005), pp. 53–70.

Foucault, M. *Discipline and Punish: The Birth of the Prison*. (New York: Random House, 1977).

Foucault, M. 'The Subject and Power', in H.L. Dreyfus and P. Rabinow (eds) *Michel Foucault: Beyond Structuralism and Hermeneutics* (Chicago, IL: University of Chicago Press, 1982), pp. 208–26.

Giddens, A. *The Constitution of Society* (Berkeley, CA: University of California Press, 1984).

Grant, D., Hardy, C., Oswick, C. and Putnam, L. (eds) *Handbook of Organizational Discourse* (London: Sage 2004).

Grant, D. and Hardy, C. 'Introduction: Struggles with Organizational Discourse', *Organization Studies* 25(1) (2004), 5–13.

Hajer, M.A. *The Politics of Environmental Discourse: Ecological Modernization and the Policy Process* (Oxford: Clarendon, 1995).

Iedema, R. 'Interactional Dynamics and Social Change', PhD thesis, Department of Linguistics, University of Sydney, 1997.

Iedema, R. *The Discourses of Post-Bureaucratic Organization* (Amsterdam: Benjamins 2003).

Iedema, R. and Wodak, R. 'Introduction: Organizational Discourses and Practices. *Discourse and Society* 10(1) (1999), 5–19.

Jupille, J., Caporaso, J.A. and Checkel, J.T. 'Integrating Institutions: Rationalism, Constructivism, and the Study of the European Union', *Comparative Political Studies* 36(1–2) (special issue) (1993), 7–40.

Krzyżanowski, M. 'European Identity Wanted! On Discursive and Communicative Dimensions of the European Convention,' in R. Wodak and P. Chilton. (eds) *A New Research Agenda in CDA: Theory and Multidisciplinarity* (Amsterdam: Benjamins 2005), pp. 137–64.

Krzyżanowski, M. and Oberhuber, F. *(Un)Doing Europe: Discourses and Practices of Negotiating the EU Constitution*. (Brussels: PIE–Peter Lang 2007).

Lakoff, G. *Don't Think of an Elephant!* (Berkeley, CA: Chelsea Green, 2004).

Lakoff, G. and Johnson, M. *Metaphors We Live By* (University of Chicago Press 1980).

Latour, B. and Woolgar, S. *Laboratory Life: The Construction of Scientific Facts* (Princeton: Princeton University Press, 1986).

Linde, C. *Life Stories. The Creation of Coherence* (Oxford University Press 1993).

Linde, C. 'Narrative in Institutions', in D. Schiffrin, D. Tannen and H.E. Hamilton (eds) *The Handbook of Discourse Analysis* (Oxford: Blackwell, 2001), pp. 519–35..

Muntigl, P., Weiss, G. and Wodak, R. *European Union Discourses on Un/employment* (Amsterdam: Benjamins, 2000).

Muntigl, P. 'The European Union: Policy-Making through Organizational Discursive Practices', in P. Muntigl, G. Weiss and R. Wodak, *European Union Discourses on Un/employment* (Amsterdam: Benjamins, 2000), pp. 1–25.

Oberhuber, F. 'Dissemination and Implementation of Political Concepts', in R. Wodak and V. Koller (eds) *Handbook of Applied Linguistics*, vol. 4: *Language and Communication in the Public Sphere* (Berlin: de Gruyter, 2008), pp. 271–89.

Orr, J. *Talking about Machines* (Ithaca, NY: ILR Press, 1996).

Panagl, O. and Wodak, R. (eds) *Text und Kontext:. Theoriemodelle und methodische Verfahren im transdisziplinären Vergleich* (Würzburg: Königshausen & Neumann, 2004).

Roethlisberger, F.J. and W.J. Dickson. *Management and the Worker* (Cambridge, MA: Harvard University Press, 1939).

Sarangi, S. and S. Slembrouck. *Language, Bureaucracy and Social Control* (London: Longman 1996).

Schäffner, C. and Wende, A.L. (eds.) *Language and Peace* (Aldershot: Dartmouth, 1995).

Schön, D. A. 'Generative Metaphor: A Perspective on Problem-Setting in Social Policy', in A. Ortony (ed.) *Metaphor and Thought* (Cambridge: Cambridge University Press, 1979), pp. 254–83.

Schwartzmann, H.B. *Ethnography in Organizations* (London: Sage 1993).

Scollon, R. and Scollon, S.W. *Discourses in Place. Language in the Material World* (London: Routledge, 2003).

Scollon, R. and Scollon, S.W. *Nexus Analysis* (London: Routledge, 2004).

Shore, C. and Wright, S. 'Policy: A New Field of Anthropology', in C. Shore and S. Wright (eds) *Anthropology of Policy: Critical Perspectives on Governance and Power* (London: Routledge, 1997), pp. 3–39.

Shore, C. *Building Europe. The Cultural Politics of European Integration* (London: Routledge, 2000).

Spradley, J.P. *Participant Observation* (New York: Holt, Rinehart & Winston 1980).

Steinke, I. 'Gütekriterien qualitativer Forschung', in U. Flick, E. von Kardorff and I. Steinke (eds) *Qualitative Forschung. Ein Handbuch* (Reinbek: Rowohlt, 2000), pp. 319–31.

Strauss, A. and Corbin, J. *Basics of Qualitative Research: Techniques and Procedures for Developing Grounded Theory* (London: Sage, 1998).

Streeck, J. 'How To Do Things with Things', *Human Studies* 19 (1996), 365–84.

Stuart, G. *The Making of Europe's Constitution* (London: Fabian Society, 2003)

van Dijk, T.A. (ed.) *Discourse and Communication* (Berlin: Walter de Gruyter, 1985).

van Dijk, T.A. (ed.) *Discourse as Social Interaction* (London: Sage, 1997).

Weimer, D.L. and Vining, A.R. 'Gathering Information for Policy Analysis', in *Policy Analysis: Concepts and Practice* (Upper Saddle River, NJ: Prentice-Hall, 2004), pp. 296–310.

Weiss, G., 'Researching the European Union. Data and Ethnography', in P. Muntigl, G. Weiss and R. Wodak *European Union Discourses on Un/employment* (Amsterdam: Benjamins, 2000), pp. 51–73.

Whyte, W.F. *Learning from the Field* (Beverly Hills, CA: Sage, 1984).

Wodak, R. *Disorders of Discourse* (London: Longman, 1996).

Wodak, R. 'From Conflict to Consensus? The Co-Construction of a Policy Paper', in P. Muntigl, G. Weiss and R. Wodak. *European Union Discourses on Un/employment* (Amsterdam: Benjamins, 2000), pp. 73–115.

Wodak, R. 'Recontextualisation and Transformation of Meanings: A Critical Discourse Analysis of Decision-Making in EU Meetings about Employment Policies', in S. Sarangi and M. Coulthard (eds) *Discourse and Social Life* (London: Longman, 2000a), pp. 185–207.

Wodak, R. 'The Discourse-Historical Approach', in R. Wodak and M. Meyer (eds) *Methods of Critical Discourse Analysis* (London: Sage, 2001) 63–94.

Wodak, R. 'Multiple Identities: The Roles of Female Parliamentarians in the EU Parliament', in J. Holmes and M. Meyerhoff (eds) *The Handbook of Language and Gender* (Oxford: Blackwell, 2003), pp. 671–99.

Wodak, R., 'National and Transnational Identities: European and Other Identities Oriented to in Interiews with EU Officials', in R. Hermann, M. Brewer and T. Risse (eds) *Transnational Identities: Becoming European in the EU* (Lanham, MD: Rowman & Littlefield, 2004), pp. 97–129.

Wodak, R. 'Mediation between Discourse and Society: Assessing Cognitive Approaches', *Discourse Studies* 8(1) (2006), 179–90.

Wodak, R. *Discursive Representation and Construction of Politics in Action* (Basingstoke: Palgrave Macmillan, forthcoming).

Glossary

address Markers of the recipient of talk, for instance in naming them, calling to them, or looking or turning towards them (see *participant roles*).

adjacency pair Two turns in conversation for which the first sets up an expectation of the second, such as question and answer, invitation and acceptance/rejection, assessment and agreement/disagreement (see *preference structure*).

affordance The affordances of a medium are what users can do with it. Typically, this term is used to compare the enabling features of different media, or to describe developments over time. For example, the interactive potential of the computer, one of its key affordances, is greater than that of books, whereas books still score higher on portability, haptic (i.e. 'touch') qualities, and reading convenience.

coherence (or textual semantics) The meaning of a text. Coherence is considered a mental phenomenon; it is not an inherent property of a text under consideration. Language-users establish coherence by relating different information units in the text.

cohesion Cohesion concerns the components of the textual surface that signal the 'text-syntactic' connectedness. The linear sequence of linguistic elements in a text is in no way accidental, but obeys grammatical rules and dependencies. All the functions applied to create relationships between surface elements are categorized as *cohesion*.

communicative dynamics The core element of focus groups crucial to the overall development of the discussion. Interactions and exchanges between the participants accumulate to the overall communicative dynamics of a focus group and are aimed at in order to yield a possibly far-reaching diversification of views and opinions (which are among key reasons for using focus-groups as a research method).

concordance A list of all the instances of a particular search word (or 'node') as they appear in the corpus, that is, with a specified number of words to the left and right. The node is placed in the centre of each concordance line, and the surrounding words are aligned. In this format, frequent collocational patterns stand out clearly. Concordances also enable the researcher to identify the semantic prosodies and semantic preferences of words in large corpora.

concordancer A computer program that produces KWIC ('keyword-in-context') concordances, lists frequencies and computes measures indicating whether certain patterns of co-occurrence are random or statistically significant.

context A concept that is an inherent part of discourse analysis and contributes significantly to how systematically it can be applied as part of interdisciplinary approaches. In the course of investigating complex social problems it is necessary to draw on multiple theoretical approaches to analyze given contexts and relate these to texts. Thus contexts are, on the one hand, structural constraints and norms, time and space; on the other hand, cognitive perceptions of a given situation by speakers, viewers and listeners: whether 'context' is included in linguistic analysis and the definition of 'context' *per se* are dependent on prior theoretical decisions.

context of situation All the factors immediately surrounding a speech event that affect the speech, such as participant roles, setting and genre.

corpus A collection of texts compiled for the purpose of analysis.

co-text Text surrounding a word or phrase under investigation.

documentary There is no fixed set of formal criteria that sets documentaries apart from other film genres. A film is regarded as a documentary when there is the explicit or implicit claim, by its producers and/or by the company that broadcasts it, that it is a documentary.

ethnography From the Greek words *ethnos* (people) and *graphein* (writing); has its roots in travel writing and colonial office reports, and was originally conceived as the study of non-European peoples and tribes. In contemporary research practice, it denotes a holistic method of data collection which requires researchers to engage with their subject at the local level and to take account of the 'natives' point of view'.

face-work The constant and mutual attention to the way each participant is presenting himself or herself in an interaction. For instance, if one participant threatens the face of the other by raising a sensitive topic, both participants conventionally try to protect the face of the other, for instance by softening the act, delaying, or giving reasons.

field Originally a closed space such as a village or an island; in contemporary ethnography it is metaphorical. Can include a variety of data from different levels, locations and situations which are drawn together by the researcher in order to understood a particular problem.

field of political action An institutionalized place of social forms of practice or framework of social interaction that allows the pursuit and realization of various political purposes by specific discursive practices; among these fields are the law-making procedure; the formation of public attitudes, opinions and will; the party-internal formation of attitudes, opinions and will; the inter-party formation of attitudes, opinions and will; the organization of international and (especially) interstate relations; the political advertising; the political executive and administration and the political control.

focus groups Social-scientific research method, frequently defined as *focus-group discussions* and widely considered as a form of group-interviewing. A focus group involves an activity undertaken by several participants; that activity might pertain to either discussing different issues right away or performing simple group-tasks which are to facilitate a group debate on a particular topic.

genre The conventionalized, more or less schematically fixed use of language associated with a particular activity and with particular functions for a specified speech community – as a socially accepted and conventionalized way of using language in connection with a particular type of social activity.

interdiscursivity Interdiscursvity indicates that discourses are linked to each other in various ways. If we define discourse as primarily topic-related, that is a discourse on X, then this discourse might refer to topics or subtopics of other discourses Y and Z.

interpretative repertoire The set of ways a speaker has of ways of explaining things, which they expect hearers to recognize; they may shift between repertoires in the course of an interaction. The same speaker may use more than one repertoire in different situations.

intertextuality This refers to the fact that all texts are linked to other texts, both in the past and in the present. Such links can be established in different ways: through continued reference to a topic or main actors; through reference to the same events; or by the transfer of main arguments from one text into the next.

metafunctions Systemic functional linguistics (SFL, a linguistic approach developed by M.A.K. Halliday and viewing language as a network of intertwined options, with each option standing for a different meaning construction) defines three distinct metafunctions of language (use): (1) ideational, (2) interpersonal, and (3) textual. The ideational metafunction of language refers to the linguistic representation of experiences, perceptions, and contents of consciousness. The interpersonal metafunction refers to the function of language as a means to establish and negotiate a relationship between text-producer and text-recipient. The textual metafunction refers to the structure and inner organization of texts as fundamental for any transfer of meaning.

modality One important criterion in everyday communication is the weight attached to a particular utterance. What is in linguistic terms called the *modality system* and marked by modal markers such as *may* or *might* can also be transferred to non-verbal semiotic phenomena. Hodge and Kress distinguish in this context between *realistic* and *non-realistic* forms of representation. Thus, verbal or (audio-)visual modality markers have a guiding function for the receivers' attribution of realistic value to a representation.

moderator/facilitator (in focus groups) A person leading an individual focus-group discussion whose position is much different from the classic role of an *interviewer*. A moderator/facilitator does not merely *ask questions* and instead steers and facilitates the process of a focus-group discussion, presents key topics/activities to the participants and is responsible for overseeing the overall development of the (*communicative*) *dynamics* taking place in the course of a focus group.

organizational discourse A field of research studied from multiple disciplinary backgrounds such as linguistics, sociology or anthropology. Organizations are conceived as practices of text and talk embedded in certain social settings, and specific characteristics and functions of linguistic exchange are highlighted such as the role of narratives and representations, the articulation of discourse with organizational practices, or the dimension of power and ideology in organizational discourse.

participant roles Erving Goffman points out that communication does not involve just a speaker and a hearer – each of these roles may have several possibilities. The speaker can be the animator (who does the actual speaking), the author (who writes the actual words) and the principal (in whose name the words are given). The hearer may be a ratified participant, addressed and taken to be the recipient of the talk, or a bystander who happens to be around and is not addressed, or an eavesdropper who is not acknowledged as present but who can still receive the message. For instance, in the Queen's Speech opening a session of the UK parliament, the Queen is animator and principal, but the staff members of the government of the day are the author; the members of the House of Lords and the House of Commons are the ratified participants, members of the public in the gallery are bystanders, and members of the broadcast audience participate as eavesdroppers.

political rhetoric The practical science and art of the use and effects of linguistic (including *nonverbal*) and other semiotic means of persuasion relating to political matters, prototypically of the effective or efficient speaking and writing by professional politicians.

politolinguistics A transdisciplinary approach to the analysis of political rhetoric that combines rhetoric, political science and linguistics (especially critical discourse analysis).

polity, policy and politics Three different dimensions of *the political*. *Polity* relates to the formal and structural framework as basis of political action; *policy* relates to the content-related dimension of political action that aims at shaping and is primarily connected with governmental action in different policy-fields; *politics* regards conflicting processes of articulating political interests and positions and of fighting for political power and influence.

populism An ambiguous term for various political phenomena such as a specific politics, movement or strategy of mobilization; in the present context conceived of as political style in the sense of a complex syndrome and functional way of political expression that relates to the contested category of *the people*.

preference structure Where one turn in conversation has two possible responses, one is often marked as preferred, and is typically given without hesitation or markers, while the other is dispreferred, and is typically given with hesitation – particles such as 'well', hedging, or an explanation. For instance, the preferred response to an invitation is acceptance; rejection may come with a delay, a 'well', a statement that one would like to accept, and an explanation of why one can't. An assessment, a statement of opinion, is typically followed by a second assessment that agrees (often in upgraded form), while disagreement may come with delay, and weak agreement followed by disagreement, which is often hedged.

presupposition In informal terms (there are formal definitions for the semantics of statements), an utterance presupposes a proposition when that proposition must be assumed to be true for the utterance to make sense. For instance, the directive 'Please tell us three instances in which you realized you made the wrong decision' presupposes that there are instances in which the decision was wrong. The question 'Why did you support the war?' presupposes that the addressee did support the war.

recontextualization By taking an argument and restating it in a new context, we first observe the process of decontextualization, and then, when the respective element is implemented in a new context, of recontextualization. The element then acquires a new meaning because meanings are formed in use.

register An identifiable variety of language use, with the lexical and syntactic choices and pragmatic conventions associated with that use. For instance, academic writing, sports commentary, political oratory, and romance novels all have distinctive registers.

semantic preference Term used to refer to semantic features shared by the collocates of a word. For example, *elderly* has been shown to be surrounded by items from the semantic domains of disability, vulnerability, care and so on.

semantic prosody A word's evaluative meaning, in particular along the bipolar dimension of 'good' and 'bad'.

synecdoche A rhetorical trope constituted by a whole standing for a part (*totum pro parte*; this is the case, if *the people* stands for just one specific social group), or, vice versa, by a part standing for the whole (*pars pro toto*; this is the case if *the citizen* stands for *all citizens*).

theoretical sampling Originally developed by Barney Glaser and Anselm Strauss in 1967, theoretical sampling is a processual method for choosing research sites and cases which is open in the beginning and becomes more focused over time. Other than probabilistic sampling, the goal of theoretical sampling is not to allow representative conclusions for a given population, but to develop the analytic concepts used in the research.

topics (of discourse) Basic text-semantic units used to summarize the meaning or a key message of a text or its part(s).

topics (primary vs. secondary – in focus groups) Two types of topics crucial for the process of semi-structuring (framing) of focus groups and their textual result. *Primary topics* are put (given) under discussion by the moderators/facilitators through a set of general frames of the discussions. *Secondary topics* are developed by participants within their utterances during discussions (in the process of *communicative dynamics*), frequently in response to the primary topics.

topoi (plural of topos) Generally used and generally accepted arguments, also called commonplaces. For instance, it is a commonplace to say that one should act on local problems before considering problems further away.

topos of the people (argumentum ad populum) An argumentation scheme in the centre of populist rhetoric that, among others, can be paraphrased as follows. If the people favours/refuses a specific political action or decision, the action should/should not be performed/the decision should/should not be taken.

transitivity Systemic functional linguistics recognizes two uses of the term: on the one hand it describes a grammatical system which construes the world of experiences through a typology of different forms of processes; on the other hand it stands for a major principle of the ideational metafunction, a principle that can in simple words be expressed through the question *Who does what to whom?*

visual semiotics The attempt to elaborate something such as a *visual syntax*, a visual meaning-making system, in analogy to, and at the same time different from, the verbal syntax.

Index